The State, Corporatist Politics, and Educational Policy Making in Mexico

The State,
Corporatist Politics,
and Educational Policy
Making in Mexico

Daniel A. Morales-Gómez and
Carlos Alberto Torres

PRAEGER

New York
Westport, Connecticut
London

Library of Congress Cataloging-in-Publication Data

Morales-Gómez, Daniel A.
   The state, corporatist politics, and educational policy making in
Mexico / Daniel A. Morales-Gómez and Carlos Alberto Torres.
      p.   cm.
   Includes bibliographical references (p.   ).
   ISBN 0-275-93484-5 (alk. paper)
   1. Education and state—Mexico. 2. Educational planning—Mexico.
3. Politics and education—Mexico. I. Torres, Carlos Alberto.
II. Title.
LC92.M4M67   1990
379.72—dc20   89-29986

Library of Congress Catalog Card Number: 89-29986
ISBN: 0-275-93484-5

First published in 1990

Praeger Publishers, One Madison Avenue, New York, NY 10010
An imprint of Greenwood Publishing Group, Inc.

Printed in the United States of America

The paper used in this book complies with the
Permanent Paper Standard issued by the National
Information Standards Organization (Z39.48-1984).

10 9 8 7 6 5 4 3 2 1

Contents

Tables

Acknowledgments

This book is the outcome of many years of work and learning that began in vast and culturally rich Latin America, took shape at Stanford University and in Mexico, and continued later in Canada. Most of all, however, this book is the joint product of a friendship.

We owe a great debt to those who made it possible for us to be what we are today. Yet this book would have been impossible without the love and support of Stephanie and María Cristina. To them, our gratitude.

We wish to acknowledge the support provided by the Department of Educational Foundations, University of Alberta, for preparation of the final draft.

Many thanks also to Manuel Figueroa Unda, our friend and colleague who coauthored Chapter four and contributed vital information. Thanks also to many others for their comments and suggestions: Martin Carnoy, Arnaldo Córdova, Anne Marie Decore, Gilberto Guevara Niebla, Elizabeth Lange-Christensen, Pablo Latapí, Raymundo Martínez, Victor Mlekwa, Juan Millán, Ray Morrow, Carlos Muñoz Izquierdo, Luis Narro, the late Carlos Pereyra, José Angel Pescador, Arturo Sáenz Ferral, Joel Samoff, Sylvia Schmelkes, and Daniel Schugurensky. Naomi Stinson prepared the camera-ready copy with enthusiasm and efficiency that deserve recognition. We thank them for their wisdom. However, responsibility for the final content of the book is ours.

Daniel A. Morales-Gómez
Carlos Alberto Torres
Ottawa and Edmonton, 1990

Introduction: The Politics of Educational Planning in Mexico

This book is a critical analysis of the conflicts and contradictions of educational policy planning in Mexico since the early 1970s. We examine the relationship among the politics of a corporatist State built on the remains of a revolutionary tradition, the current model of associated-dependent development,[1] and the process of policy formation in formal and nonformal education.

The policies implemented during the last two decades by the Mexican State to improve the role, quality, and delivery of education have become entangled in the ongoing sociopolitical and economic crisis. The contradictions that have emerged between policy and practice in education are leading to questions regarding some of the fundamental assumptions of postrevolutionary society. The hegemonic role of the State, supported by a nationalistic revolutionary rhetoric, a unique political party system, and a series of mechanisms to mediate and control social conflicts and participation, has become a fertile ground for the formation of a technocratic-political elite in government capable of controlling major decision making processes. It is this elite group that determines major policy directions. In education, it conditions the process of educational planning and the formulation and implementation of educational policies, programs, and innovations.

Through an analysis of specific cases reflecting the practice of education, we present an overview of key factors intervening in the design, planning, and implementation of educational policies. This in turn leads to a critical discussion of policy outcomes. We discuss the relationship of correspondence and contradiction between State-sponsored education and the educational needs of the model of capitalist dependent development. This leads to an examination of the process of planning in education and the effects of educational change on the poorest sectors of society. The analysis is based on a political economy of education combined with a political sociology of educational policies. The political economy of education treats education as a factor shaped by the power relations between different economic, political and social groups. How much education an individual gets, what education is obtained and the role of education in economic growth and income distribution are part and parcel of these power relations. For political economists, no study of the educational system can be separated from some explicit or implicit analysis of the purpose and functioning of the government sector. (Carnoy, 1985: 157).

A political sociology of education, starting from an explicit theory of the state that would explain the particular organization and functioning of the government sector, will constitute a valuable approach to study educational policies and outcomes.

Why a given policy is created; how it is constructed, planned, and implemented; who are the most relevant actors in its formulation and implementation; what are the impacts of such policies for both specific clienteles and society at large; and what are the key systemic and organizational processes involved in policy formulation are fundamental issues at stake for a political sociology of education (Torres, 1990).

The book does not attempt, however, to address directly the process of educational planning and educational policy making per se, but to examine how the internal dynamics of these processes are reflected in the functioning of the educational system and in educational outcomes

Before discussing some assumptions of planning and its role in policy formation in Mexican education, a question should be addressed: What is the importance of a study of planning and educational outcomes in contemporary Mexico for comparative education purposes? For a number of reasons a reader interested in comparative education may benefit from a study of Mexico's education. First, the symbolism of education in a revolutionary and postrevolutionary state can be clearly perceived and assessed in the texture and dynamics of Mexican education. Second, as long as the educational symbolism is important not only as a key component of the political rhetoric of a capitalist state but also, and above all, as a substantial means for political legitimation and cultural hegemony, the Mexican experience could be quite illuminating. Third, as one of the most successful experiences of dependent development in the periphery, the fiscal commitment of the Mexican state to educational development has been outstanding by any account. A study of contradiction and correspondence of state policies in the midst of a severe social, political, and fiscal crisis could offer several lessons on the results of disparities between growing social demands for education and diminishing fiscal resources. Fourth, the approach used in this book, characterizing the Mexican State as corporatist, provides an interesting avenue for the study of educational bureaucracies and bureaucratic policy encapsulation between compatible state institutions in the world system. That is, this approach allows for a comparative study of educational policy formation in advanced capitalist states (e.g., Scandinavian states) and peripheral capitalist states which have in common a corporatist backdrop. Finally, the peculiar political and geographical position of Mexico (the border of poor, dependent, and underdeveloped Latin America with the United States, one of the most affluent industrially advanced societies in the world) and the role of cultural nationalism and hegemony emerging from the Mexican revolutionary tradition has assigned to education—and cultural policies in general—a specific role in the constitution of the nation, the socialization of the citizenry, and the articulation of the identity of the State. The struggle for defending or altering the ideological role of education in Mexico is also worth observing. A study of conflicts and contradictions in educational planning and outcomes, or the clashes between differential factional educational bureaucracies, will offer invaluable insights in that regard.

Planning Education for Development

The modernization-oriented policies of the Mexican State until the 1970s were key factors influencing the reform of the education system and the expansion of educational services to the school-age and adult populations. Education was seen as a panacea for some of the crucial problems of national development, in particular the preparation of human resources. As in most developing countries, the government in Mexico was convinced of the potential economic benefits of investing in schooling. However, in making the society more modern and better tuned to a changing pattern of capital accumulation, key assumptions were made by politicians and by the technopolitical elite about the "power" of education as a vehicle for economic growth, political modernization, and liberal reforms.

Formal and nonformal education was not only a channel to strengthen the economic infrastructure of the country, but also a means of upward mobility. It assisted the State in its efforts to redefine and change values, attitudes, and sociopolitical behaviors and to influence the collective performance of individuals as producers and citizens. Education was perceived as a mechanism with three broad functions: It was expected to prepare citizens to be capable and willing to function within the framework of Mexico's postrevolutionary democracy; it was also expected to train the professional, entrepreneurial, and technical cadres required for the implementation of the development model and the achievement of particular levels of economic growth. In addition, education was used in the hands of the public sector as a means to accommodate the negotiation among different factions of the bureaucracy within the corporate structure of the State.

Planning education became an integral part of the government's attempts to expand education, to introduce innovations, and to implement literacy and extension programs aimed at facilitating the legitimation of a new strategy for national development. In the minds of politicians and policy makers, planning was both a reliable means to secure the achievement of political objectives and a technique to be applied independently of the contradictions of the dominant political ideology.[2] In practice, however, educational planning was used primarily as a political control mechanism rather than as a policy tool. It allowed the technopolitical elite in government to achieve short-term objectives as well as to rationalize and legitimize decisions, to reinforce or to gain popular support, and to justify strategies and actions aimed at strengthening the position of the ruling party, the *Partido Revolucionario Institucional* or Institutional Revolutionary Party (PRI). The way in which educational planning has been applied is "in many ways, a prime example of a form of legitimization that sustains an existing structure of political authority and power not through normative principles but through a set of procedural conventions" (Weiler, 1985: 394).

Despite evidence indicating that the current widespread socioeconomic and political crisis in Mexico, as in most countries in the Latin American region, will remain unchanged for several years to come,[3] no efforts have been made to integrate this fact into the planning of education or into the process of policy formation. Given the contradictions in educational policies over the last 20 years, education has not even been an effective means to minimize the reverse developmental effects of the crisis that are slowing the rate of growth.[4] One of the consequences of this phenomenon has been a growth in demands to enhance educational services for marginal-urban and rural sectors and to improve the conditions of teachers and schools in the country, particularly in the less developed states.

Educational policies in Mexico before the 1970s were based on two assumptions. First, there was the belief that an effective way to reach stable economic growth was by accommodating educational change to rapid industrialization. Second, it was assumed that the political principles guiding education immediately after the Revolution were still effective in maintaining political cohesion and generating social support. In practice, however, the economic development of the 1950s and 1960s suffered a rapid deterioration. Although industrialization brought about the diversification of the productive structure, it did not reduce external dependence and did not result in self-sustained growth as expected. In fact, like most other countries in the region, Mexico began to suffer increasing problems in its balance of payments, fiscal deficit, unemployment, and inflation. In addition, the postrevolutionary system neglected domestic agriculture which resulted in growing agricultural imports and food dependency by the early 1970s.[5] In a relatively short period of time, the socioeconomic standards of the rural and the urban poor began to worsen in terms of income redistribution, employment, housing, health, nutrition, and general consumption. To minimize the potential for social unrest associated with this situation, the government began to seek alternative solutions to these problems to reduce the sociopolitical pressures on the State.

In the early 1970s, democratic planning and social programming became distinctive features of the role adopted by the State (Suárez Gaona, 1987; Pravda, 1984). Education became instrumental in maintaining an equilibrium among the interests and class alliances necessary to regulate class conflicts. It also played a critical role in minimizing the politically negative effects of economic decisions made to control the symptoms of failure of the model of associated-dependent development. Educational policies were thus directed to areas that have the potential to improve the living conditions of the poor, workers, and peasants, and to restore some of the principles of equity and equality of the Revolution.

The role of the technocratic elite, who saw planning as a means to inject a pragmatic rationale into the development process, was critical in facilitating the changes that took place in the late 1970s and early 1980s. Development planning, including education, operated at a purely technical level and at the service of the political will. Both conceptually and as a social process, it was perceived to involve a double dynamic. On the one hand, planning was an effort to maximize the "formal rationale" of the development process, meaning the optimization of the relationships between the development means and objectives of the State. On the other hand, it was an attempt to increase the "material or substantive rationale" of development, or the relationships between the goals of society defined by the dominant political elite headed by the president and the changes required for their achievement.

The ultimate developmental purpose of educational planning was to bring together these two rationales connecting technical and political factors in the process of public policy formation and implementation. In practice, educational planning for development was a technique for the selection of means in accordance with the norms drawn from the principles of the Constitution. As a technique, that is to say as a series of procedures for political action, planning was seen as neutral: neither good nor bad in an ethical sense, but necessary to consolidate the legitimacy of the State. To be effective in fulfilling the government's objectives for social change, it was required, first, to demonstrate that the goals of the political rhetoric were realistic and attainable with a minimum social cost. Second, it was required to ensure that the means chosen to bring about change were the best available, or at least that they were the most effective to minimize potential social conflicts. Third, planning was expected to prove that the development goals and the political means leading to the implementation of social programs were compatible with the hegemonic character of the State[6] and would not interfere with the process of social reproduction.

Planning and Politics

Educational planning at the formal and nonformal levels had a series of specific tasks mostly political in nature. It was used to reassign human and material resources according to short-term development priorities. A major effort in this direction was the implementation of adult education programs. Thus planning had a central role in the formulation and implementation of intrasectoral policies, in the forecasting of manpower needs, and in the investment and allocation of human capital resources.

Planning was also a means of introducing a rationale, first, into the decision making process of the education sector, increasingly affected by the growth in public expenditures, and second, into the deliberations and negotiations required to deal with the demands from the teachers' union. Public policy formation in education became a priority target for the technical rationale that planning was expected to introduce into the financing of education and in balancing the relationship between public and private recourse to education. Educational planning was also expected to order the development of the system according to the demands of different social groups. National planning at various levels in the system became an important component in the government's attempts to control the development and role of education at the state level, but ineffective in providing long-term strategic directions to educational change. Finally, planning was expected to generate levels of decision making within the system and assist in the allocation of specialized human resources to redistribute power among different sectors of the technopolitical elite struggling for control of the process of educational change.

Unfortunately, in conceptualizing the role of educational planning, little attention was given to three interrelated factors that were to determine the effectiveness of short-term political objectives over the corporate structure of the State. No assessment was made of the existing planning capacity at different levels of government. There are in fact many examples in which the process of policy planning responded first to competing bureaucratic ideologies. In some cases, the planning function was left in the hands of senior bureaucrats with little or no formal training in public educational administration, or to individuals politically reliable but with little experience in specific areas corresponding to their sectors. In most cases, however, planning was the main function of the members of the technopolitical elite. To compensate for their lack of understanding of the role of education in the context of the corporatist State's principles of postrevolutionary Mexico, they adopted a technocratic and bureaucratic view of public policy and administration.

Decisions made in this way had long-term implications. Almost no attention was given to the broader and more complex pattern of social development and governance within which planning was carried out vis-à-vis the variety of demands from different pressure groups in society. The implementation of a system of technocratic planning required a legal, liberal-democratic framework that was absent in the Mexican system because of the predominance of presidentialism, regional corporative interests, patriarchism, and heavy political centralism. Intrasectoral planning thus became the predominant tendency, creating pockets of coordinated actions unconnected to each other.

The third factor was the lack of attention given to the feasibility of planning and to the need for continuity in the implementation of different government programs at the macro and micro levels. In the last three governments, for example, opposite tendencies dominated educational planning. Between 1970 and 1983, the emphasis was on centralization, followed by attempts to decentralize planning and decision making (Pescador and Torres, 1985). In most cases, the experiences in formal schooling, adult education, and nonformal programs have shown that intrasectoral systems were so structured that planning could play no role. Thus political agendas overcame the strategic plans for educational change.

The relationship between educational planning and sociopolitical and economic development during the 1970s and 1980s has been characterized by factors similar to those affecting broader developmental policies within the current political and economic crisis. As the Mexican model of development began to face a crisis of political definition and the government shifted away from liberal reforms, planning focused on operational aspects of educational expansion and delivery. This has brought together efforts to restructure the system in response to financial constraints, without proper consideration of longer-term developmental policies.

The political culture of Mexico, rooted in the remains of a revolutionary tradition, has been dominated by a sense of immediacy and pragmatism in determining the political priorities of each government. Every administration has focused on immediate issues of concern to the political power structure while ignoring the more critical problems affecting the broader social system. Educational planning has reflected the contradictions of the governments' political strategies between the "speed" and the "direction" of educational change. The predominant views of planning in public policy formation have lacked the long-term direction necessary to strengthen the input of education in building a sustainable sociopolitical and economic process. These have been determined by political agendas seeking rapid modernization and control over social mobilization as a means of reducing the gap between social classes. However, the expansion of formal and nonformal education has been undertaken without a strong resource base to sustain, over the long term, the improvement of educational quality, the consolidation of more egalitarian educational opportunities, or to manage and control school failure and its effects. Education continues to be of questionable quality in preparing individuals to enter the labor market. And the formal system continues to exclude a large proportion of students.

Educational planning in Mexico has thus been a means to reach the global political objectives of the corporatist State. However, it has been divorced from a more comprehensive development strategy. This has become more predominant at a time when the society is involved in a painful process redefining its basic social projects through restructuring the economy and the formation of political and class alliances to support the current model of development and establish mechanisms to maintain political stability. In practice, planning in education has not been instrumental in building a more socially effective or participatory system for decision making, or in formulating a more precise definition of the role of education in relation to the type of society the State is trying to achieve.

The expansion of educational services and the government's interest in responding to political clienteles are still central concerns of policy makers. They seek to build a bridge between the conditions of inequalities of capitalist industrialization and the government's objectives of social and economic modernization. Expansion of primary schooling and attempts to make basic education more readily available to a larger number of children and adults have been in response to widespread pressures to overcome social inequality and to the need to reach wider sectors of the population representing sources of potential social instability.

Ideologically, the changes in education have been used as a means to achieve political stability by pursuing goals of social equality, equity, and mobility. Formal and nonformal education have served to achieve short-term political objectives by responding to demands from sectors representing higher potential for social unrest and a threat to the hegemonic structure of the State. Education in all forms and at all levels has developed into a channel that allows the government to mediate conflicts in civil society, to recover political stability, and to consolidate a new approach to deal with development problems.

The evidence available after several years of these attempts shows that these efforts have not been as successful as expected. Objectives such as universal education and literacy, the possibility of reaching a more balanced pattern of expenditures among different levels of the system, and attempts to make education more relevant to the world of work have not been fully achieved. The policies implemented over the last two decades have failed to make the educational system more egalitarian in the distribution of knowledge, less discriminatory among social classes, more instrumental in creating the new scientific and technological cadres, or more efficient in performing the developmental functions that educational planners and educational policy makers had in mind. A clear indication of this situation is found in comparing educational expenditures and the actual changes in the conditions of equality of educational opportunities.

Although over the years a larger number of children have been able to access basic primary education, more adults have gone through literacy programs, more teachers with lower- and middle-class backgrounds have been trained to serve the growing number of students, and more textbooks and educational materials have been produced and made available to students free of charge, there is a wide gap in terms of equity and quality of education. The high rates of educational wastage among low-income children still affecting the system show that most of these changes have benefited middle- and upper-class sectors. Given the political and economic crisis building over the last three administrations, the changes in education have not been sufficient to strengthen the sociopolitical and economic infrastructure or to sustain the process of associated-dependent development and economic growth.

Planning and Legitimation

In a country such as Mexico, characterized by deep class differences, strong ethnic and cultural traditions, and profound inequalities in the distribution of wealth and power, education planned for the modernization of the society has contributed to increased social and economic differences.[7] Structural unemployment and underemployment, critical poverty, growing differences in productivity and income, and an asymmetrical structure in the distribution of political power and in social participation have become even more critical.

In planning education the State has failed to design, guide, and evaluate the processes of educational reform and innovations required to build a self-sustained development model. The theory, techniques, and instruments of planning used by the technopolitical elite in government have been poorly adapted to the conditions and circumstances where educational planning has been applied. At the theoretical level, the efforts to plan education have been framed in a technocratic rationale of neoclassical economic efficiency. In such a context, the short-term relationships between costs and benefits have provided the determinant criteria for policy decisions. Little effort has been made to create a balance between the urgency to solve immediate problems and the need to look at medium- and long-term challenges. Educational planning has not paid enough attention to the conditions of uncertainty prevailing in the country as a result of the breakdown of the development model of the 1960s. The technopolitical elite have ignored two central traits of the decision making practice in class societies. First, public policies in education in such a context often do not go beyond the primary stimulus resulting from needs for higher political effectiveness. In practice, they do not necessarily constitute a response to the demands for education that exist in the society at any one time. Second, the relationships between supply and demand for education in societies with structurally dependent economies are not regulated by a technocratic logic of natural equilibrium.

Little attention has been paid to another aspect of the process of policy formulation. The State in societies like Mexico is constantly seeking means to legitimize its role. This is due, on the one hand, to the permanent conditions of potential political instability resulting from the contradictions between a hegemonic political role of the government and the social demands created by a formal liberal democracy. On the other hand, this results from the incapacity to implement consistent economic policies that could favor the majority. In the case of education, the formulation and implementation of policies often respond to immediate political objectives rather than to the technical option that planners may find viable to solve existing social problems.

Educational planning under these circumstances has provided the technopolitical elite with a vehicle to legitimate political positions and maintain conditions of hegemonic ideological control. This has been essential to regulate the functioning of education, mediate conflicts within the bureaucratic structure of the education system, and maintain control over the political directions implemented in education at the state and federal levels. Educational planning has also served as a means to justify technically sound decisions to implement innovations and accommodate the educational system to changes in the economic and political structure. It has failed, however, in assisting the society to develop a flexible infrastructure and to build a system of education that could rapidly adapt itself to the changing environment of Mexico in the 1980s.

The nature of the processes of public policy and decision making in Mexico leads to arguments that educational planning, in the ways conceived and applied by the technocratic elite, has been understood as a political end in itself. A result of this phenomenon is that education tends primarily to generate political rather than human capital (McGinn and Street, 1984: 323-37). Planning has been used as a tool by which rationale results from a mechanistic problem-solving approach to social and economic conflicts. Policy makers have ignored the fact that a purely technical assessment of the crisis affecting the country is insufficient to deal with the relations of correspondence and contradiction of interests between social classes. The processes of planning and policy formation and implementation in education have thus been reduced to play a reproductive role as *organic* technical tools (Livingstone, 1976).

The logic guiding educational planning as a technique, and its use in the context of the Mexican political structure, has been primarily used to direct the evolution and role of education according to the dominant ideas of the political elite in power. The following chapters address this issue by arguing that the primary purpose of educational change, both at the formal and nonformal levels, has been to serve as an instrument of the State. Education has been an instrument to give homogeneity to the broader decisions determining the economic and political practice of the power structure controlling the State.

The Plan of This Book

This book is divided into two parts. Part one outlines a theoretical and historical framework that helps to situate the evolution of education in Mexico in relation to the changes in its political and economic structures. Part two shows how specific examples of educational policy implementation, or the lack of it, give place to specific modalities of educational practice both within the formal education system and in nonformal education.

The three case studies presented in part two reflect our broader research agenda. For any study of educational inequality, a comparison and contrast of the modus operandi of different schools catering to different social classes is relevant. With the strong drive in Mexico toward educational expansion, improving the equality of educational opportunities since the 1970s, to know the differential impact of schooling on social classes constitutes a central issue for a political economy approach. Similarly, the new role that nonformal education played in educational State policies since the early 1980s warranted a study of policy formation in this area. Unfortunately, policy studies in nonformal education are usually neglected, and this book attempts modestly to fill a gap in this regard. A study of workers' education allows for an exploration of outcomes of educational policies not immediately related to schooling. Eventually, a study of producer cooperatives may show the limits of social reproduction and state control.

The narrative thread of the book, drawing from the relationships between educational policies, political legitimation, and cultural hegemony in the context of the complex social, normative, and bureaucratic practices of the Mexican State, attempts to show the political and educational stories of Mexico: stories that cannot be understood without each other. On the one hand, the literature of politics is rarely informed by analysis of one of the most expensive, sensitive, and politically crucial areas of welfare policies: education. On the other hand, the literature of educational policy rarely draws upon the literature of politics in the study of specific cases. More often than not, policy studies in education are normative or prescriptive in character, evaluative in purpose, or simply descriptive at best of policy processes and outcomes. The attempt to bring together political theory into empirical analysis rather than grand theorizing is rarely done. Perhaps it is so because it is rather difficult to establish the exact connection between historical-structural analysis, empirical, survey-gathered data, aggregate, macro-statistical second-hand information, and middle-range political theorizing. We hope that confining most of the historical-structural analysis to part one will illuminate the empirical information, observations, and analysis presented in part two.

The first chapter of this book analyzes some of the political-economic factors that have historically determined the current process of associate-dependent development in Mexico and the way in which they have evolved and shaped the role of education in the country. It discusses the relationships between the process of economic development and educational change since the pre-revolutionary period to the present. Chapter two analyzes the process of sociopolitical change underlying the formation of the corporatist State. It reviews the process of political development, the relations of correspondence and contradiction resulting from the hegemonic role of the State, and the ways in which educational policies and practices are affected. Chapter three critically reviews the structure and functioning of the educational system in Mexico. Particular attention is given to the role of the technopolitical elite managing the system and the factors affecting its efficiency as well as the process of policy planning in education.

The fourth, fifth, and sixth chapters look at specific case studies of formal and nonformal education in Mexico as illustrations of the relationships among the predominant ideas shaping current development in the country, the process of policy formation in education, and the actual practice of formal and nonformal education. Chapter four presents the case of primary education as a manifestation of the contradictions in educational policy. It examines the reproductive role of formal primary schools in relation to the sociocultural traits of the groups receiving educational services. Chapter five focuses on some of the nonformal initiatives carried out by the government over the last two decades and discusses the process of planning and implementation of the major adult education programs directed to serve the more disadvantaged sectors of the population. It also addresses the conflicts that emerge within the State's institutional structure in the implementation of adult education policies. Chapter six goes beyond the features of the processes of educational innovations and change initiated by the government. It discusses the correspondence and contradiction between the educational principles that, according to the government, permeate the policies of the State and the practice of educating adults in the workplace. The Conclusion offers a summary of the book's theoretical arguments and some empirical findings; shows the relationships between planning, educational policies, and compensatory legitimation; and in closing explores four possible scenarios for the future.

NOTES

1. The notion of associated-dependent development was coined by Fernando H. Cardoso referring to the Brazilian model of development implemented after the 1964 military coup (Cardoso, 1974; 1975). Later, it has been used to refer to the model of development prevailing in the most industrialized countries in the region including Argentina, Colombia, Peru, Mexico, and Venezuela (Bambirra, 1976). Cardoso has argued that:

> The thesis I would like to advance . . . emphasizes that the new character of dependency—after the internationalization of the internal markets and the new international division of labor that allow for the industrialization of the peripheral economies—does not conflict with the economic development of dependent economies . . . Thus, I believe that there exists simultaneously a process of dependency and capitalist development. If this is true, the class relationships and the political process should be conceived in a very different form than they had been . . . The beneficiaries of this dependent development in principle are different than those of the theory of development of underdevelopment assumes. These are now state enterprises, the multinational corporations, and the local enterprises associated to both. These social agents constitute what I have termed in other opportunities the "triplet" of associated dependent development. (Cardoso, 1975: 112-113)

The key themes of this reconceptualization are a criticism of some "new mistaken thesis on dependency and imperialism in Latin America" (Cardoso, 1974: 5), including the thesis that capitalist development in the periphery is not viable, the thesis that dependent capitalism is exclusively based on the extensive exploitation of the labor force, the thesis that local bourgeoisies are no longer an active force, and finally the thesis that the penetration of multinational enterprises in Latin America has forced the nation-state to follow an expansionist policy regarding exports. Many scholars agree with Cardoso's views, including Hamilton (1975), Stepan (1978), and O'Donnell (1976; 1977).

In Mexico, the notion of a dependent-development model needs some qualification. Mexico is an oil producing country, and its proximity with the United States allows for tourism and oil revenue levels that can hardly be compared with other Latin American states. Similarly, the presence of inclusionary corporatist structures since the mid-1930s, and the revolutionary ideology of the State (Stepan, 1978: 73-89) pose difficult dilemmas for analyzing the development model. Finally, the external debt crisis, and the resulting capital flight after 1982, and negative rates of economic growth, modify, although they do not essentially alter, the capitalist associated-dependent development model.

2. This perception of planning was to some extent the result of a long tradition in the Latin American region. Jorge Ahumada, former member of the IMF and Director of the Economic Development Division of the Economic Commission for Latin America (ECLA), argued that "a planner cannot determine by himself social objectives. He always works for an economic system, for a form of social organization and for a political structure. Planning thus has a purely technical character, neutral, and it cannot be considered as attached to a given political, economic or social system" (1972: 4).

3. Norberto González, the Executive Secretary of the ECLA, indicated in his opening remarks to the International Colloquium on new Direction for Development Planning in Market Economies that "we are currently experiencing the most severe and prolonged crisis of the last fifty years, which has forced us to undertake a thorough reassessment of many of our long-standing assumptions concerning development. This reassessment covers both long-term development strategies and short-term economic policies on the one hand, and the role of the economic agents and the manner in which they operate, on the other" (González, 1987: 9).

4. The problems of the "crisis" affecting Latin American countries in the 1980s have been profusely discussed from the point of view of its economic implications associated with the external debt problem (Wionczek, 1985; Foxley, 1983). For an analysis of the effects of the crisis on the social sciences, see D. Morales-Gómez (1986b: 60-66).

5. The real GNP growth rates for the periods 1940-54, 1955-61, 1962-70, and 1971-77 are 5.8%, 6.0%, 7.6%, and 4.9% respectively, while the rates of growth of agriculture in the same periods are 7.1%, 1.9%, 3.4%, and –0.5% respectively. Obviously, a model that favored the urban industrial interest deeply affected domestic rates of agricultural production which eventually became negative. In fact, agricultural production between 1955 and 1977 grew less rapidly than population growth, and food had to be supplied from imports. In short, after the mid-1950s, Mexico moved from being a net agricultural exporter to a net agricultural importer.

6. Until the seminal work of Antonio Gramsci became widely available and a source of theoretical and political debate within Marxist scholarship and politics, "Marxism as a theory of domination remained poorly worked out" (Miliband, 1977: 43). The notion of hegemony, in its traditional meaning in political science, refers to the Latin term derived from the Greek which means "supreme direction," that is, the exercise of political power of the State regarding other states or political communities (Belligni, 1981: 774). The Marxist use of the concept has in Lenin—whom Gramsci considered the theoretician of hegemony (Bobbio, 1977: 167)—one of the first attempts to apply the term to political struggle. For Lenin and Soviet Marxism, as well as for Gramsci in his early writings of 1926, hegemony refers to the ability of achieving political direction in a society, usually emphasizing the conquest of political power and the role of physical force and domination in politics (Belligni, 1981: 775). A second notion emerges in Gramsci's writings compiled in his *Note sul Machiavelli, sulla politica e sullo stato moderno* (1949). The concept of hegemony in these later writings acquires a more extensive use, encompassing not only political direction but also cultural direction in society, a direction that includes intellectual and cultural reform. Hegemony in Gramsci's view is related to a world view pervasive of citizens' consciousness; a world view not as an individual fact, but as the expression of the community life of a social group; a world view, finally, that expresses itself as "common sense" which is related to, and results from, social practices (Carnoy, 1984; Torres, 1985). As cultural, moral, and intellectual direction, hegemony refers to a complex set of alliances between the dominant classes—in the historical bloc—which is at the same time

expressed in the State, and a way of life that rests on organic ideologies—in which the ideologies of the dominant classes have tremendous influence—that creates a system of values and creeds which contributes one way or another to reinforce the legitimacy of the established order and eventually further the interests of the dominant class (Gramsci, 1967). The structuralist reading of Gramsci, that of Althusser, but especially Poulantzas, speaks of hegemony as (a) the power of a class or faction within the bloc-in-power; (b) how this class or faction constitutes and articulates its interests over other classes; and (c) how it is able to articulate its corporative-economic interests as representing the political interests of the other social classes (Belligni, 1981: 774).

If the State is neither conceived as a neutral arena in which the conflicts of different political and economic groups unfold, nor as an instrument manipulated at will by the dominant class, the notion of a relative autonomy of the state, or the potential autonomy of the state (Skocpol, 1984: 53-66), becomes a central landmark in critical political theory. This notion of relative autonomy from the social classes helps explain how the capitalist states may use long-term planning to synthesize the goals of economic reproduction of capitalism as a system despite the short-term needs and disputes of individual capitalists. It also helps explain how as a macrostructure, the State—and the State personnel—may use the resources of society to create and support its coactive and administrative institutions, and eventually may compete, to a point, with the dominant classes in the allocation of societal resources. Finally, it may help understanding of how the State may develop policies and programs that, using fiscal resources, may promote interests which contradict those of the dominant classes (Skocpol, 1984: 62). It is in this sense that states can have a "high" relative autonomy from the social classes and indeed can develop hegemonic (i.e., intellectual, cultural, and moral direction) in the overall polity. The Mexican State has been for decades a good example of "high" relative autonomy based on the legitimacy of the Revolution and the peculiar organization of production and administration through corporatist arrangements (Torres, 1989). In many respects, this analysis will coincide with Stepan's claim on the ideological hegemony of the State in Mexico: "Hegemony exists in Mexico. Rule is not primarily a function of the domination of civil society by the state. Nonetheless, this hegemony itself is partially achieved by the selective use of the coercive apparatus of the state" (Stepan, 1978: 98). Similar or parallel perspectives on the Mexican State have been advanced by a number of Mexican scholars, including, for instance, Saldívar (1980), Córdova (1979), Paoli Bolio (1982: 57-78), and González Casanova (1981).

7. In 1980, ten states allocated between 7 and 20 percent of their budget to education; sixteen states allocated between 21 and 39 percent, and five states allocated between 40 and 56.6 percent. In 1976, the 2,377 municipalities in Mexico received only 1.6 percent of the total federal tax revenue for education, of which only 350 received the larger proportion of these funds (*El Nacional*, May 30, 1983).

Part I An Historical-Structural Approach to Development, Politics, and Education in Mexico

1 Socioeconomic Development Trends and Education in Mexico

INTRODUCTION

Compared with most countries in Latin America, Mexico's model of socio-economic development presents unique political characteristics. Over the years, these have directly influenced not only the trends of economic growth and the modernization strategies of the society, but also the evolution and role of education. Historically, education in Mexico has been a central factor in the reproduction of the ruling elite's control of the corporatist organization of the State. Ideologically, education has been a means to develop a sense of nation-state among a culturally and economically diverse population[1] and to counteract the social contradictions resulting from a pattern of associated-dependent development based on regressive policies of income distribution.[2] Education has also been instrumental in the process of socioeconomic modernization facilitating the reproduction of a capitalist model of unequal development at the local level (Evans, 1979; Amin, 1974). In making education a basic component of development and a key channel for the reproduction of the values supporting the social structure, the State has been able to give people the illusion of a social system in which the redistribution of power and wealth seems possible for all sectors of the population. In such a context, education is primarily a compensatory instrument of political legitimization (Weiler, 1983) and a means to reduce potential tensions among middle-class sectors that, given their relative position in the social hierarchy, need to be economically and politically mobile (Epstein, 1985: 65).

A society historically affected by deep cultural and economic inequalities, over the past several decades Mexico has followed a path of development substantially different from other countries in the region (Liss, 1984: 205-37). Affected by major political changes, by the hegemonic role of a powerful political and economic postrevolutionary elite, and by deep contradictions between the rhetoric of a "revolutionary tradition" and the praxis of a hegemonic State apparatus, the country has maintained until recently a stable political system and a relatively sustained economic growth despite its structural class conflicts (Wionczek, 1985). In this context, it is possible to argue that the crisis faced by the Mexican State today is not primarily an economic crisis but a crisis of hegemony. It shows the failure of the dominant class to use the political, moral, and intellectual leadership that emerged with the Revolution to develop a new type of society.

To understand how the Mexican development model has influenced the role of education, this chapter discusses some of the contributing factors that have characterized the evolution of the process of associated-dependent socioeconomic development in Mexico. The analysis focuses on the relationships between education and development throughout four major stages of the economic and political evolution of the country: (1) the prerevolutionary period from independence in 1810 to the Porfirio Díaz government in 1876; (2) the Porfirian period from 1877 to 1910; (3) the revolutionary period and the subsequent years of socioeconomic reforms from 1911 to 1940; and (4) the period of political hegemony and economic growth from 1929 to the present.[3]

SOCIOECONOMIC DEVELOPMENT AND EDUCATION: HISTORICAL OVERVIEW

To fully understand how the role of social institutions such as the educational system have been instrumental in the development of Mexico's corporatist State, it is necessary to look at the country's economic and social development in light of factors deeply rooted in the early evolution of the society in the 1800s.

After independence in 1810 and following the 11 years of wars against Spanish dominion, Mexico experienced a long period of deep political instability and economic stagnation. The wars of independence resulted in both the destruction of the colonial economy, based mainly on mining exploitation and agricultural production, and the massive emigration of the wealthy members of the colonial aristocracy to Spain. The economic development of the country at the time was further affected by conflicts against France and the United States that crippled the flow of foreign investment required to build a strong national economy (Cockcroft, 1974: 225-303). The new State faced, in a relatively short period of time, a declining infrastructure for developing domestic markets, a growing inability to implement an efficient fiscal system capable of supporting an integral development plan, and the increasing segmentation of the power structure as a result of the struggle for political hegemony among local *caudillos* (political and/or military bosses; González Casanova, 1965: 32-36; Leal, 1975a: 34-48). The political crisis concomitant with the formation of the new State became manifest by the inability of the ruling elite to create a stable political system. Between 1810 and 1876 more than 50 different governments attempted to control the country (Cosío Villegas, 1965).

Major Trends of the Porfiriato

With Porfirio Díaz in the presidency (1876-80 and 1884-1911), a slow process of growth and stability began to emerge which declined in the 1900s and ended with the Revolution in 1910. Díaz's power came from the support of national and foreign capitalists and from a well-implemented apparatus of political control. Two approaches were central to his government: He ignored those groups without capacity for political action, particularly the Indian and peasant populations, and coopted and/or eliminated individuals or groups that could threaten his government (Hansen, 1971: 190-203). The policies of Díaz responded primarily to the demands of the new urban industrialists closely associated with foreign capital and the large land-owners. The outcome of this strategy was the development of an even stronger group of landowners and the formation of a new military elite fully integrated into the system of domination to avoid armed opposition. In fact, Díaz consolidated his political power by granting state governorships and district political offices to military leaders and regional bosses in exchange for economic support and their commitment to political peace (Tannenbaum, 1966).

The strategy of Díaz, however, was aimed not only at those groups with political power but also at all factions of the society that could represent potential political opposition. The interests of the *mestizo* group were met by responding to their demands for social mobility. The economic interests of the conservative creole sector were to facilitate their alliances with foreign capital (Hamill, 1966). The Catholic Church, the most powerful institution at the time, was also coopted by avoiding the enforcement of postindependence anticlerical reforms and by taking care of the old conservative elite allied to the Church in the control of the countryside. Finally, Díaz also paid attention to the demands of the semieducated sector of the *mestizo* middle class by giving them access to the government bureaucracy, thus securing urban political support. If this period meant growth and stability, the benefits went to a very small sector of the population as a result of an increasing concentration of power and corruption in the political system.[4]

Five main factors characterized the process of socioeconomic development during the Porfirian period: the end of an open political crisis, the development of a relatively strong national industry, the increase of foreign investments with the formation of a foreign-national bourgeoisie, the expansion of internal and external markets with the improvement of the transportation system, and the attempt to implement a more uniform primary education system throughout the country in order to reach national unity (Vaughan, 1982; Vázquez, 1970: 97). Among the main achievements of Díaz were control of the struggles within the government and an end to external conflicts, which then permitted the country to recover foreign assistance. By the end of his government, Díaz had created an attractive system of investment to bring back foreign capital. This allowed his government to develop a stronger infrastructure in areas such as railway construction, mining, industry, and services (Rosenzweig, 1965: 405-54). The construction of the railroad system was the most important aid to foreign investment, large landowners, and the urban industrialists.[5] It facilitated economic integration of national markets in mining and agricultural production and encouraged the export of raw materials. The Porfiriato also contributed to the expansion of national textile and metal industries, giving rise to an industrial sector closely associated with foreign demands and investments (Bulnes, 1952; González Casanova, 1965). Among the major foreign investors during this period, the United States accounted for 38 percent of all foreign investment, England for 29.1 percent, and France for 27.6 percent, all of them in key sectors of the economy. Table 1-1 shows that by 1911 almost all sectors of the economy were under the strong influence of foreign capital.

There is enough evidence, however, to argue that development in this period did not substantially change the socioeconomic conditions of the urban poor and the rural population. Social peace was achieved using intimidation or the force of the federal army and Díaz's *rurales*. The press was tightly censored and corruption at official levels was high. The army was well equipped and better paid, making it an efficient means of repression. In 1900, Díaz was spending one fourth of the national budget on the military establishment. Racism became a stronghold among the intellectuals supporting the regime, particularly against the Indian population.

The concentration of land ownership was another highlight of the Díaz regime. While the *hacienda* system had existed since the first days of the colony, the abuses of the government were now exacerbated as railroad construction pushed land values up. A new land law, enacted in 1883, encouraged foreign colonization of rural Mexico, giving agricultural companies the opportunity to exploit public lands. This marks the beginning of the dispossession of the small landowners and the appropriation of the land by foreign companies or wealthy individuals. Within five years of the land law enactment, land companies had gained possession of over 68 million acres of rural land, and by 1894 one fifth of the total land of Mexico was foreign owned (Meyer and Sherman, 1979: 491). Millions of rural Mexicans were worse off financially than their rural ancestors had been a century before. While daily wages for agricultural workers remained the same during the 19th century, basic food prices went up almost six times from 1800 to 1910.

The development model implemented by Díaz represents the beginning of the process of dependent economic growth characterizing the history of Mexico until the present day. The expansion of the industrial sector responded primarily to the demands for exports, mainly to the United States, thus conditioning expansion and diversification of the national industry. During this period, the production of raw materials for internal consumption grew 2.5 percent and the production of food fell 0.5 percent per year while exports grew 6.5 percent. There was a particularly sharp decline in production of the basic dietary components of the poorer sectors of the population, such as corn and beans, which fell 50 and 70 percent respective-

Table 1-1
Major Investors in Mexico, 1911, by Category of Investment (percentages)

Category of Investment	USA		G. Britain		France		Germany		Others	
	% by Cat. Inv.	% by Source	% by Cat. Inv.	% by Source	% by Cat. Inv.	% by Source	% by Cat. Inv.	% by Source	% by Cat. Inv.	% by Source
Public Debt	11.8	4.7	16.6	8.3	65.8	36.1	-	3.0	5.2	12.1
Banks	20.4	2.6	10.8	1.8	60.2	11.0	7.2	18.3	1.7	3.9
Railroads	47.3	41.3	35.5	40.6	10.3	12.8	1.7	28.4	5.2	12.1
Pub. Services	5.5	1.0	89.1	21.4	4.2	1.1	-	-	1.3	3.0
Mining	61.1	38.6	14.3	11.8	22.0	19.8	-	-	2.7	6.3
Real Estate	41.8	6.3	46.9	9.2	8.2	1.8	3.1	9.0	-	-
Industry	16.0	1.7	8.4	1.1	55.0	7.9	20.6	41.3	-	-
Commerce	7.4	0.7	-	-	65.6	8.8	-	-	27.0	62.6
Petroleum	38.5	3.1	54.8	5.8	6.7	0.7	-	-	-	-
Total as % of Foreign Investment	38.0	-	29.1	-	26.7	-	1.9	-	4.3	-
Total	100		100		100		100		100	

Source: Calculated from Daniel Cosío Villegas, ed., Historia moderna de México, El Porfiriato, Tables 65 and 66, pp. 1154-55.

ly. According to the 1910 Census, 96.6 percent of rural family heads held no land at all; 80 percent of the total population depended on agricultural wages (which fell 15.6 percent between 1877 and 1911), and the land was concentrated in 411,096 landholding farmers and 840 large landowners (Silva Herzog, 1967). Three factors were central in determining the concentration of wealth: the structure of power of the local elites, the radical differences between urban and rural populations, and the industrial distribution of the labor force conditioned by the pattern of allocation of foreign investments (see Table 1-2).

The educational tradition that existed in Mexico when Díaz came to power was the product of an elite system based on educational paradigms imposed by the colonial powers. Changes in education after independence benefited only a small sector of the population, mainly the urban elite. Although attempts were made to introduce more liberal ideas into the education system, emphasizing for example the importance of political modernization, stability, and economic growth, most of them failed and education remained heavily influenced by the Church and the interests of the most conservative sectors of society. A large mass of population remained without access to the school system. Although at the end of the colonial period less than 1 percent of the population was literate, this pattern did not change substantially in the late 1800s.

During the Porfiriato several efforts were made toward implementing the educational reform of the 1860s. This was intended to establish free and compulsory elementary education as part of a system that would be uniform in content and available to the entire population (Vaughan, 1982). Despite these efforts, the main purpose of education was to serve the dominant conservative elite. The poorer sectors of society, particularly Indians, had limited access to schooling and in most cases their education was aimed at securing their religious and political indoctrination. Education was used to achieve the minimum degree of national integration necessary to maintain political control. Schools were assigned the "task of moulding a homogeneous people equipped with values, attitudes and skills appropriate to modernization" (Epstein, 1985: 54). A relevant characteristic of the relationships between education and socioeconomic development in this period, and found in Mexico even today, was the emphasis on designing an educational system that could be instrumental in the predominant economic and political development aims of the government. Growth and modernization were the central targets of the State, even at the expense of maintaining large sectors of the population under conditions of open political and economic inequality.[6]

The Revolutionary Period

With the Revolution of 1910 the three basic components of the development plan of the Porfirian economy (i.e., land tenure, foreign investment, and urban industrialization) went into a deep crisis initiating a new period of

Table 1-2
Distribution of the Population and the Work Force in Mexico, 1895-1977 (percentages)

Population	1895(a) % Total	1895(a) % Work	1910 % Total	1910 % Work	1940 % Total	1940 % Work	1960 % Total	1960 % Work	1977 % Total	1977 % Work
Population										
Total	100		100		100		100		100	
Urban	20.2		20.0		35.1		39.3		55.5	
Rural	79.8		80.0		64.9		60.7		44.5	
Work Force	35.2	100	34.5	100	29.8	100	32.2	100	28.5	100
Sector										
Agricultural	23.6	67.0	23.7	68.3	19.5	65.4	17.4	54.1	9.6	33.6
Industrial	5.5	15.6	5.8	17.2	4.6	15.5	6.1	19.0	7.2	25.2
Services	6.1	17.4	5.0	14.5	5.7	19.1	8.7	26.9	11.7	41.2

Sources: Calculated from (a) Fernando Rosenzweig, "El desarrollo económico de México, 1877 a 1911," Trimestre Económico, 32, (July-September, 1965), pp. 418 and 438; Nacional Financiera, S.A., La economía mexicana en cifras (Mexico, D.F., 1978), Table 1.7, pp. 13-14.

economic and political instability. The overthrow of Díaz in 1910 was led by a heterogeneous coalition of politically progressive sectors from the north reacting against the concentration of political and economic power. The expansion of the revolutionary movement involved a variety of sectors from the middle class, farmers and peasants, miners, and intellectuals. United into different armies, they formed two major groups. The northern group, politically influenced by European ideas and led by Francisco Madero, represented middle-class demands for socioeconomic and political mobility. The south-central group, clearly a peasant movement, was aimed at transforming the existing land tenure system and changing the poverty-stricken conditions of rural people.

The heterogeneous social composition of the movement and the conflicts of interests behind these groups gave rise to deep divergences between the political leaders and between the sectors involved in the movement (Adler Hellman, 1978). Between 1911 and the late 1920s the political environment was characterized by a series of conflicts. The potential impact of the institutional changes at the State level and the creation of a constitution representing the values of the movement were limited by conflicts among new power groups following the conservative or the radical political leaders struggling for control of the government. An outcome of this situation was the growing gap between revolutionary rhetoric and the changes implemented in the society. The new ruling coalition led by Venustiano Carranza, a conservative leader among the revolutionaries (Hansen, 1971; Román, 1973), included representatives of three major forces: an elite of new revolutionary generals, a small elite of capitalists who succeeded immediately after the Revolution, and members of the prerevolutionary landowning oligarchy who joined the movement. The Revolution did not produce radical changes in the class structure of society.[7] The power struggle among the revolutionary leaders diffused the pressure for change, diminished the capacity of the peasant movement to influence the process of sociopolitical change, and did not provide the working class with political equality (Alba, 1967; Silva Herzog, 1967). Despite these facts, the Revolution brought important changes in the social and economic structure of the country. The promulgation of a new liberal Constitution in 1917 created the legal tool with which a process of socioeconomic development led by the State seeking modernization of the country could begin.

An important outcome of the Revolution was the creation of the most important labor legislation anywhere in the world at the time, establishing the right of working-class children to education, defined in article 3 of the Constitution of 1917 as "socialist." Article 123 stated:

> the minimum wages for workers shall be sufficient to satisfy the normal material, social and cultural needs of a head of family and provide for the compulsory education of the children. In every agricultural, commercial, manufacturing and mining enterprise, the workers have the right to share the profits . . . A social security law is considered of public utility, and shall include disability insurance,

life insurance, insurance against unemployment, sickness, accidents and the like. (Adler Hellman, 1978: 20)

Through this legislation, the workers were provided with a set of labor guarantees by which the State became responsible not only for the protection of their basic economic rights, but also for their sociopolitical and cultural well-being. For many, however, although this represented an attempt to put into practice one of the central principles of the Revolution, it was also an example of the deep contradictions characterizing the process of social change at the time. Octavio Paz argues that the socialist character of the Constitution contradicted what in his view is the protection given by the same legislation to private property (1961: 164-71).

A second achievement of the Revolution was legislation leading to changes in the land tenure system and giving the government control over national resources. Article 27 of the Constitution indicates that

the nation shall at all times have the right to establish regulations for the private property which the public interest may dictate, such as those regulating the use of natural resources for conservation purposes or ensuring a more equitable distribution of public wealth. With this end in view, the necessary measures shall be taken to break up the large estates. (Adler Hellman, 1978: 21)

To a large extent, however, this particular effort did not change the conditions of inequality in rural Mexico. Although the *ejido* system[8] represented a major step forward in the implementation of the land reform, the economic structure of society continued to be determined by the power struggle at the political level and by the strong influence of foreign capital (García, 1976).

A third achievement of the Revolution was the creation of conditions for the development of a powerful central government in the 1920s and 1930s under the influence of the northern dynasty. This coalition controlled the demands of several groups attempting to impose their political objectives after the Revolution. Plutarco Elías Calles, a general from the northern state of Sonora, introduced the idea of an official party to integrate the different groups demanding political power. He created the corporative foundation of what has been the Mexican State until today (Cotler, 1979: 269). The National Revolutionary Party (Partido Nacional Revolucionario or PNR), created in 1929, was in fact the predecessor of the Institutional Revolutionary Party (Partido Revolucionario Institucional or PRI) that has been in power for the past 60 years.

A fourth outcome of the Revolution was an attempt to implement a series of progressive changes to modify the concentration of wealth in the hands of a small group of industrialists, foreign capitalists, landowners, and rural bosses controlling more than half of the agricultural land (40 percent was in the hands of foreign owners), and the Catholic Church which owned as much as two fifths of the nation's wealth. However, some of these changes took place over a long period of time and affected the poorer sectors of the population only marginally. Although the Revolution broke up the *hacienda* system to some extent, it did not alter the distribution of wealth in real terms.

A fifth series of changes was related to the role and structure of education in the country. Until 1910, illiteracy affected 84 percent of the total population. Although the largest proportion of illiterates was found in rural areas among the indigenous and peasant groups, in urban areas illiteracy reached half of the adult population (Vázquez, 1970: 107). Acknowledging this situation, the Constitution of 1917 introduced a series of changes. In addition to defining education as "socialist,"[9] the Constitution established that education was free, compulsory, under the control of the State, and secular, thus eliminating the control of the Catholic Church over the schools (Epstein, 1985). One direct outcome of this new legislation was the attempt to decentralize the education system. This was achieved by eliminating the Secretariat of Public Instruction, a central mechanism of political control over education established during the government of Díaz, and transferring control of education to the municipalities, one of the earliest attempts in educational decentralization in the history of Latin America. The Revolution did not succeed, however, in producing radical changes in the content of education, the curricular structures of the schools, or the actual access by the poorer sector of society, particularly the Indian population, to the educational system.

The Revolution was successful in breaking the economic structure that existed before 1910. There is no consensus, however, about its actual success in changing the conditions of economic inequality affecting rural Mexico and the poorer sectors of the urban population. In fact, it was not until later in the 1930s that some of the socioeconomic reforms proposed by the Constitution, including the redistribution of land, began to be implemented. Between 1917 and 1934 the postrevolutionary governments were primarily concerned with the consolidation of political power. Nevertheless, as discussed in the next chapter, some of the changes that took place during this period, particularly under the government of Plutarco Elías Calles, are central to understanding the character of the Mexican State organized on the basis of a broad alliance of classes, with the leadership of a newly emerging elite, and the support of subordinate classes such as workers and peasants.

The Postrevolutionary Period

Socioeconomic development in the postrevolutionary period was adversely affected by three main factors: the economic problems of the State resulting from internal conflicts, pressure from the United States to recover its economic dominance interrupted by the Revolution, and the effects of the world depression (Reynolds, 1974). In the economic sphere, the conflicts between the government and foreign investors came to a peak during the presidency of Lázaro Cárdenas (1934-40). He created strong policies in support of nationalization, labor organization, expropriation of foreign owned industries (such as oil, nationalized in 1938), and the implementation of an agrarian reform that affected one of the most important sources of wealth of the national and foreign bourgeoisie: the land tenure system (Nacional Financiera, 1974: 227). Cárdenas played a major role in the modernization of Mexican society (Brandenburg, 1964). He represented the progressive forces born with the Revolution who wanted to accommodate the demands of peasants and workers. In this context, he emphasized a development process based on heavy government intervention and control of the economy. He also gave special attention to the capacity of the State to control foreign capital and national resources, establish measures to redistribute land, and promote workers' organizations. During his regime, over 49 million acres of land were distributed among rural dwellers, twice the amount since the beginning of Revolution. His government also created financial organisms to support agrarian reform, including the Ejidal Credit Bank to service peasants in the *ejido* system.

Cárdenas, by no means a socialist himself, implemented a series of social and economic reforms seen by the most conservative sectors as an attempt to build a "socialist system" and a threat to national and foreign capital. To deal with this situation, he attempted to consolidate his power by developing a new political coalition to reorganize the PNR in order to give peasants and workers stronger political participation. The reorganization of the PNR led to a four-sector political institution named the Party of the Mexican Revolution (Partido de la Revolución Mexicana or PRM). Peasants were represented as an independent force apart from labor unions. With all sectors having equal participation in making national policy, Cárdenas sought to create a system in which the interests of different social groups would be safeguarded by their elected members and through which his policies of nationalization and land reform could find direct popular support. Although the policies of the Cárdenas government had a more direct impact on peasants and workers, compared with the other regimes that followed the Revolution, the central aim of his strategy was not exclusively oriented to increasing political equality and participation. His government had strong populist overtones and was primarily concerned with creating conditions for social peace, which in turn would allow the country to implement a model of capitalist development with a strong nationalistic base.[10]

Despite the series of economic and political crises affecting Mexico in the late 1920s and the 1930s, the changes that took place under Cárdenas provided the foundations for the socioeconomic development process that began in the 1940s. In addition to the higher profile acquired by peasants and workers in the national scenario, the formation of an integrated national ruling political party, the higher control over national resources, the relative improvement in the standard of living of the poorer sectors of the society, and the consolidation of some of the egalitarian principles of the Constitution of 1917, perhaps one of the major achievements of the Cárdenas period were the changes in education.

Traditionally, one of the most serious problems of Mexican society in terms of the country's long-term development capacity was the disregard governments had toward the abysmal educational inequalities affecting approximately three quarters of the population. Among the major obstacles faced by the postrevolutionary governments were lack of resources to implement changes in education and political disintegration throughout the country. Although the Constitution of 1917 provided Mexico with progressive legislation allowing the State to use education as a central mechanism to develop a more egalitarian social system, the efforts made immediately after the Revolution helped to expand educational services, but not to put into practice the spirit of the new "socialist" education or to integrate the rural and Indian population into the main stream of modern Mexico, an objective that became more a reality under the Cárdenas presidency.

A major effort in making education available to larger sectors of the population was the first literacy campaign initiated in 1921 under the government of Alvaro Obregón.[11] Among its main achievements were the creation of the Secretariat of Public Education, the creation of educational centers to serve the school-aged population in both rural and urban areas, the introduction of meal and health programs for schoolchildren, and the increase in the number of primary school teachers. Between 1924 and 1928, the number of rural schools increased from 1,044 to 4,392, the number of rural teachers rose from 1,105 to 4,445, and the number of students increased from 76,076 to 169,498 (Vázquez, 1970).

Although these efforts constituted the groundwork for building up postrevolutionary education and for the beginning of the new socioeconomic development model of Mexico consolidated in the 1940s and 1950s, it was not until the presidency of Lázaro Cárdenas that the country began to implement a system of socialist education aimed at breaking down the influence of the Church over the schools, developing values to promote equality in the distribution of wealth and labor, and strengthening a sense of national culture that could serve as a basis to build a society with a strong sense of political and economic independence.

Economically, development in the decade of the 1930s stagnated as a result of the 1929 depression in the capitalist world. Despite this situation, Cárdenas deepened the process of socioeconomic reforms in which context education played a major role. The implementation of a socialist system of education did not take place without opposition. Even sectors within the government had difficulties agreeing on the specific characteristics of the new education and on the depth to which socialist values should permeate the system, to the extent that Congress was not able to reach a definition of the meaning of socialist education.[12] This limited considerably the potential strength of educational reform. Based on the Constitution, it was clear that the State had the monopoly on education, and that the principles established in article 3 aimed, ultimately, at the implementation of a system of education at the service of the proletariat. In practice, however, there was a discrepancy between the rhetoric and the willingness of the political elite to actually implement radical changes that would imply a breakdown of the existing capitalist system.

The government was not able to develop a socialist consciousness among teachers. This fact has led some analysts to argue that in reality the route was more or less the same as the one traditionally adopted in Mexico with educational laws: the textbooks were changed, fliers were published about the reform, but the system continued to a large extent teaching the same (Vázquez, 1970: 177).

The Cárdenas period, however, represented a substantial change in the perception of the role of education in both sociopolitical and developmental terms. One indicator of the importance given to education was the increase in government investments in education as a proportion of the total government budget. Between 1930 and 1937, investments in education grew from 11.3 percent to 17.9 percent, keeping to an average of 16 percent during the government of Cárdenas. Once again during this period the creation of new schools, in both rural and urban areas, the multiplication of public libraries, the reduction of the illiteracy rate, and the general improvement of basic services for school-aged children were priority targets for the government. Equally important were some of the changes in the school curriculum, including the introduction of sex education and national history, and the emphasis on the sciences. As a whole, it is possible to argue that, despite the internal contradictions inherent in the process of development during this period, serious attempts were made to transform education into an expression of the values of the "socialist society" that was being developed. The values transmitted by the school system became more focused on the basic principles of the Revolution, making national and educational goals inseparable (Epstein, 1985: 56; Raby, 1974). Cárdenas was instrumental in advancing rural education, promoting a new educational ideology, and developing a system of polytechnical institutions that over the years became central to the training of working adults.

THE MODEL OF INDUSTRIALIZATION AND DEVELOPMENT

Several factors helped facilitate economic development in Mexico during and after the 1920s. These included, among others, the formation of a central political mechanism, the PNR, to mediate and control government stability; the creation of State operated financial institutions, such as the Bank of Mexico (1925) and the Nacional Financiera (1934) to promote investments in long-term activities; the creation of the Agricultural Credit Bank and the Ejidal Bank that played a key role in the process of land reform initiated by Cárdenas; and the nationalization of the oil industry (1938) that was central to the nation's development of the 1970s (Fagen and Nau, 1979: 382-427). Other factors were the expansion of the labor force, a result of changes introduced by the agrarian reform that created conditions for a large number of peasants who depended upon the *hacienda* system to become available to compete in the labor market; the increase in rural migration to urban areas that increased low-cost urban labor supply; and the successful attempts of the national economic elite and foreign capital in obstructing Cárdenas' efforts to apply more radical socioeconomic reforms (Hansen, 1971: 41-69).

During the presidency of Cárdenas, several changes began to take place in the composition of the class structure of Mexico, a phenomenon that had a strong influence over the socioeconomic policies of his government. Because the Revolution did not reduce the gap between upper- and lower-income sectors, the transformations that did occur came mainly as a consequence of changes in the rural and urban composition of the population. The major population growth took place in the three main strata of the urban social structure,[13] which as a whole represented a large increase in the supply of urban labor (see Table 1-3). However, by 1940 the middle rural sector of the population had increased 125.9 percent, while the upper and lower rural sectors decreased 54.3 and 20.8 percent respectively as a result of agrarian reform. This phenomenon did not actually change the pattern of social mobility or the redistribution of wealth. In fact, the agrarian reform resulted in an expanding proletarization of the middle-class and low-income sectors and in the creation of a sector of small landholders who kept control of the *ejidal* system (Stavenhagen, 1975: 146-63). This led Vicente Lombardo Toledano to argue that the *ejido* system had very rapidly become a modern version of the old *hacienda* system and not a form of socialist land reform (Liss, 1984: 223).

In the political arena, the government of Cárdenas also brought about changes affecting the political organization of the popular sectors. Under the leadership of Lombardo Toledano, the labor sector was organized under the Mexican Workers' Confederation (Confederación de Trabajadores de México, CTM), one of the most powerful government-sponsored organizations to which all major unions in the country were affiliated (Raby, 1974). This represented an important step in the process of "incorporation" carried out by the corporatist State. Through this process, major interest groups have been included into the governing process as a means to maintain harmony and avoid conflict (Hansen, 1971; Hamilton, 1982). Under Cárdenas' initiative, the CTM became a giant confederation, heavily dependent on government support, with the mandate of uniting workers to reclaim the rights guaranteed by the Constitution of 1917. However, after Cárdenas left office, the CTM was not able to retain its radical orientation and became more dependent on the dominant politics of the party, increasing its cooperation with the government and big business.[14]

The increasing contradictions between capital and labor that began to appear as a result of the ambiguous role of the CTM and the close association that began to develop between labor leaders and the political elite of the party made the official sector progressively less representative of workers' interests, resulting in the withdrawal of the more militant unions and federations from the CTM. The peasant sector, officially formed in 1935, was organized under a single institution, the National Peasant Confederation (Confederación Nacional Campesina, CNC). It was intended to become a strong group within the party to influence government decisions, aiming to

Table 1-3
Changes in the Composition of the Social Structure in Mexico, 1895 and 1940 (percentages)

Social Stratum	1895				1940				Proportional Change
	% over Total Popul.	% over the Strata	% over Total Urban Popul.	% over Total Rural Popul.	% over Total Popul.	% over the Strata	% over Total Urban Popul.	% over Total Rural Popul.	
Total Population	100	-			100	-			-
Upper	1.4	100	-	-	1.0	100	-	-	-27.1
Urban	.4	27.1	1.9	-	.6	53.9	1.6	-	+46.2
Rural	1.1	72.9	-	1.3	.5	46.1	-	.7	-54.3
Middle	7.8	100	-	-	15.9	100	-	-	+104.0
Urban	6.1	78.4	29.6	-	12.1	76.4	34.5	-	+98.0
Rural	1.7	21.6	-	2.1	3.8	23.6	-	5.8	+125.9
Low	90.8	100	-	-	83.1	100	-	-	-8.5
Urban	14.2	15.4	68.5	-	22.4	27.0	63.9	-	+58.1
Rural	76.6	84.6	-	96.6	60.7	73.0	-	93.5	-20.8

Source: Calculated from José E. Iturriaga, La estructura social y cultural de México. (Mexico, Fondo de Cultura Económica, 1951), pp. 28-30.

protect peasants from landowners dominating rural Mexico and incorporate peasants into the modernization programs of rural zones. However, the peasant sector never became a strong enough force to influence the systems either within the party or in the national arena. All along, its role was marginal and without influence over the process of political decision making of the State. Both the CTM and the CNC, although created to represent workers' and peasants' political and economic interests, in a short period of time became an additional arm of the government to exercise control over those sectors of the population they were expected to represent.

The military was the one sector of society that played a decisive role in Mexican politics until 1941. Following the Revolution most of the regional and national politicians were from the military ranks. The integration of the military as a sector of the official party in 1937 was in practice part of the political strategy of Cárdenas to obtain civilian control over conservative military leaders who threatened the stability of the State. This step brought the military under the direct control of the president, making possible the reorganization of the army and giving him control over a large number of high ranking officers who were acting freely at regional levels. With the military included in the PRM as a "group of responsible citizens and not as a special caste or a deliberating body" (Scott, 1964), they were forced to operate within the official political context, thus diminishing their power independent from the government. This initiative, however, had a relatively short life span. The military as a formal sector of the party ceased to exist in 1941 with the government of Avila Camacho.

The Cárdenas reorganization of the political system also gave place to the formation of the popular sector. This served as a means to give institutional character to a channel of participation for those groups not included in the other sectors of the party. In fact, the popular sector was a setting within the PRM for the political participation of middle-class people: professionals, business associations, mid-sized and large landowners, and workers. In 1943 the National Confederation of Popular Organizations (Confederación Nacional de Organizaciones Populares, CNOP) became a heterogeneous conglomerate of social groups. However, this sector did not have an institutional body of legislation to regulate its operations like the peasant and labor sectors, and therefore was more independent from government control. In the last 40 years this sector has become a channel through which industrialists and the educated professional elite participate in politics. To a large extent, this is the most influential section within the party, with access to important political offices and with power disproportional to its economic importance (González Casanova, 1970).

After 1940, with the administration of Avila Camacho, the Mexican economy began to display one of the highest rates of growth in Latin America. After Cárdenas, the Mexican government began to implement a plan of direct public investment in industrial infrastructure by applying a "bottleneck-breaking" policy covering those areas in which private capitalists were unwilling to invest. Following the 1940s the public sector accounted for over 30 percent of all fixed capital formation, and almost half of the public investment was channeled to areas such as irrigation, transportation including railroad and railway construction, and the steel and electric power industries. For some indicators of capital formation, see Table 1-4.

Over a period of approximately 35 years, the GNP grew at an annual rate of 6.4 percent, although the annual average population increase was 2.8 percent from 1940-50 and 3.5 percent in the 1970s. Economic growth before 1973 was the result of a combination of several mechanisms applied by the government to promote the expansion of national industry and to facilitate foreign investment, including specific policies to protect savings and public and private investments (Adler Hellman, 1978: 58). Private investment was favored through taxation policies on both interest earned from investments and profits from production (United States Government, 1969: 62). Taxes tended to be regressive in such a way that no substantial differences were observed from their effect over both extremes of the income continuum.

In 1941 several policies began to be implemented by which new industries and those considered to be essential for national development received preferential treatment in all major forms of taxation, including exemption from duty on imported raw materials and machinery. During the governments of Avila Camacho (1940-46) and Miguel Alemán (1946-52), new policies on investment were applied to protect national capital. Two mechanisms were used for this purpose: a system of tariff protection on domestic investment in import-substitution enterprises and import licensing to control imports. One of the results of these efforts was that the country began to regain access to international capital markets, which facilitated the process of economic growth (Zedillo Ponce de León, 1985). In a short time, however, the nationalistic economic approach encouraged by previous governments began to disappear. A new model of economic development, heavily dependent on industrialization and capital-intensive technology, with the large multinational corporations playing a central role began to emerge.

In this context, education during the late 1940s and early 1950s began to reflect the trends of the model of economic and political development. Educational changes and innovations were directed to incorporate larger sectors of the rural population into the school system. Three main changes took place during this period: Education for the rural masses became closer in its content to that delivered in large urban centers; a literacy campaign became a major concern for the government seeking to modernize large sectors of the rural population; and the overall expenditures in education grew from $74 to $208 million in a period of six years (Epstein, 1985: 56).

This represented a major shift in the emphasis given to education as a factor in the development of the human resources required to implement the new pattern of economic growth implemented between the 1950s and the early 1970s by which the Mexican economy began its full integration into the new international division of labor.

Table 1-4
Distribution of Gross Public Capital Formation in Mexico, 1935 to 1975 (percentages)

Years	Agriculture		Industry		Transportation and Communications		Social and Welfare		Acministr. and Defense		Total
	%	Change	%	Change	%	Change	%	Change	%	Change	
1935-40	17.7	-6.2	7.4	+37.8	64.9	-7.7	9.6	+19.8	*	*	100
1941-45	16.6	+24.1	10.2	+115.7	59.9	-26.7	11.5	+4.3	1.8	-16.7	100
1946-50	20.6	-19.9	22.0	+37.7	43.9	-14.1	12.0	+2.5	1.5	+113.3	100
1951-55	16.5	-30.3	30.3	+18.2	37.7	-11.9	12.3	+43.9	3.2	-43.8	100
1956-60	11.5	-10.4	35.8	+9.2	33.2	-29.8	17.7	+37.9	1.8	+61.1	100
1961-65	10.3	+8.7	39.1	+1.3	23.3	-7.3	24.4	+5.3	2.9	-34.5	100
1966-70	11.2	+45.5	39.6	-5.1	21.6	+5.1	25.7	-17.5	1.9	+15.8	100
1971-75	16.3		37.6		22.7		21.2		2.2		100

Source: Calculated from Nacional Financiera, La economía mexicana en cifras, (Mexico, D.F., 1978). Table 6.31, pp. 368-373.
*Data not available.

ECONOMIC GROWTH AND ASSOCIATED-DEPENDENT DEVELOPMENT

The economic growth that began in the 1950s marks a period of consolidation in the integration of Mexico as an associated partner in the industrial system of hegemonic countries. Over more than two decades, Mexico had strengthened its urban industrial sector, generated a dynamic of modernization heavily dependent on the international economic system, and begun a process of capital accumulation that provided opportunities of social mobility to the middle sectors of society. However, the process of growth over these years was not able to create the conditions of industrial and technological independence required to overcome its structural dependent character.

Economic development in the late 1950s was characterized by an increasing internationalization of the economy. Between 1955 and 1965 new direct foreign investments increased by 29.6 percent, and the total net foreign income on investment grew by 195.1 percent (Cockcroft, 1974: 227). By 1974, United States investments accounted for an average of 78.8 percent over total foreign investments. Foreign investments increased in almost all key areas of the economy including agriculture (66.7%), mining (53.4%), petroleum (43.9%), industry (55.3%), commerce (29.3%), transportation (41.2%), and electricity (3.2%) (Nacional Financiera, 1974: 403-404). By 1970, 89 percent of all United States investments were concentrated in the most dynamic sectors of the economy, manufacturing, and commerce (Delli Sante, 1979: 357). In addition, to protect and facilitate private investment, a policy of devaluation of the peso was also applied. This device was used in conjunction with an inflationary policy of financing debts of public sector expenditures rather than through direct taxation, thus negatively affecting real wages and annual price increases. Between 1961 and 1970 the gross domestic investment as a percentage of the gross domestic product (GDP) was 20.5 percent, while the gross national saving was only 16.5 percent. This situation remained relatively unchanged during 1971-75 with the gross domestic investment reaching 21.9 percent of the GDP and the gross national saving 18.0 percent. The relationship between savings and investment as a percentage of the gross domestic investment for these two periods was 89.7 and 82.6 percent respectively. Table 1-5 shows some general economic indicators.

The effects of the dependent character of the development approach being followed became evident in the evolution of the Mexican economy after the late 1950s. Between 1960 and 1976 the economy grew at an average rate of 6 percent annually, one of the highest in the region. Employment, however, grew only 2.3 percent per year, although the rate of growth of the labor force was 3.4 percent. Economic development during this period took place within apparently conflicting tendencies. These included both an attempt to reduce foreign control over the national economy, following the rhetoric of the revolutionary tradition in nationalist sectors of the party, and a developmental approach held by policy makers and the economic elite who operated on the assumption that without foreign capital it was not possible to achieve

Table 1-5

General Economic Indicators in Mexico, 1960-1980 (percentages)

Indicator	1960-70	1970-75	1975-80
Gross Domestic Product (GDP)	90.1	31.6	31.2
Total Consumption	91.8	34.5	24.3
Gross Domestic Investment	137.9	39.7	49.7
Service Payments on External Public Debt	230.0	130.2	649.4

Source: Elaborated with data from ECLA Economic Survey of Latin America and the Caribbean, 1984. Santiago: Economic Commission for Latin America and the Caribbean, 1985.

accelerated growth. Foreign investment, however, has been recognized as acting against the possibilities of opening new sources of employment. In fact, the labor-intensive technology introduced in key sectors of the national industry by foreign investments until 1970 had generated only 3 percent of employment, while it represented approximately 15 percent of national production.

Legally Mexico has distinguished among various types of ownership of industries and national resources as a means to regulate access of private and foreign capital into key sectors of the economy (Adler Hellman, 1978: 60-61). Perhaps the best example of these policies was the nationalization of the banking system in 1982. All these policies, however, have been contradictory in their actual implementation. In practice it is the president and his closest associates who decide what restrictions may be applied and to whom. It is precisely this margin of freedom in the hands of the political elite that provides the opportunity for foreign capital to use different means of cooptation to obtain political consent for investing in the country, a situation that became particularly evident during the government of López Portillo (Adler Hellman, 1978: 95-129; Delli Sante, 1979: 337-81; Zedillo Ponce de León, 1985).

The outcomes of these development policies have had a differential impact on the capacity of the national economy to create a solid basis for a sustained process of economic growth and for redistribution of wealth. Although these policies stimulated national and foreign private sectors to provide funds for capital formation, the emphasis on capital intensive production, requiring the import of advanced technology, contributed to a rapid increase of the national external debt and heavily affected the balance of trade as well as the unemployment situation, bringing the development process into a sharp decline.[15] Cotler argues in this regard that after more than thirty years of stability, Mexico began to suffer from the economic problem of other Latin American countries: balance of payments difficulties, fiscal deficits, and inflation, which, along with the nationalist rhetoric, led to a sharp reduction in foreign investment. All of this led to a profound crisis, so profound that at the end of 1976 Mexico faced the unprecedented situation of experiencing a spectacular run on bank deposits, an explicit threat of a coup, and a currency devaluation of nearly 100 percent. (1979: 271-72)

In fact, the cost of the heavy dependence created during this period of growth on foreign capital which led to overvalued exchange rates, runaway inflation, and low return to capital, had crippling effects on the national economy, particularly on the debt burden of the country.

Between 1954 and 1972, the net flow of the foreign public debt averaged US $218.7 million a year. It increased to something more than US $1.6 billion in 1973 alone and kept growing in subsequent years. As a consequence, the stock of the foreign public debt, which amounted to US $6.8 billion at the end of 1972, increased to almost US $21 billion by the time the Echeverría administration was over (1976) and to US $58.1 billion when López Portillo left office. (Zedillo Ponce de León, 1985: 294)

The decline in the real growth of the GDP from 8.5 in the early 1970s to 4.2 percent in 1976, brought concerns about the development policies implemented in the previous two decades. Little was done, however, to produce a radical change. Inflation rose from 5.3 to 15.8 percent between 1971 and 1976; the disequilibrium between the financial and current account became more noticeable; domestic expenditures increased to compensate for the decrease in external demand; and the overall economy became more vulnerable to the crisis in the international economic system. By the end of the Echeverría government, the net flow of the foreign public debt averaged 5.4 percent of the GDP compared to only 1 percent between 1970-72. The ratio of net flow to current account income grew from 13.6 percent in 1970 to 62.1 percent in 1976.

The year 1973, however, marked the beginning of the deep crisis of the Mexican development model. The survival capacity of the economy was characterized by massive public external borrowing, resulting in the increase of foreign public debt from $6.2 billion in 1970 to $20.8 billion in 1976. Interest payments over the same period grew from $0.2 to $1.3 billion. Between 1970 and 1976, the real GDP growth fluctuated from 4.2 percent in 1971 to 8.4 percent in 1973, back to 4.2 percent in 1976, while inflation grew from 5.3 percent in 1971 to 15.8 percent in 1976. When López Portillo came to power in 1977, the Mexican model of development was facing one of its worst crises in history. The real GDP growth was 3.4 percent and inflation was at 27.2 percent. The period that followed was characterized by a series of severe measures to bring the economy to a relative equilibrium. These efforts partially succeeded for a few years. The GDP grew to 9.2 percent in 1979, and public investment grew from –6.0 to 17.8 percent over the same period.[16] The bonanza, however, was transitory. By 1980 the GDP began to decline once again, reaching a negative growth of –0.5 percent by 1982 at the end of the López Portillo period. In 1982, inflation had reached an average of 58.9 percent, and the nominal exchange rate had moved from 22.7 pesos per US dollar in 1977 to 122.5 in 1982.

> When President López Portillo left office on December 1, 1982, the Mexican economy was experiencing a crisis even more profound than the one registered six years earlier—something inconceivable for a country that had earned US $47 billion in oil revenues and had gone through a rapid process of capital formation during the previous five years. (Zedillo Ponce de León, 1985: 317)

At the beginning of the 1980s Mexico's total external debt was $72 billion, reaching $85 billion by 1983, and $97.3 billion by 1985, the second largest in Latin America and the second largest in the world among key debtor countries with debt-servicing problems (World Bank, 1986: 208-213; ECLA, 1985). The crisis affecting Mexico in the first half of the 1980s is summarized by the World Bank:

> while the cumulative decline of Mexican per capita GDP between 1980 and 1985 has been a relatively modest 3.6 percent (much less than in many other countries of the region), the devastating extent of the recession can be amply seen elsewhere. Between 1981 and 1985, for instance, manufacturing employment declined by 7 percent, and average real wages fell by 28 percent. For those individuals who lost their jobs, the duration of their unemployment has increased; the percentage of the unemployed looking for work in Mexico City for more than nine weeks tripled between the end of 1982 and mid 1985. Reflecting such circumstances, social discontent and emigration have increased. At the same time, Mexico's ability to grow has been undermined by successive reductions in investment; gross capital formation for plant and equipment in 1984 was less than half that of 1981. (1986: 113)

In terms of income distribution, 1.3 percent of the top income bracket owned 40.6 percent of the national wealth, while the 30 percent of the low income families received only 6 percent of the national income, showing that the economic crisis had not affected the richest sector of the society. In mid-1983 the per capita debt was $1,193 US while the gross domestic product per capita was approximately $1,534 US. In the spring of 1987, the World Bank reported that open unemployment had gone up from 2.7 million in 1981 to 4.6 million in 1984, and that in 1982 the formal sector had not been able to create a single job, although 700,000 individuals were entering the labor market every year (1987: 2). By the mid-1980s, the critical economic picture of Mexico had not changed substantially. Inflation as a variation of the consumer price in 1985 was 57.7 percent, 105.7 percent in 1986, 159.2 percent in 1987, and approximately 140 percent in 1988. The average annual growth of the GDP reached 3.5 percent total and 0.7 percent per capita. And the ratio between interest paid on external public debt and exports of goods and services was 37 percent (ECLA: 1985). This leads one to assume that this situation will not change substantially in the near future. On the contrary, the chances are that Mexico will continue to face over the next several years the effects of its model of associated-dependent development (Evans, 1979).

LONG-TERM EFFECTS OF ECONOMIC DEVELOPMENT

The Mexican strategy of development of the three last decades cannot be analyzed solely from a global perspective.[17] Although the development process between the early 1950s and mid-1970s showed more positive signs than in most other Latin American countries, the distributive effects of economic growth were no different from most dependent countries where the lower income sectors did not share the benefits of modernization. According to Cotler,

> because of the dependent-capitalist character of this development, Mexico has in fact not solved the economic and social problems posed by the Mexican Revolution. One thus observes a growing relative emiseration of broad sectors of the popular classes who are concentrated in the major cities and who constitute a "marginal" population or, to put it in classic terms, a structurally unemployed population. (1979: 270)

Economic development in Mexico cannot be fully understood by looking only at economic growth aspects. The fact that the country was able to maintain a rate of growth similar to many developed economies did not significantly improve the living conditions of the majority of its population in terms of redistribution of wealth, social equality, or political participation. The distribution of economic and political power in Mexico has remained among the most disparate in Latin America (Navarrete, 1970: 18-71; Niblo, 1975: 109-24).

The efforts to improve the standard of living of low-income sectors failed to benefit the poorer half of the population that remained largely unaffected by the gains of the development process of the last three decades. In 1950, 2.4 percent of the population received 32.3 percent of the total income that year, whereas the poorest, 10 percent, received only 2.7 percent of the national income. The bottom 50 percent of the population shared 19.1 percent in terms of general income, yet the richest 10 percent received 49 percent. In 1957, this situation had changed only slightly, with the bottom 10 percent of the population receiving 1.7 percent of the total income and the top 2.3 percent receiving 24 percent. During this whole period, the lower half of the population shared 15.6 percent of the national income while the upper 10 percent received 46.7 percent. In 1963 the situation remained about the same: The poorest, 20 percent of the population, shared merely 4.17 percent of the income; 2 percent of the total income was concentrated in the poorer 10 percent and 42.5 percent was concentrated in the top 10 percent. In 1970, the distribution pattern of the monthly family income indicates that 0.9 percent of the population received over $80 US per month, 7.8 percent received $200 US or more, whereas 44.7 percent (compared with 45.9 percent in 1960) received less than $40 US per month. According to ECLA, Mexico has the most unequal distribution of income of any country in Latin America. In the early 1970s, the income of the upper 5 percent of the population was 32 times higher than the income of the poorest 20 percent, and in 1980 65.1 percent of the national wealth was concentrated on 5 percent of the population, a situation that by the mid-1980s had remained approximately the same. This regressive pattern of income distribution has severely affected the lower half of the population in absolute terms. Overall, the differences between upper and lower income groups have become wider as a result of the development process of the late 1970s and early 1980s. The extreme austerity forced on Mexico as a result of the external debt and the pressures from the International Monetary Fund have reinforced inequality.

These conditions of inequality can also be analyzed taking into account differences in the consumption habits of the population. The gap between lower and upper sectors increases even more when the distribution of wealth is considered in terms of its impact on the real purchasing power of different income groups at a time when the Mexican economy was facing a period of prosperity. Table 1-6 shows some indicators of the differences in lifestyles between urban and rural populations in 1970, as well as a series of indicators to measure a "poverty factor" for 1967 as it is used by James W. Wilkie (1967: 204-32). Over the years this situation has suffered little variation; between 1976 and 1981 the purchasing power of the minimum wage decreased 17 percent.

Table 1-6
Indicators of Lifestyle and Poverty in Mexico, 1967 and 1970

Type of Indicator	Lifestyle of Population (a) 1970		Poverty Factor (b) 1967
	Urban %	Rural %	Factor Loadings
Live in dwellings of one room	30.6	48.1	-
Live in homes with electricity	84.5	34.5	-
Cannot read or write (over six years old)	17.8	39.0	.681
Go barefoot	1.6	12.0	.134
Wear sandals	3.8	22.0	.811
Wear shoes	94.4	65.6	-
Eat only tortillas (no bread)	12.8	34.0	.857
Do not eat meat even once a week	11.0	30.0	-
Do not eat eggs even once a week	15.8	30.0	-
Living in isolated areas	-	-	.751
Without sewage disposal	-	-	.659
Speaking only an Indian language	-	-	.109

Sources: (a) Secretaría de Industria y Comercio. Dirección General de Estadísticas. *IX Censo General de Población 1970*. (Mexico, D.F., 1972); pp. 135, 273, 1081-1082.

(b) James W. Wilkie, *The Mexican Revolution: Federal Expenditures and Social Change Since 1910*. (Berkeley: University of California Press, 1967).

Assuming that these findings related to the conditions affecting the rural sector may also apply to the poorer sectors of the marginal urban population, it is possible to argue that the differences between urban and rural lifestyles are also representative of the general pattern of consumption that adversely affects lower-income sectors in general, that is to say, over 60 percent of the population. The "factor loadings" in Wilkie's factor analysis of data on poverty indicate how seven indicators relate to each other to form the poverty factor. The indicators of poverty with the highest factor loadings (people who regularly wear sandals, eat tortillas, live in isolated areas without sewage disposal, and are illiterate) summarized the variations of a larger number of factors that accounted for 58.8 percent of the variation among the seven basic indicators in Wilkie's analysis.

Another indicator to assess the degree of inequality in Mexico is the real working time required to earn the costs of subsistence. A worker's family of five in 1970 had to work 223.48 hours per month to keep a minimum level of subsistence (see Table 1-7). For a family in the lowest income stratum, the total working time available per month was insufficient to cover the costs of a minimum standard of subsistence. In real terms, there was a difference of –$7.87 (US) per month to cover the cost of living with one person working full time. This difference increased to –$13.14 (US) in 1975, assuming that the number of hours of work remained constant, and considering the change in the actual minimum salary in 1974-75 and the increase in the cost of living for a salary earner between 1970 and 1975. Although in a five-year period the minimum salary was almost half as much as the costs of a minimum level of subsistence, almost 60 percent of the average expenses of a worker's family went to buy basic food supplies, and almost 94 percent went to food and rent.

Additional indicators on poverty and social inequality in Mexico can be found in other statistics. According to the 1970 Census, 40 percent of the dwellings in Mexico contained only a single room, 36 percent did not have running water, 58 percent lacked sewage disposal facilities, and 41 percent did not have electricity. The annual inflation rate increased from 23.7 percent in 1974 to almost 63.7 percent at the end of 1985. Early in 1986 the Consumer Price Index was 65.8 percent higher than the previous year, the highest recorded in the last 19 months and only slightly lower than the 67.1 percent registered in 1984 (Expansión, 1986: 5). Between 1969 and 1970 Mexico had an average meat consumption of 30.6 kilos per year per inhabitant in comparison with 161 kilos in the United States. Only 16.8 percent of Mexicans eat eggs daily and 20.6 percent never eat meat. The consumption of milk was only 54.18 litres per person compared with 211 litres in the United States and 511 in France. The average daily diet contained only 1,115 calories in Mexico's rural areas, although the minimum healthy diet according to international standards was 2,500 calories. "If we consider the minimum diet calculated for Mexico by the National Institute of Nutrition (that assumes 80.9 grams of proteins and 2741 units of daily calories per capita), in 1975 close to 60% of the population did not have

Table 1-7

Differences in Working Time and Costs to Maintain a Worker's Family of Five in Mexico, 1970 and 1975

Family of 5 Members	Monthly Working Time		Costs in Terms of Minimum Monthly Wages (c)	
	HH:MM	%	1970 (c)	1975 (c)
Minimum Daily Diet	132.30	59.20	32.96	62.39
Minimum Clothes (a)	14.68	6.57	3.66	6.92
Rent (two-room house)	76.5	34.23	19.06	36.07
Total Working Time Necessary for Living	223.48	100	55.68	105.38
Regular Monthly Working Time (b)	192.00		47.80	92.24

(a) Calculated on the basis of a total of 35.23 hours per year, assuming that this minimum is spent once a year.

(b) Calculated on the basis of eight hours per day, six days a week.

(c) $US 1970.

1970 Calculated on the basis of the daily minimum urban wage in 1970-71 (24.91 pesos; $1.99 US)

1975 Calculated on the basis of the daily minimum urban wage in 1974-75 (48.04 pesos; $3.83 US). The costs for 1975 were calculated on the basis of the increase in the Price Index (189.3%) related to the Cost of Wage-Earner Life, Ibid., Table 6.3, p. 230.

Source: Nacional Financiera S.A., La economía mexicana en cifras (Mexico, D.F., 1978).

access to a minimum normative diet that would impede its nutritional deterioration ... In 1975, with a population of 60 million persons, there was a deficit of more than three million tons of foods" (Cordera & Tello, 1981: 23). From 1971 to 1974 the price of cereals and beans, one of the basic components of the Mexican diet, increased by 92 percent; powdered milk increased by 452 percent, and the price of tortillas increased from 0.80 to 2.40 pesos per kilo.

The economic conditions of low-income sectors can also be assessed by analyzing the evolution of minimum wages during the years in which the country was at the prime of its economic growth (see Table 1-8). Mexico has an elaborate structure of minimum wages with substantial differences between urban and rural wage rates for the same occupation that is determined with virtually no control from the workers. During the period of economic growth, the gap between average rural and urban wages increased rather than diminished. Between 1950 and 1975, urban wages were approximately 18.3 percent higher than rural wages, and between 1960 and 1975 urban wages were 22.5 percent higher than rural wages. In terms of

Table 1-8
Evolution of Minimum Wages in Mexico, 1950-1975

Years	Minimum Wages				Wage Index*		
	Monthly Urban Average	Monthly Rural Average	Differ Rural and Urban Wages %	Real Difference	Urban %	Rural %	Industrial %
	US$ 1970	US$ 1970		US $ 1970			
1950-1951	8.04	6.38	-26.0	-1.7	33.9	30.1	41.2
1952-1953	12.84	10.92	-17.6	-1.9	54.1	51.5	50.6
1954-1955	15.22	12.62	-20.6	-2.6	64.1	59.6	62.5
1956-1957	17.40	14.38	-21.0	-3.0	73.3	67.8	73.9
1958-1959	19.51	16.46	-18.5	-3.1	82.2	77.7	86.8
1960-1961	23.74	21.19	-12.0	-2.6	100.0	100.0	100.0
1962-1963	29.86	26.21	-13.9	-3.7	125.8	123.7	117.9
1964-1965	38.40	32.33	-18.8	-6.1	161.8	152.5	140.0
1966-1967	44.86	37.73	-18.9	-7.1	188.9	178.0	167.6
1968-1969	51.79	43.97	-17.8	-7.8	218.2	207.5	185.3
1970-1971	59.78	50.88	-17.5	-8.9	251.9	240.1	221.4
1972-1973	70.30	59.86	-17.4	-10.4	296.2	282.4	281.2
1974-1975	115.29	98.16	-17.5	-17.2	485.7	463.2	427.4

*1960-1961 = 100.

Source: Calculated from Nacional Financiera S.A., *La economía mexicana en cifras* (Mexico, D.F., 1978) Table 8.5.

real dollar value, minimum wages between urban and rural areas differed by $8.90 US in 1970-71, $10.40 in 1972-73, and $17.17 in 1974-75. Between 1973 and 1977 the average minimum wage rate increased by 22.6 percent, whereas the National Index of Consumer Prices increased 164.4 percent and the prices of food, beverages, and tobacco increased 141.2 percent (Trejo Delarbre, 1979: 133).

The conditions of social inequality in the distribution of income are also affected by the monopolistic role of the industrial sector, heavily influenced by foreign investment and by a pattern of concentration of capital which limit the opportunities of the larger part of the work force. To a large extent this is due to the progressive disintegration of labor organizations and the predominance of political pressures, regardless of the constitutional guarantees protecting workers' rights in collective bargaining (Vanek, 1975). Differences in wages among industries also contribute to enlarge the gap between various social groups. Some industries pay up to 10 percent over the minimum wage and employ 30.5 percent of the blue-collar workers. Other industries pay between 10 and 30 percent above the minimum wage and employ 47.5 percent of the blue-collar work force. A third group of industries pays between 30 and 100 percent above the minimum and employs 12 percent of the blue-collar workers. This situation in which workers in the same occupation and with the same educational qualifications receive substantially different salaries negatively affects workers' cohesion in terms of wage demands, owing to the tendency of these groups to defend their own immediate interests.

The way in which education evolved during the 1970s is to a large extent a result of the development objectives of the government in power. Modernization was a central idea leading the role of the education system at all its levels, particularly in larger urban centers. In practice, however, education has a differential effect on different income groups, and its contribution to economic growth in Mexico has remained one of the lowest in Latin America.[18] Expansion of the education system took place at the higher education level and benefited the middle- and upper-income sectors. Higher education continued serving approximately 4 percent of the school population while absorbing 20 percent of the education budget which in turn grew from 2.5 percent of the GNP in 1970 to 4.5 percent in 1980. Although lower income sectors also received some benefits from the reform implemented in the early 1970s, in practice the survival rates for lower income and rural children remained considerably low. In correspondence with the effects of the model of economic development, the benefits of education and its quantitative and qualitative expansion during these years satisfied primarily the demands for more and better education of the upper and urban middle class. Although adult illiteracy declined from 26 to 18 percent between 1970 and 1980, the percentage of urban illiterates grew from 39 to 45 percent, mainly as a result of the large rural migration to large cities.

At the university level the unequal character of the modernization policies becomes more evident in the educational system. Between 1975 and 1983 the enrollment rate in universities grew 90.6 percent, while at the primary education level it grew only 34.4 percent. At the secondary and postsecondary level, education focused on providing the large mass of students entering the system with technical-vocational alternatives or with options to obtain technical qualification, encouraging in this way their rapid integration into the labor market in areas required by the process of industrialization (UNESCO, 1986: 119).[19] Education in the last three decades has become a relatively inexpensive means to compensate for the lack of opportunities of social mobility outside the school. Economic development has not helped to make education more effective in reducing the gap between rural and urban populations or between lower- and upper-income sectors.

CONCLUSION

Economic development and education in Mexico have expressed the political objectives of the bureaucratic bourgeoisie controlling the State. They have been used both as mechanisms to mediate social conflicts and to reproduce the class structure and the relation among classes in a society traditionally affected by deep cultural and economic differences. Through direct control of the State, economic development has been a mechanism primarily at the service of the economic and political elite. It is this faction of the society that, as a result of the development policies implemented over the last thirty years, has been able to benefit from a larger proportion of the national wealth and that has acquired direct control over the private sector of the economy. The model of economic development has exacerbated the contradiction inherent in postrevolutionary Mexico between an economic system increasingly controlled by private interests and dominated by foreign capital, and a political system that struggles to maintain the appearance of a revolutionary tradition in which the State plays a central role in determining the development policies of the country.[20]

Perhaps more effectively than in any other country in Latin America, education in Mexico has been used more as an instrument of legitimization than as a development tool. Since the postrevolutionary period, education has served to minimize social conflicts but not to compensate the lack of real economic and political mobility of members of the lower classes. Economically, education has not been a means to feed a process of development by preparing the human resources required to maintain a relatively successful process of economic growth. Changes in primary and nonformal education have simply expanded the pool of individuals competing to enter the labor market in low-paid occupations, while the higher education system has reinforced the ranks of the new technocratic elite in government and the private sector occupying managerial posts in society. Politically, education has served to legitimize a hegemonic power structure and a nationalistic political ideology that serve as a basis to the corporatist State controlling not only political life but also the direction and distribution of the benefits of the development process. Education has helped to maintain a facade of political stability and the image of a revolutionary tradition that provides a historical frame of reference where the corporatist State can operate.

NOTES

1. Martin Carnoy argues that "the nation, as developed in the capitalist State, together with its territory, tradition, and language, is a form of unification of people divided by capitalist production into classes—segmented, separated, individualized and isolated—into a new concept of space and time, a concept that is intended to keep the dominated class from realizing who and why it is so" (1984: 121). The implications of corporatism for the constitution of the nation-state in Mexico and for educational policies are discussed in the next chapter.

2. Fernando Enrique Cardoso indicates in this regard that

associate-dependent development is not without dynamism; it is not based on ruralization at the expense of industrialization; it does not reinforce the old division of labour in which some countries only exported raw materials and imported manufactured goods.

On the contrary, the distinguishing feature of the new type of dependency that is evolving in countries like Brazil, Argentina and Mexico is that it is based on a new international division of labour. Part of the industrial system of hegemonic countries is now being transferred, under the control of international corporations, to countries that have already been able to reach a relatively advanced level of industrial development. . . . The model of associated-dependent development does have a dynamic character. It does allow for economic growth and social mobility, at least for the urban-industrial sector. (1973: 156-57)

3. These periods are distinguished for analytical purpose and should not exclude each other.

4. For a more detailed analysis of the Porfiriato, see Francisco Bulnes, *El Verdadero Díaz y la Revolución* (Mexico City: Editorial Nacional, 1952).

5. Railroads were in the hands of United States enterprisers. The so-called Mexican National Railroad Company was a mixed enterprise of Colorado investors and French and English enterprisers. See W. Raat, "Los Intelectuales, el Positivismo y la Cuestión Indígena" *Historia Mexicana* (Mexico, Editorial del Estado), p. 142.

6. José Angel Pescador in his article "El esfuerzo alfabetizador en México (1910-1985): Un ensayo crítico," indicates that during the Porfiarian period there was not a real preoccupation to promote mass education. On the contrary, during this period the tendency was to prepare a managerial elite with the highest level of education possible at the expenses of the ignorance of the larger masses (1986: 3).

7. James D. Cockcroft indicates in this regard that "the Mexican Revolution of 1910-1917 was not a bourgeois one against feudalism, nor did it succeed in more than overthrowing Porfirio Díaz and changing part of the ideology of social change. Radical changes in the class structure did not occur as a result of the Mexican Revolution, mainly because the worker-peasant thrust of the Revolution was blunted by Venustiano Carranza's victory over Emiliano Zapata" (1972: 41).

8. The *ejido* system is a form of rural community organization in which land is collectively owned and agricultural production is carried out either on a collective or individual basis.

9. Article 3 of the Constitution is still a source of major debate. Several scholars argue that, in practice, the Mexican State has not been able to implement a socialist education system in the country in spite of the official rhetoric in this regard.

10. At the very beginning of the revolutionary movement it became clear that Mexican development was not perceived as based on a socialist economic structure.

For all the main revolutionary leaders, including Cárdenas, a controlled but strong alliance with capital was seen as central to the modernization of the society (Córdova, 1974: 17-19).

11. The opportunities opened by the Revolution, particularly in regard to rural Mexico, were seriously diminished by the lack of education in the rural population to begin a process of change. Aware of this fact, the government of Alvaro Obregón began a serious attempt to change the conditions of rural education, which under the lead of José Vasconcelos takes the character of a large scale literacy campaign despite the lack of resources that limited the scope of these efforts.

12. Josefina Vázquez in her book *Nacionalismo y educación en México* argues that there were heated arguments and confusion about the meaning of the concept of socialism. For some the word socialism meant an "aggressive economic nationalism," for others it meant "seeking social justice vaguely understood within the context of capitalist institutions," and for a smaller group it meant "the application of the marxist pattern of a classless society" (1970: 174-75).

13. These were 46.2, 98, and 58.1 percent in the upper, middle, and lower strata respectively.

14. The development of this alliance among government, labor, and big business is discussed in more detail in Chapter two.

15. The role of private national and foreign investments in the process of capital formation had a direct effect on the rate of growth of the domestic product. According to the Nacional Financiera, between 1940 and 1975 the GDP grew an average of 13.9 percent in the primary sector, 31.4 percent in the industrial sector and 54.7 percent in services. In practice, however, the only sector of the economy that sustained growth during this period was the industrial sector from 24.6 percent in 1940-45 to 35.2 percent in 1975. The primary sector decreased from 19.3 percent in 1940-45 to 10.3 percent in 1970-75, and the service sector decreased from 56.1 percent in 1940-45 to 54.5 percent in 1970-75 (1978: 25-34).

16. The importance of the petroleum boom in 1978-81 for economic recovery should not be underestimated. The contribution of the oil industry to Mexico's GNP was 4.5% and oil exports produced 70% of the export revenues by the early 1980s (Labra, 1982: 57). Indeed, when the discovery of petroleum reserves in the continental platform of the states of Campeche and Tabasco was confirmed in 1979, Mexico was ranked fifth in the world in terms of the magnitude of its proven oil reserves. In only three years the production of hydrocarbons in the country doubled, and Mexico that in 1975 was a net importer of petroleum became a net exporter. The potential reserves of Mexico in millions of barrels was 200,000 by 1979, and the country was in a position by the mid-1980s to satisfy 30% of the Unites States' demand for oil.

17. Many authors have characterized this process as "unequal combined development" (Alavi and Shanin, 1982; Amin, 1974).

18. George Psacharopoulos and Maureen Woodhall in their book *Education for Development* calculate the contribution of education to economic growth in Mexico as 0.8 percent of the annual growth rate, compared to 16.5 percent in Argentina, 6.5 percent in Honduras, 4.9 percent in Ecuador, and 4.5 in Chile (1985: 17, Table 2-1).

19. Our own estimates show that between 1975 and 1983 the enrollment rate in universities grew 100.2% while elementary school enrollments grew only 30.9%.

20. A clear example of this contradiction is presented in the expanding economic role of the State acting as an entrepreneur during the 1970s. By 1979 there were 900 State enterprises in operation, including *Petroleos Mexicanos*, one of *Fortune*'s 500 largest enterprises in the world. The 27 enterprises under control of the legislative power in

Mexico in 1979 produced 30% of the GNP that year. After 1982, there has been a drastic process of economic restructuring with the privatization of public enterprises (Torres, 1989).

2 The Mexican Corporatist State, Hegemonic Politics, and Educational Policies

INTRODUCTION

There is little doubt that the Revolution of 1910 represented an important change in Mexico's economic and political life. Less evident, however, is its long-term success in changing the trends of political power and the conditions of social inequality and lack of participation.

The emerging political system that followed the Revolution was fragmented and dependent on the new revolutionary leaders who controlled the State and played a key role in developing the socioeconomic principles of the Constitution of 1917. However, it was not until the creation of the official party, the Partido Nacional Revolucionario (PNR), that a political institution was available to subordinate the autonomous social forces within the various segments struggling to control the State and thus resolve political conflicts.

In the late 1920s, after several failures to create a more stable government, members of the revolutionary coalition[1] led by Calles (1924-28) perceived the need to create an institutional mechanism with authority to channel popular political participation and led Mexico into a rapid process of political modernization and development (Portes Gil, 1954; Manjarrez, 1930). Simultaneously with the formation of the PNR in 1929, a formal pact of union and solidarity was agreed upon among the main political and military leaders. They compromised in accepting the party as the setting to unify political participation linked to the government at the state and local levels. The party provided a hierarchy controlled by the president as "supreme arbiter" of the country and a system of institutional political bargaining that set the basis for the corporatist structure of the State (Leal, 1986).

However, the political modernization of Mexican society began with the political and socioeconomic reforms brought about during the government of Lázaro Cárdenas (Pescador, 1986; Hamilton, 1982; Brandenburg, 1964).

Together with his emphasis on giving the State greater control over socio-economic development, he implemented a new power coalition by reorganizing the PNR and giving peasants and workers stronger political participation in decision making within the public sector.[2] His ideal was to create a system to safeguard the interests of different social groups and channel popular support to facilitate socioeconomic and political reforms. This system is identified in the next sections as a corporatist system.

The official party remained in power without fundamental changes from 1940 until 1990. Sectorial reorganizations took place over the years to accommodate interest groups at different points in time, including the labor sector, the military, the peasants, and the popular sector. Perhaps the most important of these changes occurred in 1946 when the party was again reorganized and renamed the Institutional Revolutionary Party (Partido Revolucionario Institucional, or PRI). This marked the beginning of the popular sector's increasing influence over government decisions[3] and the legitimation of the dominant elite under the coverage of a "revolutionary tradition." Juan Felipe Leal argues in this regard that

> the state that is born of the revolution is already a "reformed" capitalist state, "more advanced" than certain countries of late-developing capitalism and "ahead" in certain respects of the capitalist powers . . . because of the fact that it was born within the context of the structural weakness of the basic social classes, the "new order" establishes the supremacy of the state over society and it disputes, not only in a general manner—which is true of any capitalistic state—but in a specific manner as well. . . . the state assumes authority to grant recognition to and participate directly in the organization of the classes and class factions, advising them of the institutional boundaries within which disputes are permitted, with the stipulation that they are always subject to state arbitration. This final point guarantees the hegemony of the ruling bureaucracy. (1986: 33)

For the past 60 years the PRI has had a decisive role in Mexican political development. Its hegemonic role,[4] and the concentration of power in the president and a small group of leaders, has been perceived as constituting a model of government without parallel in Latin American politics (Carpizo, 1978). Some scholars have argued that the system of political succession controlled by the PRI, and more directly by the president himself as top leader of the revolutionary coalition, institutionalizes the control exercised by a wealthy and powerful elite which in practice makes all major political decisions (Pereyra, 1979: 289-305). The relationships between the PRI and the Mexican State (State bureaucracy) is the subject of much theoretical and political debate. The interpretations are so diverse that it will be impossible to summarize all of them in this work. It will suffice to mention two main contrasting positions. From a structural-functionalist perspective with strong Weberian overtones, Peter Smith's work suggests a struggle for hegemony between political and economic elites (Smith, 1979: 191-216). In short, the argument is that Mexico does not have a power elite—in the sense that there are cliques overlapping the political and economic elites sharing a similar social origin and education. For Smith, instead of a unified elite,

Mexico seems to have a fragmented power structure, with two competitive, an economic, and a political elite sharing a tacit agreement about the reproduction of capitalism in Mexico, but continuously struggling to gain control over the process of economic development and the public sector (Smith, 1979: 214-216). In this context, the political elite is itself divided between the *técnicos* or technocrats, university alumni who held virtually no prior elected office before being appointed to run a given agency in the State bureaucracy, and the politicians whose source of power relies mostly on their political (family, historical) connections within the PRI, established historical loyalties with different regional power and interest groups, who in general count on the reliance, acquiescence, and/or support of the worker and peasant sectors of the PRI. Since for Smith, Camp (1970; 1980), Levy (1980; 1986), Bailey (1986), and many other scholars the technocrats have come to dominate politics in Mexico in the last 15 years (Smith, 1986: 109), recent political literature emphasizes the subordination of the PRI to the political bureaucracy of the State which is in turn controlled by *técnicos* (Camp, 1986).

An historical-structural approach emphasizing the dialectics between economics and politics in Mexico is advanced by many scholars, including Pereyra (1974; 1981), Córdova (1972a; 1972b; 1979), Cockcroft (1974), González Casanova and Enrique Florescano (1979), Hamilton (1982), Leal (1986), Leff (1982), and Pescador and Torres (1985). For them the PRI is a mass party, and it is the hegemonic apparatus of the Mexican State in the context of Mexico's corporatist system. Córdova has argued that:

> One of the essential characteristics that defines the Mexican state is, without doubt, its *politics of masses*, in which the state establishes its power over society, and which is, at the same time, the historical result of the great political, economic and social commotion that constituted the Mexican Revolution of 1910-1917. This politics of masses has always determined the extension of state power, and its success or failure in the country. The efficacy of the state as leader of the economic and social life of Mexico has always been in direct relation to the efficacy or deterioration of its politics of masses; in other terms, to the control and ascendancy of the state over and in the bosom of wide strata of the working population in the cities and countryside. (Córdova, 1979: 9)

For this approach there is a symbiotic relationship between State and party. In the political corporatism prevailing in Mexico, the PRI does not have the constitutive features of a liberal political party. It is a mass party, and its sectors are those that constitute the party, not the individuals. Those that practice politics within the party are the mass organizations which are members of the party—as class organizations or grouped around professional interests—but which are not conceived as organs of the State as in classic fascism or European corporativism (Córdova, 1979: 22-24). The class organizations, in a sense, overlap with the party, particularly the CTM which is the largest, and the party is reduced to (a) an entity that coordinates the action of the mass organizations, and (b) a key institution at election time, although even in elections the role of the organizations is decisive, since the selection of the political positions (i.e., individual representatives to Congress of each organization once the quota of federal and State representatives or senators per organization is decided within the party structure, or governorships and even the presidency of the Republic) it is made by each mass organization and not by the bureaucracy of the party or the bureaucracy of the State (Córdova, 1979: 25). Finally, the party constitutes a key institution to convey the wishes of the president and the president's entourage regarding selection of candidates for key political (elected) positions, even the candidate for the presidency, to the rest of the political and interest groups interacting in the PRI, particularly the mass organizations.

Once again, Córdova captures the fundamentals of this position when arguing that:

> In these cases, the party is a simple transmission belt, a mediator, and when it is in a better position, a broker among different factions. In reality, it is not the party, but national or local bureaus, the local committees, because the party are the organizations . . . it is a committee that administers the questions of the corporations, that is to say, the organizations. We can call it also a Ministry of corporations, but in this case of political corporations, that is to say, with very limited faculties of simple coordination. (Córdova, 1979: 26)

Hence, for this position, although on the surface the contradictions within the PRI between *técnicos* and politicians may be important (and in several areas of the State such as education that conflict is vigorous), the key differences are in the political economy of alternative models of development (i.e., neoliberals versus revolutionary nationalists in the terminology of Cordera and Tello, 1981: 78-135). In addition, there are strong differences between sectors of the PRI since there is no identity between sectors and the organizations that constitute a given sector, and given that the real power lies only in a few organizations such as the Federation of Workers of the Federal District (FTDF) which constitutes the vital nerve of the CTM and is the most important mass organization of the Mexican State and its symbiotic party (Córdova, 1979: 28-30). Lastly, a discussion of the nature of the Mexican State and policy formation should include not only what happens at the national level or in the Federal District, but also what happens at the level of local communities, since "Despite the growing predominance of *técnicos* at the national level, the persistence and extension of political bureaucracy on the local level help explain why people here—and elsewhere in Mexico—have been, from a comparative perspective, quiescent" (Eckstein, 1988: 274).

In this book the relationships between the State bureaucracy and the ruling party are understood in terms of a historical-structural approach. There are many problems with structural-functionalist analyses of the Mexican State. Although rich in information and some interesting analyses, a number of shortcomings are noted. Prevailing methodological individualism has led structural-functionalist analyses to overemphasize in a fairly instrumentalist manner the role of human agency in the "kitchen" of Mexican politics, that is, of individuals acting almost independently of the

institutional and structural settings. In addition, it shares a strong liberal-.
pluralist view of the State by which, in the absence of the basic traits of a
democracy, the underlying feature of the Mexican State is its authoritarianism, which may be too limited as a definition or political understanding of such a complex stucture as the Mexican State. This view takes
the issue of corporatism in a fairly cursory fashion, and hence the State and
the ruling party are considered more in terms of their political representation (or lack thereof) than as constitutive factors in a process and
structure of domination of social life in Mexico. Finally, the combination of
methodological individualism (which usually takes the verbalization of individual social behavior as a proxy to explain the rationale and underlying
causality of effectively performed social action), a liberal pluralist view of the
State that results in instrumentalism, and their interpretation of social
history as the act of rational (and impassioned) human agencies, but with
little regard for historical-structural constraints, allows this approach to
grasp the most colorful contours of the folklore of the political life of Mexico
and the Mexican elites (i.e., how the elite explains how politics is conducted
in Mexico), but usually neither provides us with a thorough understanding of
its key determinants or laws of development, nor with a complete understanding of mass politics rather than elite politics.

According to Frank Brandenburg, the official party and its sectoral system
has not been in fact an effective device to represent the interests of various
groups, but a means to consolidate the power of the "Revolutionary Family,"
the group governing the country.[5] Vincent Padgett (1966) concurs that
Mexico is ruled by a "Revolutionary Coalition" of members related to a
revolutionary tradition. The PRI, in his view, is a means to promote consensus within the elite and to legitimate control over Mexican politics. Scott
(1964), in turn, suggests that the PRI is the mechanism providing an equilibrium among the interests of different groups participating in politics.
Vernon (1963) has portrayed the PRI as an undefined political institution
due to its attempts to satisfy a wide range of political interests. Lowenthal
(1987) argues that the PRI has also been a means to maintain the type of
political stability which is important for the relationships of Mexico and the
United States.[6]

Often interpretations of Mexican politics by functionalist social scientists
describe the PRI not as a mechanism representing the various corporations
in society, but as an instrument at the exclusive service of an elite led by the
president, allowing him to maintain full political control. One of the main
pitfalls of these analyses is that they downplay both the highly conflicting
process of political bargaining and contradictions within the PRI as an
instrument for political representation, not of individuals but of corporative
groups, and the crucial role played by the party and its interest groups in
public policy making.[7] Considering that until 1988 the PRI consistently
obtained the largest majority in the elections, its position of control is
manifest.[8] Under this system the president and the small group around him
are the supreme controllers of political life. This has led some scholars to

argue that the political system in Mexico is one of "six years authoritarianism" and that the only limit to the president's power is his time in
office (Scott, 1964: 38). When the president retires he continues to have a
great deal of influence on the choice of his own successor among the closest
members of the elite. Although increasingly contested in times of hard
economic and political crisis, in practice the president is the final authority
in deciding who gets what, when, and how in the political system. However,
the traditional notion of "presidentialism" as a central component of the
hegemonic role of the State is becoming less and less adequate to explain the
most recent trends in Mexican politics.

There is strong evidence suggesting that this system worked better in the
past than it did in the late 1980s. A series of events shows the difficulties
faced by the political system in the midst of Mexico's worst economic crisis.
In 1986 internal dissent in the party led to the creation of a "neo-Cardenist
faction," the so-called Democratic Faction (led by the former Governor of
Michoacán and son of President Lázaro Cárdenas, Cuahutémoc Cárdenas,
and by the former Secretary of Education and Mexico's former representative at the United Nations, Porfirio Muñoz Ledo). This faction was dis-
qualified by President De la Madrid and by the party's leader Senator Lugo
Verduzco, who after the formal announcement of the formation of this
faction had to resign to his post. The race for the presidential nomination
within the PRI also began earlier than usual. Following traditional procedures the internal dispute had always become visible in early January of the
election year. In this case, however, the open expression of internal turmoil
came in September 1986, following the unrest generated within the party by
the self-proclaimed Democratic Faction. Breaking with tradition within the
party, Salazar Toledano, the influential leader of the PRI in the Federal
District, declared four cabinet members as potential PRI candidates.[9]
Meanwhile, the Secretary of Justice announced the Secretary of Mining and
Para-State Enterprises, A. del Mazo, as the candidate of the PRI. President
Miguel de la Madrid instead selected the Secretary of Programming and
Budget, Lic. Salinas de Gortari, as his successor. The turmoil among the
ranks, however, shows that the notion of an "autocratic" presidential sys-
tem, which has never worked smoothly, is now in a process of deterioration.

The performance of the system is not only conditioned by the individuals'
possibilities to become part of the elite and receive favors from the head of
the party, but also by the capacity of the system to corrupt, coopt, or repress
those who dissent. Jesús Silva Herzog, at one time high political official and
a well-known nationalist liberal intellectual, indicates that

> politics degrades and corrupts everything. . . . There are big, medium and small
> politicians, giants and dwarfs, and one finds them everywhere: in offices and
> ante-rooms of public officials, in schools, in labor unions, in cooperative societies
> and in *ejidos*. The politician is seldom considerate and honest, he is interested
> solely in personal gain, he is the profiteer of the Revolution; on the *ejido* he
> exploits the *ejidatario*, in the labor union he exploits the workers and other

employees, and in the schools he exploits his companions. Politics is the easiest and most profitable profession in Mexico. Immorality is the most alarming in the Federal Public Administration, in the States and in the municipalities . . . Many are public officials who have made fortunes in a few months without loss of respectability. (1967: 33-34)

Thus the political system is built on the basis of an effective mechanism of political control which, associated with systematic and institutionalized corruption, determines the degree of political flexibility and participation at all social levels in a corporatist system.

CORPORATISM AND PUBLIC POLICY

A feature of the Mexican State today is its corporatist character as a mode of political organization and control. *Corporatism* in Mexico is an expression of the capitalist State and, as such, a distinctive mode for making and implementing public policy. The discussions on the character of the Mexican case are well documented and most seem to concur with the assessment of the Mexican State as a corporatist State (Pereyra, 1974, 1979, 1981; Leal, 1972a, 1975b; Córdova, 1972a, 1972b, 1976).

According to these analyses, corporatism in Mexico refers to a form of State that, being the result of a popular revolution, has a broad mass-base of popular support despite its capitalist character. The Mexican Revolution is seen in essence as a antioligarchical movement that disorganized the *latifundio* system and put an end to the oldstanding economic power of the Catholic Church. It is also perceived as both the simultaneous expression of the political reforms originated in the provincial intelligentsia, commanded by regional factions of the bourgeoisie against the central power represented by Porfirio Díaz, and the peasants' dissatisfaction with the intensifying of the capitalist mode of production in agriculture and the pauperization of the mass of landless peasants (Leal, 1975a).

The triumph of the Mexican Revolution—perhaps the first social revolution in the 20th century—brought about a new form of capitalist State in Mexico. The block in power was reorganized under the hegemonic leadership of a new civilian and military bureaucracy created by the revolutionary movement. It was this new bureaucracy and not the peasantry who in practice profited the most from the bloody civil war. The political, social, and economic reorganization that followed the Revolution did in fact redefine the existing linkages between the old block in power and the subordinate classes (Córdova, 1972b; Leal, 1986). In this sense, there was a partial introduction of a series of reformist and radical programs within the new capitalist State. They were expressed in the design of the Constitution of 1917 with its "revolutionary nationalist" and "jacobin-socialist" overtones,[10] in agrarian reform, the nationalization of the railroads, the expropriation and nationalization of the oil industry, and most recently in the nationalization of the private banking sector in 1982.[11]

The concept of corporatism is also used to refer to the incorporation of the socially subordinated sectors (peasants, workers, and middle-class sectors) into the political party apparatus and into the system of distribution of power and influence in the State. To better understand this process, it is necessary to discuss corporatism at a more theoretical level, to take thus full advantage of this model in the analysis of Mexico's political system.

Corporatism has been defined by Phillip C. Schmitter[12] as:

> a system of interest representation in which the constituent units are organized into a limited number of singular, compulsory, noncompetitive, hierarchically ordered and functionally differentiated categories, recognized or licensed (if not created) by the State and granted a deliberate representational monopoly within their respective categories in exchange for observing certain controls on their selection of leaders and articulation of demands and supports. (1974: 93-94)

Gerald Lehmbruch (1982: 6) argues that corporatism has five main characteristics: (1) Interest organizations are strongly coopted into governmental decision making (as measured by representation in advisory committees or other forms of consultation); (2) large interest organizations, in particular labor unions, are strongly linked to political parties taking part in policy formulation in a functional division of labor; (3) most interest organizations are hierarchically structured and membership tends to be compulsory; (4) occupational categories are represented by noncompetitive organizations enjoying a monopoly situation; and (5) industrial relations are characterized by strong "concertation" of labor unions and employers' organizations with government, implying that unions refrain from employing strike weapons or other conflicting tactics.

In Mexico, corporatism refers specifically to the organizational characteristics of the State[13] structure and party and political control that depends to a certain degree on popular participation and mobilization, both being carefully controlled and manipulated for nondemocratic ends (Kaufman, 1977). In our analysis corporatism does not refer to a form of State but to the organizational characteristics of the State structures and party. We agree with Stepan when he argues that corporatism "refers to a particular set of policies and institutional arrangements for structuring interest representation" (1978: 46). Indeed, we also agree with Stepan's distinction between corporatism as an elite response to crisis, as an attempt by an elite to use the State apparatus to restructure the relationships between sectors of civil society and the State rather than viewing corporatism as a function of historical continuity, and as a reflection of the way some civil societies are organized (Torres, 1984a: 107-110). Thus corporatism will not be mostly the result of cultural, legal, institutional, and administrative historical structures, although the political culture of a society may reinforce (or challenge) corporatist experiments (Stepan, 1978: 47-54). Similarly, we agree with Stepan's insightful discussion of the differences between corporatism and fascism (1978: 48-52) which is compatible with a historical-structural explanation of forms of state authoritarianism in Latin America. This approach, by considering fascism a historical category, will conceptualize the

Mexican State as corporatist but not as fascist (Córdova, 1979: 23-25; Borón, 1977: 481-528; O'Donnell, 1977: 47-87). The category of state corporatism used by Stepan and Schmitter is appropriate for the Mexican State as long as it emphasizes its character as an "inclusionary" form of corporatism, that is, "the state elite can attempt to forge a new state-society equilibrium by policies aimed at incorporating salient working-class groups into the new economic and political model" (Stepan, 1978: 74). Indeed, Mexico will be a particular case of "inclusionary" corporatism (Stepan, 1978, 89-97; Torres, 1989).

Corporatism is thus a form of political control that fulfills several functions. These include the regulation of class conflicts, the rationalization of political procedures, the implementation of political and economic decisions, and the effective execution of political control to assure the continued functioning of the State (Reyna and Weinert, 1977).

Another outstanding characteristic of Mexican corporatism is the existence and institutionalization of a powerful bureaucracy in charge of decision making. The origin of this bureaucracy, legitimized as a social category within the government, can be traced to the beginning of the postrevolutionary State. The strengthening of this bureaucracy over the years has led to the use of cooptation as a mechanism of the political system. This maintains a continual renewal of the leadership and introduces new actors in the political arena, such as some sectors of the petit bourgeoisie or the middle class.

Finally, corporatism in Mexico also refers to the formation of a strong State that controls not only political life (including dissent), but also some of the most important features of economic production. This characteristic of the corporatist State could be seen in the case of many latecomer countries entering a highly monopolized world capitalist system as a precondition to achieve sustained economic growth and development. Until the crisis of 1982, Mexico was one of the most successful and long-lasting examples of capitalist development among the semiperipheral countries of the Third World.

The legitimacy of the Mexican State can be linked to several sources. These include, first and foremost, the Revolution of 1910 that gave the State the role of principal modernizer of the country. This role, as discussed earlier, has been reinforced and expanded through the continuity of the system and the self-proclaimed historical legitimacy of the State. Other sources include a party in power for 60 years; a successful mechanism for leadership replacement and political-administrative succession every six years; a criterion of nonreelection of the president, which contributes to the reproduction of the political system and the political actors; and a sufficiently stable discipline of the working class, with a chairman of the Mexican Confederation of Workers (CTM) holding office for almost 40 years. These are not just formal, anecdotal, or peripheral characteristics of a stable institutional system. On the contrary, they are part of its central political features (Torres, 1989).

Two other contributing economic aspects have already been noted in Chapter one. The rate of sustained growth of the GNP and the success of the so-called *desarrollo estabilizador* (stabilizing development) are uncommon characteristics in dependent countries. The solutions adopted to deal with some of the basic obstacles to the growth of the Mexican economy, including the problems of agrarian reform and the industrialization bottlenecks, gave the State until 1982 not only historical and political legitimacy but also the opportunity to play a determinant role in balancing and sustaining a pace of growth underlining the process of political domination.

If Schmitter's (1974) distinction is taken into account at this point, it would be possible to argue that this is a case of State corporatism.[14] The capacity of this ideology to be flexible and adaptable to change has been quite high and effective. This has allowed the Mexican State to play a role of mediator, minimizing the role of other social institutions. In contrast to other Latin American societies for example, the Church in Mexico has not been in the past decades an alternative or a bridgehead representing vigorous factions of civil society and challenging State policies. The Church has avoided as far as possible any direct confrontation with the State in almost any matter of mutual competence. However, with the strengthening of the conservative-Catholic National Autonomous Party (PAN) since the early 1980s, the Church is increasingly on a collision course with the State.

The corporatist State in Mexico seems to have a high degree of political legitimation both from the subordinate classes and from the factions of the dominant class in power (the ruling block). The elections of July 1985 and 1986 for governors in several states and for Congressional seats showed that, despite the predictions of severe setbacks for the ruling party, the PRI was still capable of holding power and beating the opposition. This capacity to maintain its power at all costs has been challenged even more forcefully as a result of the presidential elections in 1988.[15] For the first time the country witnessed a solid campaign to question the honesty of the government in relation to stopping fraud. The issue to discuss further is the extent to which the hegemonic pattern of the State in Mexico has been sustained primarily through superstructural practices. To analyze this point, it is important to review the process of policy formation in education as an example.

HEGEMONY, LEGITIMACY, AND EDUCATIONAL POLICY FORMATION

From the perspective of the political sociology of education, Roger Dale stresses that education in capitalist societies tends to further the process of capital accumulation (furnishing the appropriate levels of knowledge and skills of the labor force), contributes to the provision of a societal context amenable to capital accumulation (contributing toward social control), and legitimates the dominant mode of production. On this last point he argues that "educational systems make a much more basic contribution to the legitimation of capitalism through the way that they make so many of its features seen absolutely normal. I propose, therefore, to label this core problem that of hegemony rather than one of legitimation (or ideology)" (1982: 146). The notion of political domination in the analysis of hegemony is based on socially diffused goals and competing class consciousness. The notion of hegemony in turn reflects a framework of competing and contrasting social classes which cannot have a common social destiny and are mediated by relationships of social and economic exploitation bearing sharp differences in power and material resources.

Ultimately, this accounts for the stability or nonstability of the political and social order. Any attempt to sort out the deadlock of a political and economic system that cannot be, in and of itself, justifiable in the view of some classes becomes the central issue. What is at stake, therefore, is not the gaining of consent but the attempt to unify values and subjective goals into a societal project.

Political domination from this perspective does not refer exclusively to a particular way of ruling a society or attaining acquiescence and consent. The focus of analysis is on how the dominant class, and any class-bound entity such as the capitalist State, operates undermining any sense of severe fragmentation of the total polity. In other words, how do the State and the ruling classes devise ideological means to exert authority that preclude resorting to legitimate violence as an organizational and ideological alternative to the existing social arrangements? And why and how are the subordinate social classes' interests and consciousness diffused to allow a given hegemonic and dominant culture to manipulate and control the subordinated political culture? In this regard, the concept of hegemony points at an issue similar to one addressed by legitimation: the ability of the State to design, negotiate, and sustain a stable political arrangement for a society fragmented in social classes, and the peculiar contribution of superstructural practices to this end.

According to Carnoy, the superstructure in society represents an active and positive factor in any process of historical development. He indicates that "[it] is the complex of ideological and cultural relations, the spiritual and intellectual life, and the political expression of those relations that become the focus of analysis rather than structure" (1984: 68).

Hegemony thus refers to the relationship between social classes. A faction of the dominant class could be thought of as exercising hegemony over other allied factions of the block in power. The actual direction of this relationship is based on the moral and intellectual leadership of the dominant faction, which in turn is generally founded on its economic supremacy in the social formation.

Hegemony also refers to the relationships between the block in power and the subordinate classes in terms of the ideological predominance of bourgeois values and norms over those of the latter. In Gramsci's formulation, hegemonic direction occurs through moral and intellectual persuasion rather than through control by the military, the police, or the coercive power of the law. He argues that "rule by intellectual and moral hegemony is the form of power which gives stability and found power of wide-ranging consent and acquiescence, every relationship of hegemony is necessarily a pedagogical relationship" (1975, Vol. II: 1321).

In Mexico it has been hypothesized that educational policies are linked to the stability of the political system. In a well-documented book on Mexican politics, Miguel Basañez suggests that there have been attempts "to explain the stability of the Mexican political system in terms of its capacity to provide the masses with social mobility and social benefits through skillful administration in agrarian, educational, labor and electoral matters" (1981: 175).

He argues that the hegemony of the political-military bureaucracy that took over the State apparatus after the Revolution was built on the basis of four premises: redistribution of land, strengthening of labor unions, massive education, and the principle of nonreelection (Basañez, 1981: 176). Each of these premises addresses differently the needs and political demands of particular social classes, sectors, or political actors. Thus "education constitutes an open access to social mobility mainly for the small, urban middle classes, inasmuch as such mobility is encountered by the peasants in the distribution of land and the workers in the security of employment" (Basañez, 1981: 178).

This hypothesis, although appealing and well documented, is not completely trustworthy. Stretching it to its limit would confine the analysis of education and hegemony to a reductionist and mechanistic approach. Education would be only a channel for social mobility for members of the middle classes or the petit bourgeoisie. This view might hold true for only a certain period of time. It would not permit us, however, to understand the proposal for a socialist education during Cárdenas' administration in the late 1930s. Although such a hypothesis could be useful to explain the development of some educational levels and modalities, like higher education, it would not help to understand the overall process of policy formation. It would not explain, for example, the rationale to launch the National Literacy Campaign during the government of Manuel Avila Camacho in 1944. This type of hypothesis does not differ substantially from other research findings in the scciology of education in Latin America, in which educational policies, particularly in the 1960s and 1970s, are explained as the State's response to pressures to enhance the social, political and occupational mobility of the middle class.

In response to the question about the features and determinants of educational policy formation in Mexico, it is possible to identify four main features characterizing this process. At the global level, the federal government has followed a policy of consistently increasing the allocation of resources in public education. This policy could be explained in the light of the hegemony hypothesis. At the intrabureaucratic and political level, education has been used to legitimize the corporatist network and the groups' interests, such as in the case of the teachers' union. Regarding the middle class, educational policies have been carefully used to counteract radical trends within a spectrum of political conflict, particularly in regard to distributive demands from several middle-class groups. Finally, it could be said that although a technical rationale operates in the formal process of educational policy formation, the underlying rationale is primarily political. Educational policy formation reflects bureaucratic dynamics and is a byproduct of politically contradictory projects within the State. A clear example of these trends is found in the adult education policies to be discussed in the final section of this chapter.

THE CORPORATIST STATE, HEGEMONIC POLITICS, AND EDUCATIONAL POLICY: FINANCING EDUCATIONAL DEVELOPMENT

In educational financing the federal government has shown a coherent and continuous commitment to increase financial resources for public education. Government officials argue that this is necessary to show the persistence, validity, and current importance of education in the "Revolutionary Program" for the masses.

Although analysts such as Basañez (1981) would argue that education is primarily at the service of the petit bourgeoisie, education is seen by the bureaucracy as an inexpensive tool at the service of the State to reach income redistribution and favor all social sectors. Although at some educational levels the middle class may be better prepared to take advantage of new developments in education, it would be misleading and perhaps naive to emphasize that the middle class is fully satisfied with the State's educational policies. If educational policies were in fact favoring the middle class, as Basañez argues, there would not be a negative evaluation of the quality of education, a criticism of the leitmotif of the expansionary publicly funded educational policies, or a persisting growth of elitist private secondary and higher education institutions to provide for the children of the dissatisfied middle and upper classes and the ruling elite.

Looking at higher education, for example, it is possible to observe the existing conflict between public and private universities. Even though private universities are quite small in enrollment and material resources compared with public universities, the latter have grown at the same pace as the former in the last few years. Between 1976 and 1981 the number of public universities grew from 95 to 159, while the number of private universities grew from 91 to 151 (Pescador and Torres, 1985: Table 6).

Analysts of education have also noticed the new initiatives of the private sector and Church-related organizations to counteract the hegemony and influence of the State in education, mainly in higher education (Fuentes Molinar, 1983: 203-241; Pescador, 1980). An example of this type of conflict in the formulation of educational policies was the polemic unleashed by the elaboration of free primary education textbooks during Echeverría's administration (1970-1976). Reactions included complaints about their "Marxist character" or their "extreme openness" in sexual matters (Latapí, 1976). Another case involved public claims and accusations from middle-class parents' associations during López Portillo's administration against some of the Secretariat of Education higher officials in charge of overseeing the quality of education and the production of books for high schools.

The importance of these issues in regard to educational policy must be seen in the context of their potential implications for education. In the academic year 1985-1986, a total of 71.7 million books were produced and distributed free of charge by the Secretariat of Public Education to primary school students and teachers. Similarly, in 1986-1987, 55 million free books for elementary education, 1.4 million monographs per state for the diversification of fifth and sixth grade curriculum, and 5 million free books for pre-school education were distributed throughout the country. The use of these books is mandatory in both private and public schools.

Another important factor to consider in the analysis of educational policies is the actual government expenditure in this sector. In 1970 from a total GNP of 418.7 million pesos, 10.7 million or 2.57 percent went to education. This increased to 39.7 million pesos in 1975, and to 276.5 million pesos in 1981 reaching 4.72 percent of the GNP. A similar situation occurred between 1970 and 1982 in terms of total government expenditures. In 1970, from a total of 109.2 million pesos, 7.1 million pesos or 6.58 percent were expended in education. This figure increased to 29.1 million pesos or 7.29 percent in 1975, and to 306.5 million pesos in 1982, a 13.83 percent of the government expenditures. Table 2-1 shows the allocation to education as a percentage of the GNP and of total government expenditures.

In recent years, federal participation in education increased sharply compared with other possible sources of educational financing. The contributions of the states and the municipalities together do not account for more than 20 percent of the expenditure in education, and investments of private sector in education have declined substantially over time. In fact private sector participation dropped from 16 percent at the beginning of the Echeverría administration to less than 6 percent at the end of López Portillo's administration (see Table 2-2).

The decrease in the private sector participation in education is not an indication of a lack of interest. On the contrary, low private participation is not the result of a massive withdrawal of funds, but the effect of an overwhelming investment of the State. The high level of investment in education by the government demonstrates the financial commitment of the State to decisively control educational policy and programs in the country. As mentioned earlier, education is seen by the State bureaucracy as a cheap and effective instrument to compensate for any change in income distribution and for any substantive transformation of the socioeconomic structure. Education at certain levels and at some points in time becomes an effective means to generate social mobility in some segments of a particular social class, such as the petit bourgeoisie. In practice, however, education plays only an indirect role in the redistribution of social goods.

Table 2-1
Educational Financing in Mexico, 1970-1982

GNP Accounted for by Public Education Spending, Government's Total Expenditure, and Total Educational Expenditure

Year	Spending Total $	Education $	Education %	Expenditure Total $	Education $	Education %
1970	418,700	10,743	2.57	109,238	7,188	6.58
1971	452,400	12,561	2.78	121,331	8,724	7.19
1972	512,300	15,341	2.99	148,768	11,058	7.43
1973	619,600	19,832	3.20	204,033	14,091	6.90
1974	813,700	26,671	3.28	276,483	19,311	6.98
1975	988,300	39,707	4.02	400,549	29,152	7.27
1976	1,228,000	56,632	4.59	486,126	39,776	8.18
1977	1,674,700	81,363	4.86	686,558	57,258	8.34
1978	2,104,550	97,680	4.64	926,034	72,748	7.85
1979	2,738,981	137,043	5.00	1,124,269	97,354	8.66
1980	4,276,490	194,648	4.55	1,169,172	125,354	10.72
1981	5,858,225	276,509	4.72	1,440,724	196,492	13.64
1982	-	-	-	2,216,316	306,522	13.83

Source: Calculated from José A. Pescador "El balance de la educación superior en el sexenio 1976-1982," *Foro Universitario*, No. 28, March 1983, Tables XII and XIV.

If educational policies in Mexico are analyzed from the perspective of the "ethical State" in Gramscian terms (Torres, 1985), it is possible to argue that they are not aimed at serving only the middle class by creating new channels of social mobility or even by responding politically to its demands and pressures. Education, in the view of one of the most prestigious intellectuals of the PRI, is oriented toward enhancing the multiclass orientation of the State's welfare policies. These in turn are said to have predictable effects in the transformation of the social structure in the ongoing revolutionary programs of the government (Reyes Heroles, 1983). The State bureaucracy therefore sees education as an instrument of compensatory legitimation having similar effects to distributive welfare policies.

An example of the way in which the State views education can be found in the evolution of the elementary school system. Between 1970 and 1982 elementary education accounted for more than 70 percent of the total student enrollment, employed more than 50 percent of the teaching force, and included more than 80 percent of the schools in Mexico. By 1986, elementary education concentrated 37 percent of the educational expenditure (267.3 million pesos). Despite these facts, and studies showing that in countries like Brazil and Colombia public financing of elementary education

Table 2-2
Total National (estimated) Expenditures in Education (million of current pesos)

Year	Budget SEP (1)	%	Budget states (2)*	%	Budget municipalities (3)	%	Exp private (4)	%	Total (5)	%
71	9,445	65.5	2,518	17.4	217	1.5	2,250	15.6	14,430	100
72	11,760	66.5	3,189	18.0	275	1.6	2,450	13.9	17,674	100
73	15,140	69.2	3,817	17.4	329	1.5	2,600	11.9	21,886	100
74	20,795	68.1	5,811	19.0	432	1.4	3,500	11.5	30,538	100
75	31,115	71.7	7,396	17.1	637	1.5	4,200	9.7	43,348	100
76	42,496	72.4	9,486	16.8	849	1.4	5,500	9.4	58,691	100
77	61,761	73.5	13,569	16.2	1,169	1.4	7,500	8.9	83,999	100
78	77,563	72.6	18,676	17.5	1,609	1.5	9,000	8.4	106,848	100
79	103,776	72.0	26,133	18.1	2,252	1.6	12,000	8.3	144,161	100
80	139,465	72.5	34,839	18.1	3,002	1.6	15,000	7.8	192,306	100
81	219,935	75.8	47,587	16.4	4,101	1.4	18,500	6.4	290,123	100
82	385,000	79.4	67,900	14.0	5,800	1.2	26,200	5.4	484,900	100

* It includes the D.D.F (Department of the Federal District).

For (1) i) from 1971 to 1981: "Cuenta de la Hacienda Pública Federal" 1971 to 1980, SHCP and SPP;
ii) 1982: Estimated by the Dirección General de Programación.

For (2) i) from 1971 to 1982: "Gasto de los gobiernos estatales en educación," Dirección General de Programación (SEP), 1982.
For (3) i) from 1971 to 1976: *Diagnóstico del sistema educativo nacional*, Chapter 10, Dirección General de Planeación Educativa (SEP), 1977.

ii) from 1971 to 1976: Estimated by the Dirección General de Programación (SEP).

For (4) i) from 1971 to 1977: "Producción estatal de servicios" Dirección General de Programación (SPP), 1979.
ii) from 1978 to 1982: Estimated by the Dirección General de Programación (SEP).

Source: SEP Memoria 1976/1982, Volume I, *Política educativa*, Mexico, 1983: 489, table 9.1

has strong positive distributive effects (Jallade, 1974, 1976, 1977), some critics argue that in Mexico elementary education is not aimed at being an effective means to eliminate social and class inequality but rather to reproduce it. Although elementary education has reached all social sectors and all regions, it "has had differential outcomes that benefit particularly those social groups located in the intermediate and higher levels of the social stratification scale, especially those groups living in urban areas in the more developed regions of the country" (CEE, 1979: 1-2).

Educational financing in general has been used to counteract radical trends emerging from the political conflict permeating society. In this sense, educational policies and programs are used as powerful tools for the political cooptation of leaders, and to eliminate sources of dissatisfaction and conflict in certain social sectors.

An example of this phenomenon is the educational policies formulated during the Echeverría period. These were carefully designed to counteract political unrest in the universities after the student movement of 1968 and the crisis of 1971.[16] Educational policies in this period were used as a means to create a distance from the preceding policies implemented by Díaz Ordaz, who was seen as a conspicuous representative of an international capitalist model of development with strong authoritarian overtones.[17] Several studies have shown that during the government of Díaz Ordaz educational expenditures dropped sharply at the cost of educational enrollment. Total enrollment in education dropped from 64.4 to 43 percent compared with the preceding López Mateos government (1958-64), and educational and federal expenditures in education grew only 79 and 74 percent respectively, compared with 228 and 254 percent during López Mateos (CEE, 1971: 121-127).

It could be said that the Díaz Ordaz administration represented an impasse in terms of educational policies. Echeverría in turn not only reversed the financial setback of the previous administration, but actually returned to the financial standards set up by the government of López Mateos. Under Echeverría, federal expenditure in education increased from 9.4 million pesos at the beginning of his administration, to 30.7 million pesos by the end of his administration in 1976, representing an increment of 225 percent, while total enrollment grew only 38 percent (Centro de Estudios Educativos, 1976: 121-126).

Educational financing under the Echeverría government was meticulously used to satisfy most of the demands of intellectuals and scholars. Some of these included opening new teaching positions in higher education through the creation of the National Metropolitan University (UAM) in Mexico City and expanding the capacity of the system at that level to incorporate a growing educational demand, showing thus its first signs of massification. Other features of his administration, such as the amnesty offered to leaders of the 1968 student movement, and the growing incorporation of younger technocrats into his government even at the Cabinet level, were part, in Offe's terms, of a heavy reliance on the modes of State intervention (Offe, 1984).

The evolution of education in Mexico has been the result of a deliberate political project of the State. As part of the revolutionary image the State attempts to maintain, public education has been a means to compensate for other benefits the majority of the population cannot enjoy. To some extent also, the expansion of education has been instrumental in coopting political unrest and in keeping the political support of the largest and most powerful labor organization in the country, the teachers' union.

The Teachers' Union and Educational Policy

The National Union of Educational Workers (the Sindicato Nacional de Trabajadores de la Educación or SNTE) has been an important actor in the process of educational policy formation since its creation in 1943. This union was conceived as an organization with strong popular support to serve as an instrument of mobilization and as an intermediary between the popular masses, especially the peasants, and the State.

In contrast to the experience of most countries in South America (Núñez, 1986), the teaching profession in Mexico has been more an alternative for employment and social mobility of peasants than for members of the middle class. The teaching profession in Mexico differs from that in other parts of Latin America by having a heavy representation of males, not only in managerial positions, which is the case in the rest of the region, but also as rank-and-file teachers. The proportion of male teachers is higher in the rural and less developed parts of the country. This phenomenon has important implications in terms of labor opportunities available for males from a peasant or working class background.

Traditionally, the SNTE has functioned as an intermediary and instrument for the organization of the teachers' political constituency (Pescador and Torres, 1985). This role has been strengthened by the evolution of Mexico's development strategy and by the policy of incremental growth followed in education. The teachers' union has become increasingly important in the process of political bargaining in the educational arena. The main political groups controlling this union have also emerged as powerful groups within the Mexican State. Currently they constitute a central force in the formulation of educational policies and within the ruling party. The SNTE is also relevant in labor politics because of its large number of members and its character as an experienced intermediary between concrete segments of civil society. This leads us to conclude that under the present circumstances the teachers in general, and their organization as a union, have emerged as an important corporative entity. Until the early 1980s, the teachers' union constituted a firm and unchallenged support for the general processes of policy making and mass mobilization of the State. In 1989, however, important changes have occurred leading to the democratization of the union, which eventually may alter the relationships between union and State. The growing opposition to Revolutionary Vanguard, the political group that controlled the SNTE for the last two decades, was successful in overthrowing the leader of Revolutionary Vanguard Carlos Jonguitud, and the democratic teachers through mobilizations and strikes in the spring of 1989 succeeded in obtaining a salary increase of 25 percent—well above the ceiling imposed by the government's social pact between workers and capital.

The SNTE is the largest union in the country and perhaps one of the largest in Latin America. In the 1977-78 academic year, the SNTE had 548,355 members distributed in 55 sections throughout the country (see Table 2-3). It is also among the most financially powerful unions in the country. In 1982, the SNTE received in membership fees alone approximately $48 million. Politically, it is the core of the State Workers' Federation (the Federación Sindical de Trabajadores del Estado or FSTE) and the central faction of the "popular sector" of the PRI. The involvement of the teachers' union in the political system is impressive. The SNTE has seated 1 governor in the state of San Luis Potosí, who is at the same time the principal leader and lifetime president of the union; 1 federal senator; 11 federal representatives to the last Congress; slightly more than 100 local representatives for the state congresses, and several alternate representatives and senators. As Table 2-3 shows, the principal educational employer in Mexico is the Secretariat of Public Education (SEP). Teacher employment in the private sector is nonsignificant and the states have only one fifth of the total teaching force.

In organizational terms, the SNTE is very hierarchical. The center of power rests in the hands of the General Secretary of the National Central Council who screens the policies and demands of the organization. Traditionally, the principal bargaining areas of any union have been labor conditions, including salary, labor legislation, and social benefits for the members. The SNTE is no exception. The main areas of the union's concerns have been employment and internal promotion policies as well as supervision mechanisms; administrative reforms; rotation of teachers' positions; and the quality of teachers' training, including the quality of teachers' colleges, curriculum, and administration. It is important to highlight that in contrast

Table 2-3
National Union of Workers in Education: Membership, 1977-1978

Total of Sections	System	No. of Schools	Total Membership
36	Federal System	49,706	439,435
4	Federalized	107	2,573
18	State System	11,760	105,041
1	Private System	51	1,307

Source: María de la Luz Arriaga "El magisterio en lucha," in *Cuadernos Políticos*, Mexico, No. 27, 1981: 81.

to other professions, on graduation from the teachers' colleges, primary and secondary teachers almost automatically get jobs with the Secretariat of Public Education. According to an agreement with the union, the Secretariat of Public Education is under the obligation to allocate to teachers' college graduates a minimum of 22 teaching hours per month, the equivalent of a part-time job.

During the last few years, there has been growing dissatisfaction among teachers at the grass-roots level with their national organization. In 1979, a massive protest involving approximately one tenth of the membership of the SNTE gave place to the formation of the National Coordination of Educational Workers (Coordinadora Nacional de Trabajadores de la Educación, CNTE) as an independent teachers' union challenging the hegemonic leadership of the SNTE. The principal regional focus of such discontent is found in the states of Oaxaca, Chiapas, Morelos, Guerrero, Hidalgo, and the Estado de México. Most of these states, with the exception of the last, have large indigenous populations, are very underdeveloped compared to the rest of the country, and in some cases have been centers of more liberal political activity for decades. This movement of democratic teachers, although internally divided politically, made important gains in 1989.

The emergence of the teachers' union as a center of power is the result of the need of the corporatist State to reach a higher degree of political legitimation while devising a coherent framework for controlling labor leaders and articulating demands and support in the process of educational policy making. The obstacles the State has been facing to achieve these objectives more effectively are related to the complexity of the State. Increasing bureaucratic encapsulation of policy making, the growing complexity of civil society, and the sophistication of social demands from different interest groups and class factions have lead to a persistent conflict of interest between the SNTE and the Secretariat of Public Education.

This conflict has its major manifestation not only in key areas of policy making and policy operation, but also within the union itself, in the trends toward its redemocratization (Arriaga, 1981; Fuentes Molinar, 1983: 79-101). Although the teachers' union has not been in a position to exert a priori influence legally or politically on the process of educational policy, the SNTE has used the strategy of influencing policy decisions a posteriori. The SNTE has organized systematic nationwide boycotts of controversial decisions made by the SEP, which include obstructing the implementation of such policies. Among the areas of conflict have been the opposition of the SNTE to the plans and programs of teachers' colleges; the appointment of delegates to the General Delegations of the SEP in the states; the appointments of higher officials in the general administrative and political structure of the SEP; and the administrative decentralization of the SEP that began in 1977 and which implies high risks for a centralized union.

Also important in this regard are the position of the SNTE in relation to the organization, administration, academic projects, and political control of the National Pedagogic University;[18] the expansion of the preschool system during the López Portillo administration (1976-82), particularly as this related to teacher training and hiring policies; the creation of the National Mass Literacy Campaign (PRONALF) and the National Institute of Adult Education (INEA);[19] and the process of bargaining with the Secretariat of Public Education over labor conditions, wages, and social benefits for teachers.

A hypothesis to explain the differences between the teachers' union and the Secretariat of Public Education, which were publicly evident between 1977 and 1982, indicates that these are due to opposite political strategies. From the point of view of the union, this means a traditional strategy of political clientelism[20] expressed by its programs, which do not correspond to the strategy of modernization and administrative reform of the Secretariat of Public Education. This view indicates that conflict of interest and power in the process of policy formation is the factor that has given shape to the principal decisions in education. It also shows that the overall performance of the actors involved has followed the rules of the corporatist process of bargaining. It has taken the issue away from the State boundaries to resolve it within the overall political strategy and practice of the ruling party. However, this process has not been free from conflicts and contradictions, nor without impact on the policies and the overall quality of education (Pescador and Torres, 1985).

Bureaucratic Rationale and Adult Education Reform

Most State bureaucracies in developing countries tend to overemphasize the value of technical remedies to problems such as illiteracy resulting from underdevelopment, social inequality, and poverty. However, new policies on adult education advanced by the Mexican State between 1981 and 1982 were more than a technocratic attempt in policy planning to deal with an educational modality misrepresented at the level of policy formation in an educational system strongly oriented toward basic formal education for children.

A substantial proportion of the hidden curricula in adult education was structured around bureaucratic dynamics and the political agenda of the Mexican State. In fact, the new adult education policies not only followed a technobureaucratic rationale, but were structured according to the political rationale of the corporatist State. Adult education policies became part and parcel of the State rationale leading to the development of a system of education capable of including a large mass of adults. These were the members of the most disadvantaged sectors of society, distant from the mainstream mechanisms of political representation. In such a context, adult education became a means through which the State attempted to develop a constituency instrumental in the development of new means for political legitimation and controlled political participation.

Although dissent to State practices and policies and political struggle in Mexico have been mostly related to organized labor and students' political activism, the potential conflictive role of disenfranchised and impoverished adults should not be too quickly dismissed (Eckstein, 1988: 274-278; 1989, 12-25). Three arguments support this point. Larger, more encompassing political alliances, including the urban poor, eventually emerged as social movements after the earthquake of 1985. They are starting to alter the standard patterns of political negotiation and strife in Mexico (Eckstein, 1988). In addition, following Claus Offe, it may be argued that growing informality in relations of production may lead to decommodification of important sectors of the labor force, related to what Eckstein has called "incomplete proletarianization" (1989: 18). This decommodified form of labor which cannot fully exchange its value in the market may become a source of political conflict of some kind (Torres, 1990). Finally, in looking at new policies of compensatory legitimation attempting to create new channels for political participation, the anticipatory role of the capitalist State in policy formation should not be overlooked (Torres, 1988).

Looking at the organizational aspects of policy formation, although current adult education programs are narrower in scope and less effective than those carried out under Echeverría and López Portillo, they share a similar rationale. One of their purposes is to serve as a policy laboratory. Through them, the State can implement in the educational system some of the main directives from the administrative reforms and deconcentration carried out by the public sector. However, it is important to indicate that although in the last 60 years Mexico organized an educational system that included 24 million students, it was not until 1975 that the State publicly became responsible for educating adults. The National Law of Adult Education required the State to offer basic education services to the illiterate population 15 years of age and older, which in 1982 was close to 6.5 million.

During the Echeverría administration, adult education regained momentum when the National Law of Adult Education was passed in 1975. One of the outcomes was the creation of the National System of Adult Education (Sistema Nacional de Educación de Adultos, SNEA). During López Portillo's presidential term, a national literacy campaign began in early May 1981 and the National Institute of Adult Education (INEA) was created as a decentralized branch of the Secretariat of Public Education. The Institute was responsible for undertaking research, designing experimental programs in adult education, and coordinating an extensive network of services of primary and secondary basic education for adults. The magnitude of these policies becomes more evident considering that in Mexico there are 52 different indigenous spoken languages besides Spanish; that approximately one million people neither speak, read, nor write Spanish; and that approximately 28 million people 15 years and older have not yet finished their primary and/or secondary education.

The political-administrative organization of the National Literacy Campaign reflected both the interbureaucratic and political struggles taking place within the Secretariat of Public Education and the way in which adult education was used as a policy laboratory to achieve political objectives

(Torres, 1984a). Several factors tend to reinforce this perception. Early in the Campaign, it became clear that the process would not allow a massive participation of human resources connected to the teachers' union. The control over the type of groups involved in the Campaign helped to minimize, in the view of the Campaign's higher officials, the possibility of transferring the ongoing power conflicts manifest in the formulation of educational policies, first into the Campaign and later into the Institute. Another factor was the hiring of nonpermanent personnel. Both decisions were seen as a means to minimize the replication of the conditions that existed in the formal education system which gave place to a self-expanding and ever-enlarging bureaucracy.

Several other steps were used from the beginning to maintain control over the process of adult education policy formation and implementation. These included the definition of policy based on administrative decentralization, linear planning, and a fast and supposedly effective new method for literacy training implemented by the new technocracy in charge of the programs of adult education. In addition, the hiring of university and occasionally high school students as volunteers was another means to make the program cost-effective and to keep the teachers' union away from the Campaign. This option implied the use of nonspecialized personnel, who in some cases had higher educational credentials but lacked experience in teaching adults.

Organizational decentralization in policy implementation also affected the power of the teachers' union. Because the union is a highly centralized and hierarchical organization with power residing in the hands of the Executive Council based in Mexico City, its capacity to advance a consistent policy that could address what was happening in the states was severely jeopardized. The union was prevented by several handicaps from confronting and bargaining over adult education policies. Since the new system of adult education was set up, the technocratic outlook of the Ministry of Education concerning adults overran the strategies of political clientelism of the union.[21]

In retrospect, the policies of adult education appear to be an attempt to put into practice an ideal technocratic outlook of policy planning, policy making, and policy implementation. The higher officials of the National Institute of Adult Education were part of the bureaucratic cadres connected with the Secretary of Public Education. They were trained at the university in technical and administrative professions heavily influenced by theoretical approaches based on the use of system theory, complex organization, linear planning and programming, and scientific administration (Torres, 1984a).

CONCLUSION

Historically, education in Mexico has displayed some of the main contradictions of the State. Perhaps more than in any other area, the process of educational policy formation has served as a means to expose the clashes between factional bureaucratic ideologies, political projects, and antagonistic political groups.

During the past decade educational policies have been used in Mexico as a State response to counteract some of the radical trends resulting from the political conflicts in society. Education has been used to regulate the hegemonic relations between the State and society in various ways. In some cases, it has been used to compensate for the lack of more substantial distributive reforms. In others, it has served to counteract dissatisfaction and political unrest of different sectors, including university students, intellectuals, and some factions of the middle class.

Adult education has been effectively used to reach and eventually to control sectors of the labor force that are neither employed (and therefore mobilized and controlled through corporatist labor unions) nor organized in civil associations (and therefore mobilized and controlled by the ruling party through State welfare agencies). Adult education has been used in an attempt to increase the socialization of these sectors, making them employable and thus furthering the legitimacy of the State and preventing potential unrest. Adult education policies have also been used as a policy laboratory in which to test organizational processes, administrative methods, and political reactions from powerful interest groups such as the teachers' union.

NOTES

1. L. Vincent Padgett indicates that the Revolutionary Coalition that rules Mexico includes a "cluster of groups and leaders" whose political prominence is directly or indirectly connected with the "revolutionary" struggle and the victories won in that struggle. There are men and groups that given their connections with the Revolution have some influence, or at the very least, hope to gain influence in decision making within the system (1966: 34).

2. Samuel Huntington (1968) indicates in this regard that the capacity of the official party to assimilate new groups into the political system has been one of the factors contributing to Mexico's political stability and economic development.

3. The three wings of the PRI are workers, peasants, and the popular sectors. Peter Smith, in his documented study on *The Labyrinths of Power* in Mexico has argued that: "Whatever the true proportions of party membership, it is clear that the popular sector—presumably the smallest of all—has dominated congressional delegations of the PRI. [Between 1943 and 1976] the popular sector has generally received more than half of the deputy seats" (Smith, 1979: 227).

4. The hegemonic role of the official party is understood as a sociopolitical condition in which all aspects of political life of Mexican society are (1) determined by a single political group and, (2) conditioned by the ideology of a power elite that determines the degree of autonomy of the political system. In this context, the concept of hegemony refers to a form of order in which a certain way of life and a given set of ideas play a dominant role in the society, giving way in turn to a particular perception of reality which is diffused throughout all its institutional and private manifestations, informing with its spirit all social relations, particularly within intellectual and moral connotations. For further references see also Marx and Engels (1970); Livingstone (1976: 235-250) and Gramsci (1975).

5. According to Brandenburg, "the Revolutionary Family is composed of the men who have run Mexico for over half a century, who have laid the policy-lines of the Revolution, and who today hold effective decision making power." In his view, the Revolutionary Family operates at three levels. At the top, there is a selected group that decides on the major orientation of Mexican economic and political life with the president as the head of the family. A second level is composed of top representatives of the power elite loyal to the supreme chief, the president. Finally, a third level includes the high ranking officials of the PRI (1964: 3-6). One of the most astute political analysts of Mexico, however, has argued that

> The idea, repeated so many times, that the governing bureaucracy of this country constitutes a "revolutionary family" only has served to hide the specific features of the formation of political power in Mexico. [This notion of a "revolutionary family"] suggests, in effect, a degree of homogeneity that in fact cannot be granted by virtue of the different commitments acquired by this bureaucracy with the various groups and classes in the process of configuring the social pact needed to end the civil war unleashed in the second decade of this century, and thus proceed to restructure the state. The dissimilarity and commitments contracted with the dominant social bloc and with the subordinated classes has been progressively accentuated during the long decades that have elapsed since then. (Pereyra, 1982: 155)

6. See Lowenthal, *Partners in Conflict. The United States and Latin America* (Baltimore, MD: Johns Hopkins University Press, 1987).

7. Hansen argues that the official party is used by the power elite to control Mexican politics at two different levels: "At the first level the PRI is used as a mechanism to attain majorities in municipal, state and national elections. At the second, it is used to control the various sectors of the party itself; the PRI structure provides access to large organized groups which can furnish the party with electoral majorities without granting those groups anything that could be reasonably labelled effective representation" (1971: 122).

8. Given the system of internal nominations for major political offices, including the presidency, it has become a norm in Mexican politics that when the PRI announces its candidate, public interest in knowing who will be the next president ends.

9. The four candidates were M. Bartlett, Secretary of the Interior; M. González Avelar, Secretary of Education; R. Beteta, president of PEMEX; A Del Mazo, the Secretary of Energy, Mining and Para-state Enterprises.

10. This refers particularly to the content and orientation of articles 3, 27, and 123 of the Constitution (Pereyra, 1979: 23).

11. In 1982, Mexico faced its worst economic crisis in history. The country's interest burden rose from $5.4 billion in 1980 to $10 billion in 1982. New foreign investments fell by 50 percent bringing the economy of the country to a solvency crisis.

12. Schmitter has identified the following corporatist experiments in government: Sweden, Switzerland, The Netherlands, Norway, Denmark, Austria, Spain, Portugal, Brazil, Chile, Peru, Greece, Yugoslavia, and Mexico; he also claims that part if not a substantive portion of the interest groups' universe in the United States, Great Britain, West Germany, Canada, and France can be characterized as corporatist (1974: 11n). Most recently, Lehmbruch, analyzing the European context, has ranked Austria, Sweden, and The Netherlands as "strong corporatism," West Germany and Great Britain as "medium corporatism," and France as "weak corporatism" (1982: 16-23).

13. At the descriptive level, the argument here follows Hans Weiler's analysis when he argues that the State may be understood as "the totality of public authority in a

given society (government or otherwise), regardless of the level—national, sub-national, or local—at which it may operate" (1983: 259).

14. The understanding of Mexican corporatism stated here is based on quite different grounds from Schmitter's definition and analysis. Following Stepan's (1978) comments on the Mexican case, Schmitter's (1974) model and definition

> presents an ideal type and no regime necessarily fulfills all his criteria. For example, most writers would probably consider Mexico one of the most fully structured corporatist regimes in Latin America. However, even when we look at urban labor, which we could expect to be the most fully institutionalized sector of the corporatist state, we find a situation that differs in four of nine of Schmitter's criteria. The *singular* criterion does not apply, since Mexican labor, even at the peak levels, has been represented by two or three organizations since the 1940s. The criterion of *compulsory* membership occasionally does not apply, because the *singular* criterion does not apply. The *non-competitive* criterion does not fully apply, because due to their somewhat greater autonomy and militancy, the "non-official" union has presented greater threats to the regime, and as Brandenburg indicates, have been able to extract somewhat more resources from the political elite than their official competitors. The criterion of *representational monopoly* granted to organizations is also not applicable. Normally, the government, in its continuous attempt to coopt or to contain the rival unions grants them seats on major commissions and in Congress. (1978: 68-69)

What remains is the notion of a corporatist system that works through negotiations and bargaining from accepted, "legitimate" associations or corporations representing vested interests in a given issue, rather than labor confrontation. The State pursues two contradictory logics of development, one supporting capital accumulation and private enterprise surplus, and another supporting measures that reinforce the legitimation of the system but contradict the surplus-oriented facade. The revolutionary origin and revolutionary legal foundations of the Mexican State have contributed to the development of a unique mode of policy making. This model balances negotiations with repression, investment with cooptation, and the formation of political consensus through alternative systems of political representation at the grass-roots level with political manipulation and electoral corruption.

15. The PRI was almost defeated in the 1988 elections, barely achieving absolute majority, winning 50.4 percent of the vote. Cuahutémoc Cárdenas, from a left-leaning alliance, obtained 31.1 percent (an impressive showing for a leftist coalition) and Manuel Clouthier from the right-wing oriented party PAN (Partido de Acción Nacional) obtained 17.1 percent of the vote. The remaining 1.4 percent was obtained by the candidate of the PRT or Trotskyist Party (Partido Revolucionario de los Trabajadores), Rosario Ibarra de Piedra, and by Gumersindo Magaña, the candidate of the far-to-the-right-wing party, PDM (Partido Demócrata Mexicano). After the election, the PRT and the PDM lost their electoral registration because they did not achieve the minimum of votes prescribed by electoral law.

16. The student movement of 1968 was one of the major cases of student unrest in Mexican history. The government used strong repression that resulted in the massacre—never fully documented—of more than 500 students in Tlatelolco. The crisis of 1971 also involved repressive actions from the government in the Casco de San Cosme, an area of downtown Mexico City.

17. The model of development advanced by Díaz Ordaz was severely criticized on several occasions, though not essentially modified, by Echeverría himself.

18. A nonautonomous university created in 1978 with the explicit intention of upgrading the quality of teachers' training but with the implicit long-term purpose of transforming and overriding the traditional teachers' colleges—which include non-university postsecondary education controlled for many decades by the union.

19. This, which included among its purposes the training of adult education teachers, would keep this training process away from the teachers' union's sphere of influence.

20. Frances Rothstein has defined clientelism or patron-client relationships as "a form of politics in which ties between leaders and followers are personal. The patron grants favor in return for political support, material goods and or other services" (Rothstein, 1979: 25).

21. This does not mean that government technocrats were more concerned than the teachers' union with democratic participation. In both cases their concern was with the need to identify more effective means for social and political control. The growing importance of the movement of democratic teachers between 1979 and 1989 obviously alters the framework of policy negotiation in Mexican education. Some studies are appearing which explore the political implications of the democratic movement in Mexico (Street, 1984; 1989).

3 The Educational System: Its Structure and Internal Conflicts

INTRODUCTION

The general process of change brought about by the Revolution between 1910 and 1921 had major effects on the basic institutions of Mexican society. Particularly important was the impact of the Revolution on the institutional structure of the educational system. In 1921, the government created the Secretariat of Public Education[1] as one of the means to implement some of the major policy directions established by the Constitution of 1917.

The Secretariat of Public Education was designed to be responsible for implementing the fundamental principles outlined in the third article of the Constitution that represented the cornerstone of the new education system. This article established four principles around which the new education in the country was to be restructured: free delivery of instruction throughout the nation; secularization of education in all public institutions of learning; limitation of all religious associations or ministries of any religious creed to create or manage schools of primary instruction; and establishment of new private primary schools only with approval of the State and under direct official supervision (Gill, 1969: 21). The Constitution aimed at the creation of a free, compulsory system of education with no involvement from the private sector. Schooling was organized under a centralized federal system that was expected to control the resources, the administration, and the curriculum. This new system permitted only limited freedom to municipal and state governments in the implementation of their local systems of education. However, it provided the State with a strong mechanism of control over the delivery, the content, and the management of education.

This chapter analyzes the evolution of the educational system in Mexico that began with the creation of the Secretariat of Public Education. Emphasis is given in the discussion to the factors that affected the efficiency of the system over time. The chapter also focuses on the role of decentralization as a key State policy approach for the development of education in the country. Attention is given to the evolution of the educational system from the point of view of both the role of the State in the process of policy planning leading to the expansion of education and the conflicts affecting the educational State bureaucracy over the last decades. The chapter concludes with a general discussion of the major contradictions found in the process of educational planning in Mexico.

THE EVOLUTION OF THE EDUCATIONAL PROFILE IN MEXICO

José Vasconcelos, the first Secretary of Education,[2] undertook as one of his first official tasks the diagnosis of the education system. He was seeking to identify major gaps and to create a reliable database that could allow the government to take well-documented steps to restructure education. One such attempt was the organization of a general survey of educational resources in Mexico City. The results of this review showed an abysmal picture even for the conditions of Mexico at the time.

The education system was found to lack the capacity to absorb the existing primary school-aged population. Of 160,000 children the system was providing services to approximately 60,000 students due to a lack of places in primary schools. Those attending school were receiving education that did not meet the minimum criteria to allow them to become productively integrated into society later in life (*El Universal*, February 9, 1922). Vasconcelos also relied heavily on the results of a census carried out in the Federal District. This census showed that of 118,133 children between 4 and 14 years of age, 47,621 or 40.3 percent could not read and write. Of those who were literate, 55,057 were enrolled in private schools (Pescador, 1986: 9).

A first response to the problems affecting education was the design and organization in 1921 of an aggressive literacy campaign complemented by an increase in the number of public libraries all over the country. However, the challenges faced by the newly created federal system of education were immense. Several factors contributed to make the task of the Secretary of Education a major enterprise. Among them, the most important were the large size of the country (1,972,000 square kilometers); a society devastated by a prolonged civil war that had resulted in more than one million dead and an equal number migrating to the major urban centers; a population of over 14 million scattered around the territory but with a large proportion concentrated in two major cities, Mexico City and Guadalajara; and a demographic structure characterized by a very young population.[3]

Demographically, this situation did not substantially change over the years as far as its effects on education were concerned. The challenges faced by the government immediately after the Revolution became even more acute with the impressive population growth that took place over the next five decades (see Table 3-1). After 1940, the population doubled every two decades reaching over 74 million in 1980. This, together with large flows of migrants from rural to urban areas, aggravated the situation. One of the most important effects of this phenomenon was the change in the configuration of the rural-urban population structure. Although by 1910 the rural areas in the country comprised 71.3 percent of the total population, 50 years later only 49 percent of the population was living in rural areas (Secretaría de Industria y Comercio, 1970: 17). Another effect was a change of the ethnic and multicultural configuration of the population. By 1980 more than 52 indigenous languages were spoken in Mexico by over five million people. Over one million of this indigenous population spoke no Spanish.[4] The age composition of the population was also an important intervening factor in the government's plans to restructure education. By the mid-1970s, approximately 47 percent of the population was less than 15 years of age, and 65 percent was less than 25 years old, a situation that has changed only slightly in the early 1980s according to the National Census of 1980.

Chapter one shows that between 1910 and 1920 Mexico was involved in a bloody, cruel, and destructive Revolution that left deep scars on society. From the Madero revolt against Díaz in October 1910 to Venustiano Carranza's ascent to power in March 1917, it has been estimated that one

Table 3-1
Population of Mexico, 1895-1987

Year	Increment	Total	Males	Females
1895	100	12,632,427	6,280,506	6,351,921
1900	108	13,607,259	6,752,118	6,855,141
1910	120	15,160,369	7,504,471	7,655,898
1921	113	14,334,780	7,003,785	7,330,995
1930	131	16,552,722	8,119,004	8,433,718
1940	156	19,653,552	9,695,787	9,957,765
1950	204	25,791,017	12,696,935	13,094,082
1960	276	34,923,129	17,415,320	17,507,809
1970	382	48,225,238	24,065,614	24,159,624
1980	549	69,392,835	34,748,224	34,644,611
1981	564	71,283,520	35,694,625	35,588,895
1982	579	73,187,936	36,647,922	36,540,014
1983	594	75,107,285	37,608,729	37,498,556
1984	610	77,042,773	38,577,617	38,465,156
1985	625	78,995,602	39,555,169	39,440,433
1986	641	80,970,198	40,543,663	40,426,535
1987	657	82,965,759	41,542,712	41,423,047

Source: 1895-1970 data, Secretaría de Industria y Comercio. *Agenda estadística 1974* (Mexico, D.F. Mexico 1974), p. 12 and Secretaría de la Presidencia de México, *Mensaje presidencial 1980.* (Mexico, D.F., Mexico 1980); SPP-Conapo-Wade México. Estimaciones y proyecciones de población, 1950-2000, SPP, Mexico, 1983.

out of every eight Mexicans was killed. Overall, between 1.2 to 2 million Mexicans lost their lives during this period.

Despite these facts, the Revolution brought important changes to the social and economic structure of the country. A new type of nationalism became manifest through many forms of social and cultural expression, including the arts and general education. In many cases, this was a result of an attempt to preserve the country's indigenous cultures. Public libraries were built with the purpose of making means of education more widely available to the general population. Murals were painted as a form of popular art by the now-famous Orozco, Siqueiros, and Diego Rivera working under the protection of Vasconcelos. Vasconcelos' crusade for increasing the number of schools has been seen as an effort to coopt and centralize the working class. His open support of popular culture and the fine arts has been contrasted with the role of Anatoly Lunacharsky, the first commissar of the Soviet Revolution (Vázquez, 1970: 159). Vaughan (1982) contends that Vasconcelos used the arts to dampen revolutionary agitation and to elicit loyalty to the postrevolutionary state. She argues that

> Mexican educators sought to create through the schools a modern society manipulable by a bourgeois elite. In primary education they sought to increase workers' productivity by imparting manual skills and scientific attitude toward the world, by imposing industrial discipline and conscientious attitudes toward work, and by dampening class consciousness to ensure loyalty to the nation state. (in Parker and Parker, 1985: 409)

While acknowledging this criticism, it is important to emphasize that for the first time rural dwellers were taken into consideration in planning education. Federal funds for public education were increased substantially, especially during the Obregón regime at the time of the creation of the Secretariat of Public Education.

Among the legacies of the Revolution were the establishment of compulsory and free education; the introduction of a nationalist approach in the school curriculum, reflected later on in the free-textbook policy (Neumann and Cunningham, 1982); and the attempt to make education a means to compensate for conditions that impeded the postrevolutionary society to become as egalitarian as expected.[5] Perhaps two of the main achievements in education were the establishment of a long-standing literacy training tradition and the creation of a strong system of rural education.[6]

An important phenomenon to keep in mind in the evolution of education in Mexico is the pattern of growth that characterized all levels of the system. During the late 1960s and early 1970s the educational system suffered a considerable expansion including the massification of higher education. Two factors contributed to the expansion of education: the large number of school-aged population and the rapid growth of the economy. By 1960, 54.35 percent of the total population was under 20 years of age, representing a considerable demand on the educational system. At the same time, the country had reached a period of economic stability and a pace of growth that contributed to the allocation of resources to education.[7]

The general rate of growth of the education system between 1950 and 1970 was higher than 100 percent in all levels with the exception of preschool education. By the early 1980s, there were more than 24 million students in the educational system with roughly 800,000 teachers (Pescador and Torres, 1985: 88). The level of education that expanded the most was higher education. By 1964 there were 80 private and public universities throughout the country with a total enrollment of 116,628 students, compared with only 71,524 students six years earlier in 1958. However, 20 years later in 1982 there were 315 universities (148 private and 167 public) with an enrollment close to 1.2 million students. Only the National Autonomous University (UNAM) had approximately half a million students including university high school students (*Preparatoria*), undergraduates, and graduate students.[8] Expansion in the education system is presented in Table 3-2.

The Extent of Schooling Efficiency

The experience of countries in the developing world shows that an educational system capable of including all or almost all school-aged children cannot be created overnight, nor can it be made effective and efficient simply by political will. The experience of Mexico is no different. In spite of the pattern of continuous expansion of modern schooling in Mexico, the system is still plagued by a number of problems that have persisted during the last four decades. Dropouts and attrition remain critical problems for policy planners. There is still a pattern of uneven development in education. Some of the most backward regions and states in the country, such as Chiapas and Oaxaca where the bulk of the indigenous population lives, are at an enormous disadvantage compared with larger urban centers such as the Federal District. Table 3-3 shows some of these differences among the states and the Federal District in elementary education.

Examining the evolution of students cohorts between 1965 and 1974, repetition and dropping out appear as critical problems. Table 3-4 shows the situation for four different student cohorts. The greatest dropout and repetition rates are observed in first grade. An average of 30 percent of students is lost when they move from first to second grade. The other levels have an attrition rate of 10 percent. Overall, these figures show that 61.8 percent of the students have left school or repeated at the end of the primary cycle. This situation changed only slightly with the implementation in 1978 of a system of automatic promotion from first to second grade. Rather than solving the problem, this approach moved the critical dropout point to the upper levels of elementary education. The rate ten years later shows only a minimum improvement compared to other countries in the region.[9] Between 1985 and 1986, schooling efficiency reached only 51.3 percent in elementary education and 74.4 percent in junior high school (De la Madrid, 1986: 64-75).

This picture is even more critical regarding figures on dropout and repetition rates in rural and urban areas. Data available for the periods 1962-67

Table 3-2
Mexico: Enrollment by Educational Level (selected years)

Level	1958	1964	1970	1976	1977	1978	1982	1985-86
Total	5,184,122	7,744,050	11,538,871	16,608,676	17,487,970	18,295,700	23,587,858	25,579,266
Pre-schooling & Elementary	4,772,495	6,844,625	9,648,328	12,776,101	13,219,058	13,788,300	17,005,231	18,258,293
Jr. High and High School	347,728	782,797	1,563,325	3,127,328	3,502,830	3,686,800	5,508,026	6,064,792
Higher Education*	63,899	116,628	327,218	705,247	766,082	820,600	1,074,601	1,256,181

* It includes teachers colleges (normal superior) and agencies in charge of teacher training, especially higher education institutions and universities.

Sources: For 1958-1982: Pescador, J.A. & C.A. Torres, Poder político y educación en México, Mexico, UTHEA, 1985: 89; For 1986, calculated from Jorge Padua "La crisis y la política educativa en México: Evaluación de algunos problemas y perspectivas para el futuro" Congreso Internacional sobre educación política. Política educativa en tiempos de crisis. Educación política ¿Una alternativa? Villahermosa, Tabasco, Mexico, February 11-13, 1987, mimeographed.

Table 3-3
Elementary Schools Comparing the States and the Federal District Schools
According to the Highest School Grade Offered

Place	Total	I	II	III	IV	V	VI
National	76,282	1,981	3,683	5,348	7,314	8,503	49,457
Federal District	2,864	9	19	26	25	37	2,748
States	73,418	1,972	3,664	5,322	7,289	8,466	46,709

Source: SEP *Estadística básica del sistema educativo nacional.* Inicio de Cursos
1981-1982. Dirección General de Programación, Mexico, 1982, p. 58.

Table 3-4
Evolution of Student Cohorts, 1965-1974

Student Cohorts	Years of Schooling					
	I	II	III	IV	V	VI
1965-1970	100	67.0	57.0	46.0	39.0	33.0
1967-1972	100	70.8	60.9	51.2	44.3	38.8
1968-1973	100	71.8	62.7	53.1	46.1	40.5
1969-1974	100	71.0	62.7	53.1	46.4	40.5
Average	100	70.1	60.8	50.8	43.9	38.2

Source: Based on data from Secretaría de Industria y Comercio *Agenda estadística*
1974, México, 1974. Calculated by Manuel Figueroa; *Methodological*
Explorations on Schooling and the Reproduction of the Social Division of Labor:
A Case Study in Mexico City, Mexico. Ph.D. dissertation, Stanford University,
California, 1982.

and 1963-68 show that the greater impact in terms of educational attrition
is found in rural areas. In these cases the rates climb to roughly 92 percent
for both cohorts, with the highest dropout rate on the first step of the ladder
where the rate is 38.8 percent and 37.5 percent respectively (see Table 3-5).

This overview leads us to conclude that although education has been one of
the most pressing demands on the Mexican State as a result of the mandate
left by the Revolution, the years of educational expansion have not given the
results expected. The efforts to expand education were meant to address the
problems of educational inequality in regard to access and permanence in
the school system. Although school enrollment in the last three decades grew
by a factor of three, while the population of school age grew only by a factor
of two (CEE, 1982: 364), there are still serious problems of distribution of
educational opportunities. After examining the trends of educational expan-

Table 3-5
Students' Urban and Rural Survival Figures, 1962-67 and 1963-68

Cohorts		Years of Schooling					
		I	II	III	IV	V	VI
1962-1967	Urban	1000	730	693	644	595	552
	Rural	1000	493	313	177	113	77
1963-1968	Urban	1000	741	714	667	629	573
	Rural	1000	509	318	193	115	80

Source: Solari, Aldo "La desigualdad educativa en América Latina" *Revista Latinoamericana de Estudios Educativos*, Vol. X, No. 1, 1980: p. 17.

sion and efficiency, one of the leading educational researchers in the country concludes that

> it has been proved that access to and permanence in the educational system has not been equitably nor randomly distributed. Those who have benefited from the educational expansion are the groups at the intermediate and higher levels of the social stratum, those that live in urban communities, and especially those who live in communities in the regions with higher relative development. (Muñoz Izquierdo, 1973)

An independent assessment of this situation indicates that in spite of educational expansion, "the academic performance of students is directly proportional to the position they occupy in the social stratification or in the "continuum" of urbanization and regional development" (CEE, 1982: 364).

Educational Decentralization

On May 31, 1983, President De la Madrid announced the launching of an over-comprehensive educational reform labeled "Educational Revolution" aimed at the decentralization of the educational system. He stated

> We will push forward with the decentralization of national life. . . . Responding to a national claim, I made the decision to promote the transfer of the preschool, elementary, secondary and further education from the federal Government to local governments, as well as transferring the corresponding financial resources . . . the Federal Government will maintain the rectorial and evaluative functions through the Secretariat of Public Education. The labor rights of the teachers and the teacher's unions's autonomy will be scrupulously respected. (*El Día*, December 2, 1982)[10]

The system implemented by Vasconcelos in 1921 was centralized in character, nature, and organization to avoid the risk of its fragmentation after the Revolution. During the government of Porfirio Díaz a weak educational system had been organized around the municipalities with a decentralizing purpose and orientation. Sixty-two years later, a government of the Mexican Revolution concluded that the need for a fairly centralized education system was over, and that it was advisable to initiate a process of educational deconcentration and decentralization at a time of financial austerity.

The proposal for the decentralization of education was not well received by some of the key educational actors. The teachers' union, for example, felt that in spite of the assurance given by the president, their privileges and space for maneuvering would be seriously curtailed if the project were to be carried out (Pescador and Torres, 1985).

The challenge of decentralizing a heavily bureaucratic system of education became the concern of many. Decentralization, in practical terms, implied transferring the control of the federal government to the states of many key areas, including the control over resources. In 1983, the educational resources controlled by the government represented 60 percent of the total budget (132,000 million pesos), 77 percent of the total personnel (485,000 employees), 93 percent of the schools (62,000 schools), and 85 percent of the student enrollment which represented over 12 million children and youth (Pescador and Torres, 1985: 59). From the point of view of administrative control, it also implied a substantial change in the role of the SEP. In 1982, the SEP was an enormous bureaucratic structure which included 7 undersecretariats, 44 director-generalships, 304 managerships, 6 councils, in addition to other internal structures. In terms of employees, the SEP had under its control close to 800,000 staff and over 10,000 civil servants (Ornelas, 1988: 107).

Despite the opposition, the project of decentralization got under way. By 1986, the configuration of the educational system from the perspective of the use of resources and distribution of power was entirely different than five years earlier. In fact, the administrative units of the Secretariat of Public Education had less control over the resources, and they were slowly but consistently being transferred to the control of the states through Units of Decentralized Educational Services that by 1986 accounted for 46 percent of the total education budget. By 1985, agreements for the coordination of educational services had been signed with 15 out of the 31 state governments. By 1987 all the agreements had been signed by the remaining State governments.

Table 3-6 shows that the previously powerful Sub-Secretariat of Planning saw its power undermined receiving only 1 percent of the budget and many of its functions transferred to other units, in some cases outside the Secretariat of Education. Even the very powerful *Oficialía Mayor*, where the administration of the system was based, saw its position undermined with fewer resources under its control.

Table 3-6
Secretary of Public Education, Budget, and Distribution per Agency, 1985-1987

	1985	%	1986	%	1987[a]	%
Unit of Decentralized Educational Services for the States	550,491	41.4	976,735	46.3	1,109,439	41.4
Under-Secretariat of Planning	13,374	1.0	11,373	0.5	19,282	0.7
Under-Secretariat of Elementary Education	64,009	4.8	91,977	4.4	149,483	5.6
Under-Secretariat of Secondary Education	56,205	4.2	91,059	4.3	111,067	4.1
Under-Secretariat of Higher Education and Scientific Research	16,991	1.3	26,777	1.3	28,932	1.1
Under-Secretariat of Education and Research in Technical Education	90,151	6.8	147,326	7.0	170,287	6.4
Under-Secretariat of Culture	38,875	2.9	52,638	2.5	70,392	2.6
Under-Secretariat for Sports*	5,571	0.4	-		-	
Oficialía Mayor (Central Administration)	106,598	8.0	106,678	5.0	227,601	8.5
Entities Coordinated by the SEP	387,615	29.2	603,782	29.0	792,255	29.6
Total Sector	1,329,880	100%	2,108,345	100%	2,678,738	100%

Nat. Inst. Adult. Educ. INEA**	23,413	29,888	34,684
Universidad Pedagógica*** Nacional (National Pedagogic University)	4,594	6,424	7,281
National Politechnic Institute	46,216	81,036	95,624

*Was eliminated by Presidential Decree in 1986.

**Percentages of the total of the Sector Education, Culture, Recreation and Sports that includes also the Secretariat of Public Education as part of this sector.

***It corresponds to a percentage of the total expenditure of the Secretariat of Public Education and not of the Sector as such.

aAuthorized.

Source: M. de la Madrid Hurtado, *Cuarto informe de gobierno, 1986, educación.* Presidencia de la República, September 1986 and M. de la Madrid Hurtado, *Quinto informe de gobierno, 1987, educación.* Presidencia de la República, September 1987.

Basic Trends in Policy Planning in Public Education: Educational Expansion

A general overview of some of the major trends in policy planning during the administrations of Echeverría and López Portillo helps one understand some of these most recent developments in education. Overall, the annual growth rates in education between 1970 and 1983 had a steady increase in all major areas of the system including student enrollment and the number of teachers. Particularly relevant in both administrations was the increase in the number of schools that almost doubled during this period.[11]

Under the government of Echeverría (see Table 3-7), secondary education, especially the *Bachillerato* and teachers' education; higher education; and medium-terminal education all showed the increasing importance given to educational policy formation. Although during the López Portillo administration some of these trends were reversed (see Table 3-8), it is possible to argue that there was a basic continuity in public policy in education in both administrations with only some minor shifts in emphasis. In the government of López Portillo, preschool education, for example, received special attention and showed the highest annual growth rate in number of teachers and number of schools, with a fourfold increase in student enrollment. The support for terminal education was also high, particularly at the medium-terminal level.

In accordance with one of the main priorities of the Mexican State, primary education was consistently supported during these two administrations. Between the periods 1970-76 and 1977-82, elementary education averaged 4.4 and 4.9 percent respectively in student enrollment, compared with a rate of population growth of 3.2 and 2.8 percent. With López Portillo the pace of growth began to show signs that in some areas the educational system was achieving its maximum expansion. The government proclaimed that the educational system had been able to reach almost all the school-aged population between 6 and 12 years of age. Enrollment in teacher education programs decreased two thirds in its annual growth. Similarly, secondary and higher education also averaged a slightly lower rate of growth than under the previous administration.

An important factor to take into account in assessing the characteristics of educational expansion is teachers' employment. According to the data in Table 3-7, the annual growth of the educational bureaucracy during that period was higher than the growth rate of student enrollment. This in turn helps to explain the consistent growth over time of the ratio between student enrollment and personnel in the system. However, this does not necessarily represent an improvement in educational quality, including the student-teacher ratio. The expansion of the personnel in the system represented a substantial increase in the areas of school administration and State bureaucracy. Although there are no data available on the allocation of new personnel in regard to the proportion between teaching and administrative positions and its effects on student retention, there is a strong indication that education was still seriously affected by high dropout rates and high

Table 3-7

Mexico: Basic Indicators in Education During Luis Echeverría Administration (school years of 1970/1971-1976/1977)

School Level	Student Enrollment		Annual Rate of Growth	Schools		Annual Rate of Growth	Teachers		Annual Rate of Growth
	1970/71	1976/77	%	1970/71	1976/77	%	1970/71	1976/77	%
Total	**11,538,871**	**16,444,632**	**6.1**	**51,829**	**71,899**	**5.5**	**331,669**	**528,835**	**8.5**
Elementary	9,648,328	12,634,120	4.4	45,151	60,119	4.7	204,525	288,664	5.9
Pre-schooling	400,138	607,946	7.4	3,077	4,619	7.2	10,524	15,712	7.0
Primary	9,248,190	12,026,174	4.3	42,074	55,500	4.6	194,001	272,952	5.8
Secondary	1,437,655	2,915,803	14.7	5,000	8,821	10.9	90,551	173,602	13.1
Basic Level	1,102,217	2,109,693	13.1	4,123	7,227	10.7	67,738	125,614	12.2
Bachillerato	279,495	670,129	20.0	646	1,267	13.7	17,683	38,416	16.7
Teachers Education	55,943	135,981	20.4	231	327	6.0	5,130	9,572	12.4
Higher Education *	271,275	569,266	15.7	385	606	8.2	25,056	43,114	10.3
Terminal	181,613	325,443	11.3	1,293	2,353	11.7	11,537	23,455	15.0
Elementary **	147,752	244,382	9.3	1,069	1,993	12.3	7,392	15,539	15.7
Medium Terminal	33,861	81,061	20.0	224	360	8.7	4,145	7,916	13.0

* Includes *Normal Superior* (Secondary School Teachers' Training College)

** Technical Training

Sources: 1970/71 Developed by the Secretariat of Programming and Budget, National Coordination of the System of National Information, using data from the Secretary of Public Education.

1976/77 Secretariat of Public Education, *Memoria 1976/82: Política educativa* (Vol I), Mexico, September 1983: 379-390.

Table 3-8

Mexico: Basic Indicators in Education During López Portillo Administration
(school years of 1976/1977-1982/1983)

School Level	Student Enrollment		Annual Rate of Growth	Schools		Annual Rate of Growth	Teachers		Annual Rate of Growth
	1976/77	1982/83	%	1976/77	1982/83	%	1976/77	1982/83	%
Total	16,444,632	24,019,331	6.6	71,899	124,640	10.5	528,835	889,710	9.7
Elementary	12,634,120	17,005,231	4.9	60,119	103,949	10.4	288,664	475,680	9.2
Pre-schooling	607,946	1,766,000	27.2	4,619	24,040	60.1	15,712	55,026	35.7
Primary	12,026,174	15,239,231	3.8	55,500	79,909	6.3	272,952	420,654	7.7
Secondary	2,915,803	5,163,896	11.0	8,821	15,898	11.5	173,602	286,985	9.3
Basic Level	2,109,693	3,718,090	10.9	7,227	13,196	11.8	125,614	203,545	8.9
Bachillerato	670,129	1,255,626	12.5	1,267	2,206	10.6	38,416	70,757	12.0
Teachers Education *	135,981	190,180	5.7	327	496	7.4	9,572	12,683	4.6
Higher Education *	569,266	1,074,601	12.7	606	993	9.1	43,114	80,359	12.3
Terminal	325,443	775,603	19.8	2,353	3,800	8.8	23,455	46,686	14.1
Elementary **	244,382	431,473	10.9	1,993	2,804	5.8	15,539	21,229	5.2
Medium Terminal	81,061	344,130	46.4	360	996	25.2	7,916	25,457	31.6

* Includes *Normal Superior* (Secondary School Teachers' Training College).

** Technical Training.

Source: Secretariat of Public Education, *Memoria 1976/82: Política educativa* (Vol I), Mexico, September 1983: 379-390.

repetition rates, particularly at the lower levels of the system. According to Pescador, only 53 percent of the children entering grade one were able to finish grade six of primary schooling (1982b: 363-384).

In terms of policy planning in public education, the trends that affected the educational system during these two administrations show that educational expansion was the manifestation of a highly complex process in policy formulation. The quantitative growth of the system brought about a number of changes in the capacity of the school system to reach wider sectors of the population and increase educational services. However, the quality of education was not substantially improved, and in some instances the system became even more administratively complex.

The Corporatist Educational Bureaucracy: Technocrats versus Normalistas

The emphasis on the quantitative expansion of education resulted in a massification of the administrative structure, which became much larger and complex than in the 1960s. Table 3-9 presents a general overview of the growth of educational bureaucracy during the governments of Echeverría and López Portillo. This phenomenon is particularly relevant.

Educational bureaucracy in Mexico is not only important as a policy making setting given the corporatist structure of the State, but also because of what it represents: a distinct social group, a category within the State, and a large source of employment. Using a functionalist sociological approach, Camp (1970) carried out a comparative analysis of the bureaucracy in Mexico by studying the role of the *técnico* (technocrat) in policy making. He concluded that the bureaucracy plays an increasingly important role in national policy making, and that it is an important factor in moving the policy making process toward greater representation and democracy. The top-level decision making process in the country is no longer as highly centralized as in the past, having become more dispersed throughout the administrative system. He indicates in this regard that

Table 3-9
Enrollment and Educational Bureaucracy, 1970-1982

Indicators	1970/1971	1976/1977	1982/1983	Echeverría 1970/1976	López Portillo 1976/1982
Enrollment	11,538,871	16,444,632	24,019,331	6.1%	6.6%
Personnel	331,669	528,835	889,710	8.5%	9.7%
E/P	35	31	27		

Source: Tables 3.7 and 3.8.

data from a large number of cabinet and department heads show a continuous rise in the number of technically qualified persons in top positions of the government. The top level bureaucrat in Mexico is characterized by his youth, his urban background and orientation, at least four years of college from the National University, a degree in a field other than law, teaching experience at the National University, and his recruitment from a core region of Mexico. (xii, 1-6)

It is also important to differentiate between the "organic bureaucracy" represented by top officials, and the "subordinate bureaucracy" represented by intermediate and lower level functionaries. This distinction helps to understand the trade-offs and conflicts among different strata in the bureaucratic structure, and the conflicts originating elsewhere that affect the bureaucracy. It is also important to bear in mind the historical and material framework within which the bureaucracy becomes an administrative setting, particularly in regard to the processes of recruitment and political legitimation. The Secretariat of Public Education is one of the few government departments in Mexico which since the 1930s applies its own mechanism—the teacher training colleges or *normales*—for recruiting and training its personnel.

An important characteristic of the educational bureaucracy emerges from the relationships between *normalistas*, those trained in teacher training colleges and closely associated to the official teachers' union, and the technocrats, people with university education and related to the Secretariat of Education. There is a widely held belief in Mexico that over the years there has been a progressive shift in political control of the medium and upper levels of the Secretariat of Public Education from the *normalistas* to the technocrats. This has implications that go beyond the administration of the system. In fact, there is clear differentiation between both groups in terms of their socioeconomic background. *Normalistas* come from lower socioeconomic strata, even from peasant origin. They have been trained in colleges rather than universities and the Secretariat of Public Education represents their principal labor market and their main channel for upward mobility.

In most cases *normalistas* occupying the highest ranks in the Secretariat of Education are teachers with substantial work experience in the schools. Although they have administrative experience, this is mainly the result of their roles as teachers rather than an outcome of formal training. Technocrats, on the other hand, do not necessarily have teaching experience in primary or secondary education, nor do they necessarily have formal training in educational policy planning or administration. In most cases they have training in business administration, law, engineering, or physical sciences. They come from the provincial petit bourgeoisie and the urban middle class. Usually, they are younger than the *normalistas*, occupying similar ranks or levels and sharing common values in areas related to administrative efficiency, productivity, and order.

The evolution in the human resources pattern of employment in the Secretariat of Public Education also reflects the influence of education and welfare policies in relation to the emphasis on developing a planning and policy making capacity at the State level in the public sector. Tello argues that the creation of employment in education, health, agriculture, and energy production accounted for more than four fifths of the total State employment increments (1979: 190). More than half of the increment in the federal government corresponded to education. Tables 3-7 and 3-8 show the continuation of a similar trend between Echeverría's and López Portillo's administrations in public sector employment, this, despite minor differences between the two periods such as the slower growth in enrollment in teachers' education during the government of López Portillo, which could be explained by an expected lower rate of growth in primary school enrollment.

The second half of the government of López Portillo represents a good example of the commitment of the Mexican State to allocate financial resources to education. Table 2-1 shows that by the mid-1980s approximately 5 percent of the GNP was allocated to the education sector. In practice, however, this was the manifestation of a policy pattern followed between 1970 and 1982. In these 12 years financial allocations to education grew between 2.5 and 5 percent of the GNP.

Federal allocations to education followed a similar pattern. Federal funding of education increased over the period in comparison to the performance of other sources of educational financing. In 1982, approximately 14 percent of the total federal expenditures were in education. The contribution coming from the states and the municipalities together did not account for more than 20 percent of the total educational expenditures at the time. Simultaneously, the involvement of the private sector dropped from 16 percent at the beginning of the Echeverría government to less than 6 percent at the end of the López Portillo period (see Table 2-2).

CONTRADICTIONS OF EDUCATIONAL PLANNING IN MEXICO: CONCLUSION

This chapter has discussed some of the main trends in educational development in postrevolutionary Mexico since the creation of the Secretariat of Public Education in 1921. One of the main features in the evolution of the educational system over the last six decades has been the impressive growth and expansion of every level in the system.

This phenomenon is to some extent unique to the developing world. Boli, Ramirez, and Meyer (1985) would suggest that educational expansion in a country like Mexico has been the result of a growing secularization and specialization of the capitalist State that has taken command of the society. It has been argued in this chapter that there is evidence indicating that educational expansion in Mexico has been a response to the mandate of the Revolution. The Constitution of 1917 established public and free education as a symbol of a new ideology seeking more egalitarian means to distribute wealth and power. This was conceived as a necessary complement to other steps toward the legalization of and support to trade unions, and to the land

and political reforms (Fuentes Molinar, 1983; Basañez, 1981; Pescador and Torres, 1985; Latapí, 1980).

The expansion of the education system that took place between 1940 and 1970 was facilitated by a unique socioeconomic environment characterized by a high and persistent growth of the economy, a series of regressive income distribution policies, and by a relatively stable political system.[12] The large investment in infrastructure to support the growth in student enrollment and number of schools was possible at the expense of controlling the salaries of university and school teachers and administrators. It has been estimated that real salaries for teachers, for example, dropped by approximately 60 percent. Aboites has indicated that between 1925 and 1960 it took educators almost 40 years to reach the salary level they had in 1921 (1984: 63-110; 1986: 84-88). Considering the level that teachers salaries could have reached if they had had normal growth, the value of the salary of one teacher allowed the government to hire three teachers during 1950-65. The lack of reaction from the teachers' sector to this situation could be seen as a result of the vertical and horizontal corporatist system of control under which teachers in the country operate. The fact that during this period the government was able to compensate for the investments in expanding the system by controlling the growth of salaries is a manifestation of both the powerful links between the State and the National Teachers' Union, and the ideological influence of the revolutionary tradition portraying teachers as the builders of the nation.

During the second half of the 1970s, teachers saw a rapid improvement in their economic condition as a result of the effects of the oil boom and the increase in international borrowing. In real terms, the government was able to raise teachers' salaries to levels well above those in the 1920s. This, however, drastically changed after 1982. By 1985, the value of teachers' salaries was only two and a half times the value of the minimum salary in the country, and between 1982 and 1986, real salaries in the education sector lost 55 percent of their value (Aboites, 1986: 85).

This process of economic deterioration for the teaching profession was particularly acute in the universities. In the salary negotiations at the UNAM and at the UAM during 1987-88, the union representing support staff (secretaries, janitors, etc.) obtained salary increases that brought some of them to salary levels 10 and 20 percent higher than those of the lower rank academic staff. In a period of only four years, the salary of an associate professor lost two thirds of its real value, from 10,728 pesos to 4,142 pesos per month (Aboites, 1986: 85). By the early 1980s, the salaries of university professors were 40 percent over the minimum salary. When the minimum salary in the country was increased in 1986, its nominal amount surpassed some of the nominal salaries of the lower categories of the assistant professor level in public universities in the Federal District.

The rapid process of educational development and the massification of the educational system took place under strict State control. In practice, this meant the control of the process of financing education and administering the federal resources to promote expansion and diversification of the system, keeping it away from the influence of the private sector. This approach allowed the State to deal with education as a political project to fulfill its revolutionary mandate. In such a context, policy planning in education has been instrumental in the hegemonic role of the corporatist State.

It has been argued that educational policy planning in Mexico is primarily oriented by a political rather than by a technocratic rationale (McGinn and Street, 1982; 1984). Existing evidence shows that policy planning is a conflictive process taking place in a highly complex arena. In the early 1970s, the Teachers' Union began to lose ground in their ability to command the process of policy planning at the national level.[13] In part, this became manifest during the government of Echeverría, when the union began to lose its ability to place teachers in the highest positions in the Secretariat of Public Education due to the introduction of a new technocracy with a different political outlook and commitment. The confrontation that began to take place between this new technocracy and the teachers' union has been in part the result of the modernization of the system. A more modern and complex educational system raised new demands on those working in the sector. It required a new cadre of human resources with greater organizational and administrative skills, and with the ability and flexibility to deal with the complexities of greater social demands. It also implied the introduction of a new bureaucracy with different loyalties and different networks of interest representation. The modernization of the system also made the State redefine the roots sustaining the legitimacy of a tradition in which education continues to be seen as directly connected to revolutionary ideology. The option selected was to strengthen a new scientific policy planning expertise capable of commanding the model of educational development.

Several specific outcomes show the importance given to this approach. The provision of education per se continued to be a top priority of the Mexican State. This was achieved through a reduction of expenditures while simultaneously increasing the outcomes of the educational system.[14] A higher degree of efficiency in the allocation of resources in order to increase the outcome of the system required government planners to adopt a different approach to policy negotiations. Technocratic planners ought to have a free hand to direct the future expansion of the system and to control its dynamics of growth and change.

The process of educational decentralization undertaken by the government since the early 1980s is, to some extent, a last resort implemented by the technocratic elite to be able to control a system that has become highly bureaucratic in its decision making processes. Decentralization was expected to make possible the adjustment of priorities by redefining the use of resources while at the same time giving a new orientation to political negotiations with the teachers' union in the planning of education. This also helped the government to deal with a growing dissatisfaction in a civil society increasingly preoccupied by signs of deterioration in the sociopolitical system, including the poor performance of the economy and the political erosion of the basic institutions of the Revolution. Regarding the latter, a particular source of concern has been the decline of the educational system reflected in increasing problems related to the equality of educational opportunities, the quality of education, educational wastage, and a diminishing private rate of return. These problems were aggravated by the reduction of jobs in the public sector, particularly after 1986. The dismissal of public sector functionaries, particularly during the last two years of the government of De la Madrid, has severely affected the most educated sectors of the middle class.

Despite changes in the government's approach to education, the issue of quality remains a low priority in the day-to-day agenda of policy planners. The results of educational expansion have not produced a more egalitarian system or an improvement in educational opportunities despite the increase in the financing of education. The major beneficiaries of the expansion have been the social classes and groups located in the urban centers and in the more developed regions of the country. The upper and middle sectors of the social strata have benefited the most from the expansion in education. Dropout rates and attrition of schoolchildren from the popular classes remain very high, particularly in rural areas.

The following chapters examine some of the effects of the evolution of educational policy in Mexico within the primary school system and in the areas of adult and workers' education.

NOTES

1. The Secretariat of Public Education constituted the equivalent of a Ministry of Education. Created on September 28, 1921, it was headed by José Vasconcelos as the first Secretary of Education. In the Presidential system in Mexico, cabinet members are labeled secretaries (of the president) rather than ministers. This title provides a formal guarantee of obedience to the president and to a certain extent eliminates the formal freedom of action a minister is perceived to have in Western political systems. In practice, however, every secretary of the state has, in his or her own area of public concern (i.e., health, education, labor), as much power within the inner circle of the president as any minister of the state in other societies.

2. José Vasconcelos, a famous Mexican philosopher and former president of the National Autonomous University at the time of his appointment, has an impressive record as an educator. As president of the university he created 198 libraries throughout the country, 64 of them in local municipalities, 80 in workers organizations, and 54 in public schools. After he was appointed as Secretary of Education he continued this work by expanding the number of libraries to 671 and leading a campaign to produce 100,000 books to promote reading among the population (Pescador, 1986: 7).

3. In 1921, Mexico had a total population of approximately 14,334,780 inhabitants, 800,000 less than the figure reported by the census of 1910, not counting the population growth over the period.

4. Most of the population in Mexico resides in three large urban centers: the Federal District, Monterrey, and Guadalajara. According to data available for 1980, close to 23 percent of the total population was living in the Federal District. At the same time,

however, Mexico has still a large number of rural communities (over 2,500 of them) with less than 500 inhabitants.

5. Inequalities in postrevolutionary Mexico are striking. In terms of income distribution, in 1980, 5 percent of the population concentrated 65.1 percent of the national wealth. Approximately 1.3 percent of the top bracket of the population owned 40.6 percent of the nation's wealth. At the other extreme, the capacity of the workers to benefit from the national income was diminished. In 1950, 30 percent of low-income families received 8 percent of the national income. In 1977, the same group was receiving only 6.5 percent. For the period 1977-81, this rate went down to 6 percent (Secretaría de Programación y Presupuesto, 1983: 117).

6. With the creation of the National Commission for Free Textbooks in 1959, the Mexican State expanded even further Vasconcelos' original initiative to improve the reading and writing skills of the population. With this step, the State also attempted to promote a sense of nationhood and assist the poorest sectors of the population unable to acquire books for their children. Between 1959-64, the State produced 107,155,755 textbooks for primary education. In 1967 it distributed free of charge over 46 million textbooks, between 1976-77 the National Commission distributed 78 million, and in 1982-83 it reached 93 million.

7. According to a report from the Chase Manhattan Bank, the real GNP expanded at an average annual rate of 6.2 percent, while prices rose only 2.4 percent (Gill, 1969: 9).

8. Despite skyrocketing costs everywhere, higher education in Mexico is still free. According to *The Wall Street Journal*, the approximately 300,000 undergraduate and graduate students at the UNAM pay only a symbolic fee. A year of university education starts at 13 cents; thus a student can complete medical school for less than $1.00 US. The student unrest witnessed in 1986-87, however, shows that conflicts and contradictions of public higher education are mounting.

A series of factors have contributed to making university education explosive in spite of the guarantees students have. Due to the expansion of higher education during the 1960s that led to the massification of universities (between 1964 and 1982 enrollment grew 13.1 percent per year), there was a proliferation of parallel channels of higher education. This added to the economic crises of the early 1980s that brought about severe unemployment for university graduates, reduction in services, and a substantial decrease in the university teachers' salaries (Aboites, 1986). All these factors contributed to an already critical situation. *The Wall Street Journal* reports that the highest paid tenured professors in 1986 were making less than $5,000 a year. This resulted in higher numbers of university professors not coming to class, a deterioration in the hiring practices, and a series of abnormal situations in regard to the student-teacher ratio in some university departments. At the same time, fewer than half of the undergraduates entering the National University between 1972-81 were able to finish their studies, and nine out of ten students dropped out (*The Wall Street Journal*, October 31, 1986).

9. In terms of dropout rates in the mid-1970s, Mexico was doing better than Brazil (82%), Colombia (67.7%), Guatemala (75.2%), and the Dominican Republic (73.4%), but it fell behind Argentina (40.7%), Costa Rica (20.6%), Uruguay (35.2%), and Venezuela (45.7%).

10. Cited by Ornelas, 1988: 105.

11. According to a study of the Centro de Estudios Educativos, a private research center in Mexico, the geometric yearly rate of growth in student enrollment was 7.6

percent during the government of López Mateos, 5.8 percent during the government of Díaz Ordaz, and 7.1 percent during Echeverría's administration (CEE, 1975: 119).

12. It should be remembered that after the Christeros War, there was a long period of social stability with only some sporadic social conflicts. The only major social uprisings that had national impact were the rail workers' rebellion in 1958-59 and the student unrest in 1968.

13. Confrontations between the Secretary of Education (SEP) and the Teachers' Union (SNTE) have included several areas of policy such as employment and promotion of teachers; administrative reform within the SEP; issues related to quality of education, particularly the quality of instruction in teachers' training colleges (the stronghold of the Teachers' Union); the appointment of directive personnel in schools and in the upper echelons of the SEP administrative structure, including the decentralized units in the states; and, finally, working conditions and salaries. During 1970-1988 three specific areas of policy were at the center of the conflict and negotiations between the SEP and the SNTE. These included the reform that overhauled teacher training with the creation in 1978 of the National Pedagogic University (Universidad Pedagógica Nacional, UPN), a nonautonomous university in charge of upgrading qualifications of inservice teachers and offering university degrees at the undergraduate and graduate levels for inservice and preservice teachers; the new policies in adult education and the organization of the National Institute of Adult Education (INEA) without participation of the Teachers' Union; and the process of administrative, financial, and political decentralization of the SEP undertaken by President De la Madrid as an "educational revolution." A detailed study of these issues, particularly the conflicts related to the UPN and educational decentralization, is found in Pescador and Torres (1985: 14-33). Chapter five provides a discussion of the INEA and adult education policies.

14. For instance, the cost per student in the UAM (Metropolitan Autonomous University) in current prices was 31,980 pesos in 1974 when it was created; ten years later, per capita cost was estimated at 9,750 in current pesos. This cost reduction came about in spite of the fact that in 1974 the student population was 3,300 students and by 1984 this figure had grown to 33,000. Teacher-student ratios increased from 5:5 in 1974 to 12:88 in 1984 (UAM *Organo Informativo*, Vol. IX, January 14, 1985).

Part II Case Studies

4 Educational Inequality and Occupational Future: The Case of Primary Education in Mexico City

INTRODUCTION

This chapter discusses the role of the formal primary school system in the reproduction of the social division of labor inherent in the model of associated-dependent development in Mexico.[1] Specifically, it deals with the relationships between the school and the sociocultural traits of children from different socioeconomic backgrounds. The general framework for the analysis of these relationships is provided by the model of economic and political development of the country and by the main features characterizing the evolution of the educational system after the Revolution.

This case study looks at elementary education in Mexico City. It attempts to explain the dynamics determining current educational policies and the steps taken by the government toward their implementation. It focuses on the role played by the schools which in turn determines the general role of education within the development model. The emphasis on studying the school as a single unit, carrying out concrete actions within the spectrum of social institution performing an ideological role, responds to an interest for reaching a better understanding of two specific issues. One is the need for consistency between the approaches to education adopted by different types of schools vis-à-vis the role of schooling as a distinctive component in the reproduction of existing conditions of inequality in the society at large. The other is the need to find a more comprehensive framework which could place schooling within the broader sociopolitical paradigm determining the process of social reproduction in the relationship between education and work.

SCHOOLING AND WORK: EDUCATIONAL AND OCCUPATIONAL FUTURE

Over the years, there has been extensive debate about the ways in which schooling reproduces conditions of social, cultural, and economic inequality that exist in the society at large. In so doing, the school not only discriminates among children on the basis of their socioeconomic and class background, but also conditions their future opportunities in life, particularly in regard to their further education and to their opportunities in the world of work.

Carnoy and Levin have argued in this regard that

> schooling practices are inseparable from class and social conflicts, passing as they do through the prism of school bureaucracies—the administrators and teachers who represent formal authority to both students and their families. School bureaucracies are part of the State, which form the larger context in which class and social conflicts are related to school practices. (1985: 110)

They studied the process of differential reproduction using ethnographic methods comparing two first-grade classrooms, one in an upper middle-class neighborhood and one in a lower middle-class sector. The samples were controlled by gender and race, making certain that both variables were differentially represented in each neighborhood type. The focus of the study was on occupational values, distinguishing four attributes related to different levels of the work hierarchy. These were external versus internal standards of authority, future versus present orientation, verbal self-presentation skills, and emphasis on cognitive skills and achievement (Carnoy and Levin, 1985: 114).

After spending hundreds of hours of ethnographic observation in both schools, they concluded that the most prominent pattern discerned from the data is that in all four occupational dimensions the occupational interactions in the two first-grade classrooms reflected a similar socialization pattern. Upper-class students were being prepared to perform roles at the top of the work hierarchy, while the lower-class students were educated to perform roles in the lower and middle portion of the job spectrum. These authors argued that "this pattern seemed to hold despite the diversity of the dimensions themselves, and it supports our views that school practices are carried out in the context of a class structure. Schools differentiate the socialization of the young for work along lines that conform to parents' occupational roles" (Carnoy and Levin, 1985: 128).

The findings of this study stressed several important issues. First, the study of the classrooms showed that the systematic differentiation toward work begins as early as in the first grade of primary education. In practice this is the outcome of the fact that each social class is immersed in a particular educational context in which children are prepared to follow similar occupations to those of their parents (1985: 141). Second, the study showed that the expansion of schooling takes place within the boundaries of social conflicts which in turn respond to the ways in which the society is structured in terms of class, race, and gender (1985: 142). Third, the study indicated that school administrators, teachers, and parents contribute to the reproduction of "capitalist relations of production and the division of knowledge associated with segmented labor market occupational role" (1985:

142). Finally, the authors also showed that the underlying conflicts in capitalist social formations generate resistance to these practices of social reproduction in the school structures and practices. They indicated in this regard that

> the historical expansion of schooling, even with its insidiously structured practices, has produced an institution that is more democratic and less biased than the workplace. Historically generated by these contending dynamics, the partial autonomy of schooling from the workplace has come to mean that the output of the educational system does not necessarily conform to the needs of the capitalist workplace, nor to the reproduction of capitalist relations of production. It also means that the amount of resources devoted to schooling may be inconsistent with capitalist reproduction. (Carnoy and Levin, 1985: 142-43)

The main purpose of this chapter is to explore some of the hypotheses presented by Carnoy and Levin regarding the occupational and educational future of low-, middle-, and upper-class students in a very large urban conglomerate such as Mexico City. In many respects it is an attempt to look at the role of the school in relation to the most abject family poverty and family affluence in a dependent society. Conventional survey and interview techniques were used in gathering data. The main focus of this case study was on the modus operandi of schools in Mexico, as this relates to the linkages among a model of qualification-determination of the labor force, the occupational and educational background of parents, and students' linguistic proficiency, work aspirations, and socioeconomic status. The five schools selected for the study present an overview of the mechanisms for knowledge and information delivery (in terms of quantity and quality), types of classroom communications, and discipline. To a large extent, the research findings tend to support the conclusions of Carnoy and Levin.

SCHOOLING AND INEQUALITY IN PRIMARY EDUCATION

The study of inequality in society has been approached from at least two different directions. Some studies have focused on the issue of inequality based on the methodological contribution of the political economy of education. Other studies have focused on the internal mechanisms of social and economic reproduction of the social division of labor operating within the school. In the former, the emphasis has been on the impact of capitalism as the prevailing mode of production in the society and its institutions. In the latter, the emphasis has been centered on understanding the role of specific organizational and instructional functions of the school which are oriented to maintain the status quo. In the first case, schooling is just one among many vehicles in a society to provide children with the required means for the functions they must perform as producers. In the context of capitalism, these are the same means required to maintain the unequal conditions inherent in the model of associated-dependent development. In the second case, schooling is an internal means for the reproduction of inequality among social groups. These views are complementary and it would be practically impossible to study the functioning of the school without understanding the role that it plays in society.

One of the general assumptions of the study presented here is that schooling in Mexico is part and parcel of the dynamics regulating a society divided into classes. In such a context, the school plays a mediating role by preserving the composition of the existing social classes and by attempting to diminish the conflict among them. An essential component in this equation is the relationship between education and inequality. This is built on the basis of both the differential roles that social classes play in the control of the means of production and the role that social institutions play to ensure the reproduction of the socioeconomic and political system.

The school in capitalist societies performs two distinct tasks. These include, first, the certification of social agents by providing them with the credentials required to perform in the socioeconomic structure and, second, the allocation of individuals within the social division of labor according to their class origin (Carnoy, 1976; Bowles and Gintis: 1976; Apple, 1982). The school thus performs a "distributive task," allocating individuals and groups to different levels of the already defined positions in the social structure.

Three main processes in capitalist societies relate to the reproduction, maintenance, and perpetuation of inequality: the process of production where the roots of inequality are located; the process of reproduction carried out by social institutions such as the school; and the process of distribution of human resources in the social division of labor. There is a close relationship among these three. Changes in the process of production determine the changes in the content, delivery styles, and basic philosophy of the education system. This in turn generates changes in values, norms, and behaviors in the productive site through the distributive process. The cycle is then completed by the changes that occur in the education system in response to the new needs of the productive process.

Within this framework, the reproductive process that takes place in the classroom structure is not a consequence of a maladjustment of the educational system, but a reflection of the structural class factors interacting in society at large (Bernstein, 1971; Baudelot and Establet, 1975; Young, 1971; Apple, 1979). This leads to arguments that in societies like Mexico, characterized by deep class differences at both the political and socioeconomic levels, the school system delivers to students a differential set of traits and skills that are functional to their class integration into the social divisions of labor. This role of the school responds to a double dynamic: On the one hand, it corresponds to the requirements of a society organized according to a pattern of domination and subordination of social groups that perform differential functions in a given productive structure. On the other, it regulates the distributive process taking place inside the educational system itself which determines the prevailing notions of success and failure in life. This dynamic of the school is in turn reinforced by the existence of differences in the quality of processes, content, and rewards to which students are exposed in their classroom interactions.

Each type of school is supposed to have a modus operandi determined by the role that the social class it represents plays at a given time in society (Meyer, 1977). Thus schools serving children from families in the lower socioeconomic strata prepare their students for those positions that are outside the commanding posts in society. Given the skills, attitudes, and perceptions developed by working-class schools, the future location of those children on the social ladder is further limited by their actual chances of acquiring the proper educational credentials required for upward mobility. In the same vein, schools serving middle- and upper-class students prepare children to perform "successfully" in life according to the standards defined by the dominant groups. Thus the schools play a double reproductive role: They reproduce classes across generations and they reproduce class relations.

PRIMARY SCHOOLS IN MEXICO CITY: A CASE STUDY

To study the differential modus operandi of schools in Mexico, a *qualification-determination* model was developed. This approach integrates in one single sequence two clusters of variables: schooling variables and socioeconomic and cultural variables.

One of the variables studied was "student linguistic proficiency." Based on Bernstein's findings on the existence of distinctive linguistic codes for different social classes (1976: 76), an attempt was made to determine if differences existed among students' oral proficiency and language skills in the case of primary education in Mexico according to the type of schools they attended. Thus students in low-income or working-class schools were expected to manage a more restricted code of language and meanings than students attending middle- or high-income schools. Given the characteristics of the teaching-learning process in working-class schools, it was expected that students faced a low need for verbalization, a situation that responded to their own social conditions outside the school but that was reinforced by the educational system.

Within the same perspective, it was expected that middle- and upper-class schools develop a more elaborate linguistic code among their students. This was reflected in both a richer and more complex speech structure, composed of a wider range of alternatives for their verbal expression, and a stronger tendency to abstract and work with the analytical meanings attached to concepts. It was also expected that middle and high schools would present different ways of managing those traits through the teaching-learning process and teacher-parent interactions. In the case of middle-class schools, it was expected that the environment would be more repressive and controlled in terms of classroom conditions for oral expression of students, limiting thus the process of communication to formal aspects of the interrelations between teachers and students. In upper-class schools, the environment was expected to be favorable to the oral communication of students as a result of more dynamic classroom interactions.

Information was gathered through different means. Two successive interviews with students were used to measure language proficiency. The focus of the first interview was to informally determine the level of the student's oral proficiency. The second interview with the same students was used to determine the value of the children's proficiency. A second source of information was the teacher. Each student selected for the interviews was described by the teacher in terms of the linguistic proficiency he or she displayed in the classroom. This information was used for comparative purposes. A third source of information was the results of the verbal skill section of the Spanish Standardized Wechsler Maturity Test (SSWMT).[2] In this case, proficiency was divided into three levels: high, normal, and low or scarce. The SSWMT was used to determine discrepancies between the other two approaches to measure oral proficiency.

Another variable measured in the study was the students' work aspirations, understood as the perceptions children have about their own future. It was assumed that the children's views were shaped by the family environment, the media, and the kind of attitudes and behaviors taught and reinforced by the school. The job categories used to identify general types of occupations were those defined in the 1970 National Census. Ten categories were identified: farm worker, artisan, employee, merchant, industrial worker, technician, secretary, servant, housewife, and professional.

A variable was also created to determine the students' socioeconomic status. This variable included family income, occupation of the head of the household, and living conditions of the family in terms of the number of family members living under the same roof, telephone, servants, and automobiles. This variable permitted the determination with a certain degree of accuracy the class stratum occupied by the student's family. Income was defined as the wages or salaries earned by the head of the household. Data were obtained from school files for each family unit and from teachers and school principals. Three broad income categories were defined for the study. Families in the low-income bracket were those receiving up to $320 US per month. Families in the middle-income bracket were those earning up to $1,250 US per month. And high-income families were those receiving more than $1,260 US per month. This breakdown was consistent with the overall criteria for the distribution of income in Mexico at the time of the study.

In each school, parents' education and professional level of the head of the family were also included as indicators to assist in the identification of the type of school according to the socioeconomic status of the students. Seven occupational categories were created for this purpose: unskilled, semiskilled, skilled, white collar, manager, professional, and "home." Unskilled grouped those heads of family working in jobs that did not require learned skills or who were working primarily in the informal sector. Semiskilled were considered to be those individuals in occupations requiring certain basic skills to perform the job, such as bus drivers and construction workers. In most cases these individuals have only primary education. Skilled workers were those heads of family in occupations requiring complete primary education or a set of specific skills acquired through formal training, such as policemen and industrial workers. White collar were considered to be those in occupations requiring formal schooling and some type of formal training, such as those associated with commerce, banking, private industry, and secretarial positions. In the context of Mexico's occupational strata, managers were considered to be those who were self-employed and have their own business. Professionals were those having higher education credentials or technical certificates.

The Schools Selected for the Study

A total of five primary schools were studied. According to the socioeconomic background of the children attending the schools, two of them were considered to be lower- or working-class schools, one was classified as middle-class, and two were regarded as upper-class schools.[3]

Both working-class schools shared common characteristics. In one, the distribution of heads of family by profession included 76.3 percent of semiskilled or skilled workers, 12.4 percent unskilled without a steady income, 8.2 percent white-collar workers, and only 3.1 percent professionals. In the second school, the occupational characteristics of the heads of family were similar. Among them, 90 percent were semiskilled or skilled and 4.3 percent were unskilled workers. In the first school, the average number of members living in the same house was eight, while in the second school the number was 10.

Among the students from the middle-class school, 57 percent of the parents were professionals, 17 percent were managers or owned their own business, and 14.3 percent were skilled workers. Only one case was found of a semiskilled worker and this corresponded to a student whose father was an employee of the school. All parents in this school, with the exception of one, belonged to the middle-income bracket. A substantial difference was found in the occupation of the mothers of students in this school compared with those of children in the working-class schools. Close to 32 percent of the mothers were professionals and 2.9 percent were white-collar workers, while 65.7 percent were staying at home. The average number of persons living in the same house was five, and 82.9 percent of the families reported owning at least one car. Only 20 percent of the families reported not having external help (servants) at home.

The family situation of students attending the upper-class schools was as follows. Overall, 86.9 percent of the household heads were professionals, 8.7 percent were managers, and only 4 percent were skilled workers. In the last case, these corresponded to parents who were employees at the schools. In one of the schools, approximately 88 percent of the families were in the high-income bracket, and only 10.9 percent were in the medium level. A minimum percentage of heads of family were in the lower-income bracket and corresponded to those employed by the schools. Among the mothers of students in these schools, 47 percent stayed at home, 41 were professionals,

3.3 percent had their own business, and 7.7 percent were considered to be white-collar workers. This also had a direct implication in the mothers' income. Among them, 50.8 percent reported to have no income, 20.8 percent were in the high-income bracket, and 27.9 percent were in the medium level. External help (servants) was employed by 87.4 percent of the families, and 95.1 percent of the families reported having at least one car. In the second upper-class school, 97.6 percent of the households were in the high-income bracket, and 77.1 percent of the heads of family were professionals. Mothers' occupations in this case included 16.9 percent professionals, 3.6 managers, and 2.4 percent white-collar workers, while 77.1 percent were staying at home. Approximately 76 percent of the mothers received no income. Among the families of this school, close to 80 percent reported having servants, and 97.6 percent reported owning at least one car. Tables 4-1 and 4-2 show the general distribution of heads of households by type of occupation and by income level respectively according to the type of school.

According to these data, it is quite clear that in upper-class schools the majority of heads of family are professionals. Middle-class schools followed a similar pattern although on a smaller scale. In the case of working-class schools, the large majority of heads of family were semiskilled and skilled workers. An equally uneven distribution of income was found among schools. In this regard, the type of population served by each school corresponded to one of the original assumptions of the study.

This situation has a strong influence on the students' occupational aspirations that were expected to be influenced by the family environment and income, and by the environment of the school. In the working-class schools, the proportion of students selecting professional careers was higher than expected, but still lower than in middle- and upper-class schools. This, however, is to a large extent determined by the actual school conditions that have different effects on the students in terms of their actual chances of pursuing their aspirations later in life.

Another characteristic among the schools was shown by the analysis of "school authority." This was defined as the leadership and administrative style imposed or generated by the authorities of the school (principal or governing body). The study of this variable resulted in some revealing information. In the practice of the schools, there were three types of administration or authority patterns, each corresponding to the social class most heavily represented at the school. The working-class public primary schools followed a pattern of "bureaucratic administration." The internal authority structure of these schools serves as an intermediary between the upper levels of the State bureaucracy regulating the overall primary school system and the students, teachers, and parents. The main role of the school administration was to translate and implement the instructions of the Secretariat of Public Education into practices. The middle-class private school followed a "self-contained" approach to administration. This was characterized by a strong sense of order and discipline, a rigorous attitude toward teachers and parents, and a nearly utopian sense of values and

Table 4-1
Head of Household Occupation by Type of School (percent)

	Unskll.	Semiskll.	Skll.	W.C.	Mng.	Profss.
L.C.S.I	12.4	76.3		8.2	0	3.1
L.C.S.II	4.3	90.0		4.6	0	1.1
M.C.S.		4.1	14.3	8.6	17.0	57.0
U.C.S.I.			4.4		8.7	86.9
U.C.S.II			1.2		21.7	77.1

Table 4-2
Head of Household Income by Type of School (percent)

Type of School	Income		
	Low	Middle	High
Lower Class School I	85.5	14.5	
Lower Class School II	89.7	10.3	
Middle Class School		95.7	4.2
Upper Class School I	1.1	10.9	88.0
Upper Class School II	1.2	1.3	97.6

beliefs that students were expected to acquire and follow. The school administrators in this instance concentrated their roles on decision making without major interference from parents or from the State bureaucracy. The upper-class schools followed an "achievement oriented" pattern of administration. This administrative style was primarily academic, with a focus to encourage educational innovations and a comprehensive approach to working relations among the different sectors of the school population. The decision making processes, while centered in the person of the principal, were at the same time diffused through other levels of the school structure.

An additional characteristic observed among the schools was the flow of communication. In the working-class schools communications were unidirectional in correspondence with the authority structure. Parents had few opportunities to actively participate in the educational process affecting their children or in decisions pertaining to how the schools were run. The center of administrative control was located outside the schools, in the central office of the Secretariat of Public Education. This situation had several implications including those related to hiring practices. Teachers were assigned very much on a first-come-first-served basis without participation of the school community in their selection. In the middle-class school the communication process was also unidirectional. The center of authority was the principal, who was responsible for making decisions about educational programs, teacher hiring, and internal organization. The hiring process was "normative," heavily based on teaching credentials and attitudes of teachers' loyalty to the principles and values encouraged by the school authority. Parents were not encouraged to participate. The rationale supporting this approach is that the school philosophy expects parents to accept the rigid principles of discipline and respect for the authority of teachers and school administrators. As a result, parents were mostly passive and supportive of the decisions made by the school concerning the education of their children.

The upper-class schools were found to be open and "bidirectional" in their communication style. These schools operated on the basis of committees responsible for discussing educational and policy issues with the aim of assisting the administration of the school. Overall, teachers were satisfied with the openness and participatory approach used by the schools' administrators, despite the fact that they were hired following an "elitist approach" that relies on higher education credentials, family background, psychological stability, and accepted personality traits. In addition, the academic environment in the upper-class schools was highly supportive of educational innovations. Parents were involved in a structure very similar to those found in North American schools regarding parents' participation in school affairs. Parents' councils were responsible for assessing proposals submitted by the school administration. These councils were also involved in deciding on matters raised by the parents themselves through individual committees per grade. However, one of their primary concerns was the financial soundness of the school.

In terms of educational content and available resources, working-class schools depended on the national public educational system. In practice they did not have room for decisions concerning the procedures and methods for allocation or distribution of resources. In fact, they followed the same rules applied throughout the country in all public schools. Each school was expected to use the official textbooks prepared by the government for each primary grade and distributed to students free of charge. Official curriculum guidelines, also determined by the government, ensured that the curriculum content at each level was the minimum required by the Secretariat of Public Education in all public primary schools throughout the country. Teachers were expected to provide students with additional materials in each subject matter to complement the textbooks. In practice, however, in both working-class schools, the official textbook was the main and in some cases the only source for teaching, either because of financial limitations of the schools or simply a lack of motivation of the teachers. Knowledge transmission was limited and determined by the textbook, although it was considered to be the minimum required to provide students with a sound education. In this regard, students from the working-class schools were at a clear disadvantage compared with children from middle- and upper-class schools.

In the middle-class school, knowledge and information delivery were higher in quality and quantity. This was facilitated by the use of a wider variety of materials and textbooks in each grade. This school did not use official textbooks. Other educational materials were provided by the school, and students were also expected to contribute by acquiring materials considered to be necessary for the teaching-learning process. In upper-class schools, knowledge transmission was achieved with the assistance of an abundance of materials provided by the students and the school. Students were encouraged to go through the official programs in the shortest time possible. This was intended to develop additional skills by achieving objectives complementary to the regular curriculum. The school played a central role in developing additional curriculum content to help students obtain a broader and more comprehensive education.

Classroom communications varied from one type of school to another. Teacher-student interaction in working-class schools was limited to oral individual or group participation in specific lessons. This was to a large extent determined by the lower level of oral or verbal ability of students, but also by the delivery methods used by the teachers. By carrying out a teaching-learning process based on a narrow approach to classroom interactions, the school tended to reinforce some of the existing deficiencies among students concerning their ability to communicate.

Discipline in the working-class schools was almost nonexistent. Students were left on their own. In most of the classrooms visited, there was no effort by the teachers to enforce the basic discipline required to facilitate an adequate learning environment. Contrary to what was expected, the assumption that knowledge transmission among working-class schools took place in an environment where basic common rules of behavior were clearly established did not find support. Lower-class schools were found not to follow methodological rules or pedagogical principles that could ensure the effective acquisition of knowledge, such as being on time, observing rules of good behavior, preparing lessons, doing homework, and respecting basic social contracts implemented throughout the school. Similarly, no dogmatic disciplinarian rules were found to be applied in these schools by the teachers or the school administration. The absence of some of the most common forms of school discipline characteristic of almost all traditional educational systems seems to have a direct effect on the quality of the learning processes taking place in these particular schools. This was, to a large extent, a deviation from one of the working hypotheses that working-class schools were enforcing a strong and rigid authoritarian mode of discipline as a means to train, beginning from an early age, the future cadres of the labor force.

The middle-class school showed a high degree of internal order and rigid discipline in regard to the expected behaviors of students. They were able to participate in classroom activities only at the request and under the guidance of the teacher. Most of the time the class was silent and the children were asked to repeat different drills aloud and in perfect order. Contact between teachers and students was formal and based on a clear understanding of the differences separating them within the school structure. These perceptions reinforced some of the original assumptions regarding this type of school. Middle-class students are supposed to be educated according to high standards of academic performance; at the same time, they are taught to be obedient, respectful of order and discipline, and prepared to execute orders. This, to a large extent, shows a correspondence with the role expected in a class society from the members of the middle class, who at the level of the productive system tend to occupy middle management positions.

In upper-class schools, communication within the classroom was encouraged by the teachers who constantly demanded participation from students. Teachers were concerned with developing oral skills, a task directly reinforced by the families. As will be discussed later, oral proficiency among first graders, for example, was the highest compared with students in similar grades in other types of schools. Upper-class students used a highly elaborated and rich set of symbols that were communicated through oral capabilities (Bernstein, 1971).

SPECIFIC FINDINGS

A first step in the study was to introduce an objective measure to assess the intelligence of all first-grade students in the sample to compare the teachers' opinions about their students' intelligence. The Modified Standardized Goodenough Test of Maturity-Intelligence (MSGTM-I) was used for this purpose.

Working-class Schools

Five first-grade classrooms were selected from the working-class schools of the sample. This included 69 students from two first-grade levels in one school and 97 students from the second school. The first group of students were 59.4 percent male students and 40.5 percent female students. The second group had 53.6 and 46.3 percent of male and female students respectively. Table 4-3 shows the distribution of students in both schools by level of intelligence. For both schools, the test shows a near normal distribution.

Table 4-3 shows the distribution of these students according to the level of language proficiency associated with their level of intelligence. On average, 11.6 percent of students had high proficiency in oral language, while an average 49.1 percent present a low level of language proficiency. Contrary to the distribution by level of intelligence, the distribution of students in this case was swerved toward the lower level.

In terms of work aspirations, an important percentage of children from these schools wanted to become professionals. This, to some extent, contradicted one of the assumptions derived from the theoretical framework

Table 4-3
IQ and Oral Proficiency in Working-class Schools

		Low	Medium	High
MSGTM-I	School 1	20.2	63.7	15.9
	School 2	22.6	51.5	25.7
Avrg.		21.4	57.6	20.8
Oral Prof.	School 1	47.8	39.1	13.0
	School 2	50.5	39.1	10.3
Avrg.		49.1	39.1	11.6

sustaining that lower-class children aspire to occupations similar to those of their parents, in this case most of them low-skilled workers. Distribution by occupational aspirations among first-grade students in the working-class schools of the sample: On average, 42 percent of students from both schools wanted to become professionals, 22.4 percent aspired to be technicians, and 21 percent wanted to be skilled workers.

Teachers' judgments about the academic competence of their students in these schools were based primarily on the observed oral skills of the students. This was determined by the perceptions that teachers in lower-class schools seem to have about the intelligence of their students. According to such perceptions, teachers tend to expect less from poor students in terms of knowledge and acquired information, thus reinforcing the idea of the self-fulfilling prophecy concerning the learning capability of working-class children (Rist, 1970).

The comparison of the teachers' perceptions of students' intelligence with the results of the MSGTM-I test shows that teachers tend to have a biased view of their students' IQ capacity. There is strong evidence indicating that teachers in these schools see students of working-class background as less intelligent. This perception seems to be related to the indicator most directly available to the teachers to assess students' capacity. Most teachers focus on the students' oral proficiency in the classroom. Thus teachers tend to assume that those students with poorer oral proficiency have lower intelligence levels (see Table 4-4). This explains the finding indicating that the correlation between teachers' perceptions of intelligence and oral proficien-

Table 4-4
Comparison between MSGTM-I and Teachers' Perceptions, of Students' IQ
in Working-class Schools

I.Q. Level		Low	Medium	High
MSGTM-I	School 1	15.9	63.7	20.2
	School 2	25.7	51.5	22.6
Avgr.		20.8	57.6	21.4
Teacher Expec of I.Q.	School 1	43.4	31.8	24.6
	School 2	48.4	39.1	12.3
Avrg.		45.9	35.5	18.4

Table 4-5
Oral Proficiency as a Predictor of IQ in Working-class Schools

Levels		Low	Medium	High
Teacher Expect. of I.Q.	School 1	43.4	31.8	24.6
	School 2	48.4	39.1	12.3
Avrg.		45.9	35.5	18.4
Oral Prof.	School 1	47.8	39.1	13.0
	School 2	50.5	39.1	10.3
Avrg.		49.1	39.1	11.6

cy is higher than the correlation between actual IQ measures and the teachers' expectations of intelligence (see Table 4-5).

Middle-class Schools

The middle-class school in this study had two first-grade classrooms with a total of 71 students, 50.7 percent of whom were males and 49.3 females. According to the MSGTM-I, 22.5 percent of the students were in the high percentiles of the intelligence scale and 19.7 percent were in the lower level. Considering the variable on students' language proficiency, the distribution was similar to that provided by the measure of intelligence. As expected, in both cases there was a near normal distribution, and there appears to be a high correlation among the scores for low, medium, and high intelligence (19.7, 57.7, and 22.5) and oral proficiency (14, 50.7, and 35.2) among the middle-class students of the sample.

The data on the students' occupational aspirations tend to confirm one of the original assumptions of the study. The large majority of students wanted to become professionals or technicians (71.8 and 16.9 percent respectively), following the occupational pattern of their parents.

The comparison between teachers' perceptions of students' intelligence and the objective measure of IQ shows some interesting findings (see Table 4-6). It seems that teachers in this school tend to underclassify their students in terms of intelligence compared to the objective test. Contrary to what was found in working-class schools, the teachers' perceptions of intelligence in this school were negatively correlated to the students' oral proficiency (see Table 4-7). A possible explanation for this result can be found in the type of environment of middle-class schools. Despite the higher levels of oral proficiency compared with working-class schools, teachers may be restricted in their perceptions of oral proficiency in connection to intelligence by the high level of discipline, which in turn limits the students' oral expression. Under such circumstances, the most immediate indicator of students' capacity for the teacher is their academic work rather than their oral proficiency.

Upper-class Schools

A total of 266 first-grade students were surveyed from two upper-class schools. In the first school, with 118 first graders, 53.4 percent were males and 46.6 percent were females. In the second school, 47.2 were males and 52.7 percent were females.

According to the measure of intelligence, an average of 15.5 percent of students were in the lower level of the IQ scale, 60.6 percent in the middle level, and 23.8 percent in the high level. In terms of oral proficiency, the average distribution of students showed that a large proportion of students (65.3 percent) was in the high level of oral proficiency, while only an average of 4.6 percent of students were in the lower level (see Table 4-8). Once again in this case, there was no correlation found between the measure of IQ and

Table 4-6

General Comparison between MSGTM-I and Teachers'
Perceptions of Students' IQ in Middle-class Schools

	Low	Medium	High
MSGTM-I	19.7	57.7	22.5
Teachers' Perceptions	29.5	59.1	11.2

Table 4-7

Oral Proficiency as a Predictor of IQ in Middle-class Schools

Levels	Low	Medium	High
Teacher Expect of I.Q.	29.5	59.1	11.2
Oral Prof.	14.0	50.7	35.2

oral proficiency. This tends to reinforce the assumption that oral proficiency seems to be primarily determined by the socioeconomic status of the student rather than by the level of intelligence.

The distribution of students by occupational aspirations showed that the majority of students tend to select professional or technical occupations (the average was 86.2 and 4.4 respectively). This result follows a similar pattern to the one found in middle-class schools.

The comparison of teachers' expectations regarding students' intelligence with the actual measure of IQ indicated that there is a closer correlation between the two in the case of upper-class schools (see Table 4-9). Important to notice, however, is the fact that contrary to the findings in the other schools, oral proficiency in upper-class schools was not a good predictor of students' intelligence (see Table 4-10). A possible explanation is that in these schools teachers usually have access to objective information about the students' IQ independently of the students' performance in the classroom. In fact, the teachers know the MSGTM-I scores of students from the beginning of the school year and these schools also have psychological services to students within the system.

Conclusion

Teachers' perceptions of students' intelligence across schools tends to be more accurate among schools serving students from higher socioeconomic backgrounds. The lack of objective indicators of intelligence in schools serving children from lower socioeconomic status makes teachers look for infor-

Table 4-8
IQ and Oral Proficiency in Upper-class Schools

		Low	Medium	High
I.Q.	School 1	13.5	65.2	21.3
	School 2	17.5	56.0	26.3
Avrg.		15.5	60.6	23.8
Oral Prof.	School 1	2.6	36.4	61.0
	School 2	6.7	23.6	69.5
Avrg.		4.6	30.0	65.3

Table 4-9
Comparison between MSGTM-I and Teachers' Perceptions of Students' IQ in Upper-class Schools

I.Q. Level		Low	Middle	High
MSGTM-I	School 1	13.5	65.2	21.3
	School 2	17.5	56.0	26.3
Avrg.		15.5	60.6	23.8
Teacher Percp. of I.Q.	School 1	12.7	47.4	39.9
	School 2	15.5	62.8	21.6
Avrg.		14.1	55.1	30.7

Table 4-10
Oral Proficiency as a Predictor of IQ in Upper-class Schools

Levels		Low	Medium	High
Teacher Percep. of I.Q.	School 1	12.7	47.7	39.9
	School 2	15.5	62.8	21.6
Avrg.		14.1	55.2	30.7
Oral Prof.	School 1	2.6	36.4	61.0
	School 2	6.7	23.6	69.5
Avrg.		4.6	30.0	65.3

Table 4-11
Work Aspirations by Type of School

	Working-Class School	Middle-Class School	Upper-Class School
Professional	42.0	71.8	86.2
Technical	22.4	16.9	4.4
Secretarial	9.1	0.0	0.0
Skilled Work	21.0	5.6	0.0
Housewife	5.1	5.6	6.5
Merchant	0.0	0.0	2.7

mation about students' intelligence in aspects such as their oral proficiency (such as in working-class schools), or their academic performance (such as in the middle-class schools). It also appears that oral proficiency is closely related to the students' socioeconomic status. According to the findings of this study, oral proficiency tends to improve according to the higher socioeconomic status of the school. A different tendency was found in regard to the value of teachers' perceptions of intelligence as a predictor of students' IQ. The relationship between teachers' perceptions of intelligence and oral proficiency was found to be more relevant in schools serving students of low socioeconomic status. The opposite was found in regard to the actual value of IQ and the teachers' perception of it. This is weak among working-class schools and increases in middle- and upper-class schools.

Language proficiency tends to be overconsidered in working-class schools, although it is a weak predictor of children's capacities, particularly among the high intelligence groups. One of the outcomes of this situation is that working-class children tend to be underclassified by their teachers in the assessment of their performance. The ratio between IQ measures and language proficiency by type of school shows that the role of language proficiency in working-class schools is considerably more determinant than in upper-class schools.

The comparison among schools in regard to occupational aspirations also shows some interesting tendencies (see Table 4-11). It seems that occupational aspirations among primary school children is largely determined by their socioeconomic background and the type of school they attend. Both in middle- and upper-class schools there is a clear emphasis in the selection of professional occupations. This is also found in working-class schools, particularly in regard to professional and technical occupations, although in a lower proportion.

Overall, the analysis shows that, across the board, the internal performance of schools, the perceptions determining teachers' relations with students, and students' performance at school are heavily determined by the intrinsic characteristics of the educational institution, which in turn is conditioned by the socioeconomic characteristics of the population of the school. Each of the schools studied represented specific socioeconomic groups in Mexico City. It was interesting to observe that while the correlation between income and type of school was clearly established ($r = 0.825$), the introduction of language proficiency as a sociocultural variable into the relationship made the correlation even stronger ($r = 0.936$). This confirms that the socioeconomic and sociocultural variables influencing the education of children from different class backgrounds do not act separately, but in an interactive fashion. The school, in turn, tends to reinforce the social and cultural traits of particular social groups.[4]

NOTES

1. This chapter is drawn from the dissertation research carried out by Dr. Manuel Figueroa Unda (Stanford University, Stanford, California, 1982). The final draft of the chapter of this book was prepared by Daniel A. Morales-Gómez and Carlos Alberto Torres.

2. Like any standardized test, the SSWMT is culturally biased. It is usually skewed toward middle- and upper-class cultural capital. It was used with great caution as an intervening element to assess the linguistic proficiency of students. However, it did not provide the only criterion for such assessment. There is an expected level of proficiency in Spanish that is attested in the Free Textbook for Elementary Education of the SEP. The SSWMT takes this into account to some extent.

3. The working-class schools were public schools in the Mexican education system. The middle-class and the two upper-class schools were private. In all cases studied,

teachers working in these schools had at least the Elementary Teaching Credential obtained at normal schools (*escuelas normales*).

4. A study of this kind has several limitations. Perhaps the most important is that it offers only a snapshot of the complexities of education in Mexico by sampling few schools attended by children from different social classes. Because education is a process, its outcome and role in social reproduction cannot be fully measured at a single point in time. To overcome this limitation, it is convenient to replicate this type of study to produce a follow-up after several years. This would enable comparison of findings throughout the students' time in the education system.

5 Nonformal Education and Literacy Training: Policies and Practice 1970–1988

INTRODUCTION

After the Revolution, the Mexican State developed a complex and diversified schooling system capable of serving 24 million students in the early 1980s. However, it was not until 1975, with the enactment of the National Law of Adult Education,[1] that the State formally assumed responsibility for educating adults 15 years of age and older.

One of the unexpected outcomes of rapid economic growth and social modernization was the growing pressure of the high illiteracy rate over the actions of government policy planners. A UNESCO study showed that by 1970 the average adult illiteracy rate in Mexico was 23.8 percent (20.5 percent males and 26.9 percent females), below the 28.1 percent average for Latin America (UNESCO, 1982). By 1980, the regional average had changed to 19.3 percent (17.8 percent males and 25 percent females), while in Mexico it had been reduced to 15 percent (12 percent males and 17.6 percent females). Although this figure was impressive, the absolute number of illiterates in 1982 reached 6.5 million. Accounting for the rate of population growth, this figure had remained more or less constant during the preceding two decades. This led to arguments that Mexico's literacy rates ranked very low compared with other countries with similar industrial development trends in the region, despite its sustained process of economic development in the 1960s and 1970s.[2] Table 5.1 shows the absolute numbers and the illiteracy rates according to estimates from census data.[3]

Literacy in Mexico is a complex issue. As noted earlier, close to one million people do not speak, read, or write Spanish (Solana, 1980: 26). By 1980, approximately 22 million people over 15 years of age had not yet finished their primary and/or secondary education. Among them, 60 percent resided in more than 40,000 small rural communities with populations of 500 or less (Pescador, 1982a).

Table 5-1
Absolute Illiteracy in Mexico: Population 15 Years and Older[1]
(selected   years)

Year*	No of Illiterates	Rate of Illiteracy % of the Adult Population
1930	6,403,001(1)	63.6
1940	6,234,000	53.9
1950	6,518,000	43.6
1960	6,678,000	34.5
1970	6,694,000	25.8
1980	6,435,721(2)	16.3
1981	6,371,780	15.7
1982	6,012,324	14.3
1983	5,564,307	13.0
1984	5,011,228	11.5
1985	4,413,329	9.9
1986	3,669,365	7.7

(1) Data from the National Census of Population. (*) As of December of each year.

(2) Data is a political prisoner of governments. In comparing three sources of data in order to obtain a series like the one presented here, several problems should be noted. First the data from the presidency of the Republic for 1980, which has been estimated from the Census, is higher than the one portrayed by the Agency for the Literacy Training from INEA (i.e., the difference is approximately 150,000 adults). This difference will remain for the year 1981. Second, the data presented in Miguel Alonzo Calles for 1985 is higher (i.e. approximately 3,000 individuals) than the one presented in the INEA. The one reported here for that year is the one provided by INEA.

[1] These figures refer to absolute literacy in Mexico according to estimates from census data. It is not possible to estimate accurately functional illiteracy, marginal illiteracy, or semiilliteracy in Mexico.

Sources: For 1930-1970 Miguel Alonzo Calles, former General Director of the National Institute of Adult Education (INEA), cited by José Angel Pescador (1986); for 1970-1981 Quinto Informe de Gobierno, 1981. Presidencia de la República, Sector Educativo. 1982-1986 INEA, Dirección de Alfabetización, Programa de Acción de Alfabetización para 1986, mimeo, November 1986, anexo A. INEA, Plan de Acción del Programa de Alfabetización para 1987. Dirección de Alfabetización, January 1987, page 89, annex 3. INEA, Acción educativa 1981-1986, SEP México, 1987. INEA, Serie histórica 1981-1986, INEA, Mexico, 1987.

Since the postrevolutionary period, there has been a series of attempts to deal with the needs for literacy training and basic adult education. A landmark among developing countries in the region was the literacy campaign carried out between 1944 and 1946, as a result of which 828,029 adults became literate. This has been considered to be an achievement given Mexico's population of 24 million people at the time (Vidal, 1981: 122).

These efforts, however, practically vanished over time. One of the successful experiences, the *Misiones Culturales* (Cultural Missions), which had as main objective the training of rural teachers, was reaching almost 650,000 students when it was cancelled at the end of 1938 (Vidal, 1981: 122). Reinstated later by Secretary Jaime Torres Bodet in 1943, it became a largely symbolic institution without practical impact after the 1950s.

Between 1950 and 1970, few resources were devoted to adult education. The situation was aggravated by a lack of continuity in adult education policies. Many kinds of institutions and agencies related to adult education were created and eliminated during this period, and others were radically affected by changes in their management. The example of the general Directorate of Adult Education in the Secretariat of Public Education is a case in point. In 1979 alone it had four different directors.

The purpose of this chapter is to discuss some of the major adult education initiatives in the country that took place between 1970 and 1988. Special attention is given to analysis of the institutional structures created to deal with adult education problems, their performance, and the policy directives that led to their implementation.

THE NATIONAL SYSTEM OF ADULT EDUCATION (SNEA): 1975-1981

Adult education gained some momentum by the end of the government of President Echeverría (1970-76). He argued that the education of adults was a key component of the new model of development.[4] Even though the National Law of Adult Education passed in 1975 had an overall short-term impact on educational policies, in practice it produced minor changes and only a slight reorganization of services. One of its specific outcomes was the creation of the National System of Adult Education (SNEA).

During the mid-1970s and until the creation of the National Program of Literacy Training (PRONALF) in 1981, the main agency in charge of adult education services within the Secretariat of Public Education was the General Directorate of Adult Education. Its services were provided through the National System of Adult Education (SNEA). This system's most important services were the Centers of Basic Education for Adults (CEBAS), the Cultural Missions, the Telesecondary Schools, the *Salas de Lectura* (Reading Rooms or Libraries for Adults), the Night Primary Schools for Adults, the Night Secondary Schools for Adults, the Night Secondary Schools for Workers, and the open distance education system for primary, secondary and high school (*preparatoria*) for adults.

The CEBAS were devoted primarily to literacy training and intensive primary education for adults. This service was organized for adults in urban areas following the calendar of the regular school system. In 1970 a total of 24,625 students graduated from the CEBAS, and by 1980, 983 centers were operating in Mexico with a total enrollment of 99,903 students.[5] The Cultural Missions, one of the oldest adult education services in Mexico and

Table 5-2
Open Primary and Secondary School for Adults, 1980

	March 1980		Jan-March 1980		Jan-March 1978		1979 (1)		1980 (1)	
	OPA	OSA	OPA	OSA	OPA	OSA	OPA	OSA	OPA	OSA
Students of First Enrolment	2.4	6.6	6.0	20.6	4.5	22.6	65.8	229.2	71.8	248.2
Students who have taken an examination	4.7	17.1	11.3	46.3	8.2	54.6	43.3	211.4	11.3	453.0
Examinations solicited	15.3	49.2	36.4	136.4	28.4	178.2	143.3	666.2	36.4	136.4
Examinations accredited	5.2	23.7	5.2	23.7	2.1	7.0	61.1	172.5	5.2	23.7
Students who receive a certificate	0.387	0.649	0.611	0.291	0.474	1.256	3.8	6.6	0.3	1.3
Communities served (nationwide)	164	244	269	351	162	336	444	621	269	361

(1) is accumulative since 1976; thousands of persons;

OPA = Open Primary Schools for Adults;

OSA = Open Secondary Schools for Adults.

Source: Carlos A. Torres "La educación de adultos en México: Problemas y perspectivas" *Cuaderno de Trabajo* No. 1, Dirección General de Educación de Adultos (DGEA), Secretaría de Educación Pública, Mexico, March 1980, p. 11.

Table 5-3
Student Enrollment in the National System of Adult Education (SNEA):
Annual Enrollment and Rates of Growth (year base: 1975=100)

Year	Absolute	Accumulative	% Growth Absolute	% Growth Accumulative
1975	99,815	99,815	100	100
1976	631,729	731,544	+533.1	+633.1
1977	406,645	1,138,189	+307.4	1,040.3
1978	78,816	1,217,005	−21.0	1,119.3

Source: Oscar Cuellar *El Sistema Nacional de Educación para Adultos: Evolución del registro y características de la población inscrita (1975-1978)*, November 1981, (mimeographed) p. 5, Table No.1.

perhaps in Latin America, operate exclusively in rural communities and focus on basic training and basic education. In 1980 there were 215 Cultural Missions in 645 rural communities throughout the country, employing 1,700 teachers and serving an estimated population of 202,800 persons. The Telesecondary Schools were divided into a federal-controlled and a state-controlled system. By 1980, there were 2,297 federal teleclassrooms in ten states, and 335 teleclassrooms controlled by and operating in four states. These systems had a total of 2,692 teachers and 79,415 students, and during the 1979-80 school year they produced 22,095 graduates. The system of Reading Rooms (*Salas de Lectura*) or Libraries for Adults operated throughout the country as a mobile library service for rural communities. In 1978-79, they were established in 99 rural communities serving 73,245 readers. The system of Night Primary Schools was organized into 450 schools with an enrollment of 65,621 students. Finally, the Open System, including primary, secondary, and high school services, was the most prominent adult education service at the beginning of 1980s. Table 5-2 shows data for this particular service for adults at the primary and secondary levels.

These data show that the efficiency of the open system for adult education has been quite low. The percentage of examinations solicited and approved in relation to the total enrollment shows that a very small percentage of students were able to finish successfully. If total enrollment is compared with the potential demand for this service, it can be argued that only a small number of those in need of the services were able to receive it. There is also a trend indicating that the efficiency of the system increased at the higher levels of education particularly in regard to literacy training, thus favoring the small proportion of adults able to reach such levels. In fact, the lowest levels of adult education were those with the lowest efficiency in terms of the rate of enrollment vis-à-vis the number of graduates.

The National Service of Adult Education (SNEA) was created in 1975 as an integral part of the Secretariat of Public Education dependent on the Sub-Directorate of the Open Education System. In addition to open primary and secondary education, the SNEA also comprised literacy training identified as "introduction to primary education."

The enrollment profile of the SNEA between 1975 and 1978 shows that the system had a sharp decline. In fact, the total number of students enrolled in 1978 represented only 80 percent of the total enrollment in 1975 (see Table 5-3).[6] This casts some doubt on the overall efficiency of the system and its capacity to attract students.

By level of education the distribution of students shows some clear trends (see Table 5-4). Enrollment in literacy training increased only 5.2 percent between 1976 and 1978, while primary education, representing 53.9 percent of the total enrollment in 1976, dropped to 38.5 percent two years later. As indicated earlier, secondary education clearly gained importance in terms of

Table 5-4
Enrollment at the SNEA: Distribution by Levels, 1976-1978

Year	Literacy Training Absolute	%	Primary Education Absolute	%	Secondary Education Absolute	%	Total %
1976	117,910	14.2	448,233	53.9	265,586	31.9	100
1977	56,092	13.8	178,244	43.8	172,309	42.4	100
1978	15,278	19.4	30,380	38.5	33,162	42.1	100
Total	189,278	14.4	656,857	49.9	471,057	35.7	100

Source: Oscar Cuellar *El Sistema Nacional de Educación para Adultos: Evolución del registro y características de la población inscrita (1975-1978)*, November 1981 (mimeographed) p. 9, Table No. 2.

Table 5-5
Adult Education: Satisfaction of Potential Demand, 1976-1978

Level	1976	1977	1978
Literacy Training	1.51	2.22	2.42
Primary Education	3.73	5.22	5.47
Secondary Education	4.05	5.97	6.34
Total	3.23	4.64	4.91

Source: Oscar Cuellar, *El Sistema Nacional de Educación para Adultos: Evolución del registro y características de la población inscrita (1975-1976)*. November 1981, (mimeographed), p. 17, Table No. 6.

enrollment by increasing from 31.9 to 42.1 percent during the period. According to Cuellar's (1981) analysis of this situation, if 1976 is considered as a base year, the changes become negative over time. In terms of relative decrease in enrollment, between 1976 and 1978, literacy training shows a loss of 87 percent, primary education 93.2 percent, and secondary education 87.5 percent. Overall, the best performance in regard to enrollment was secondary education, and the least efficient was primary education.

To assess the system's effectiveness, enrollment can also be contrasted with the potential demand for the SNEA services. During this three-year period, less than 5 percent of the total population representing the potential demand for adult education in the country was registered in the system (Vergara, 1981: 154). If enrollment is broken down by level as a percentage of the potential demand, it is found that literacy training attracted only a handful of potential students (see Table 5-5).

These data suggest that, given the potential demand, the services provided by the SNEA system to the adult population were in fact minimal. However, the situation is even more critical if one looks at the clientele who demanded these services. A general review of enrollment data shows that there was a slightly larger proportion of males (52.03 percent compared with 47.97 percent of females). In both cases, 60 percent were younger than 31 years of age, with a mode in the age group of 15-20 years old (Cuellar, 1981: 20-22). In the group of youngest students, 52 percent were women. The average schooling level of those enrolled in the system was four years of completed primary school (Vergara, 1981: 16), and almost 80 percent of SNEA students had had at least one year of completed formal primary schooling. These findings are consistent with those showing the inability of the system to attract illiterates.

Regarding occupation and areas of economic activity, a great number of the students were housewives, and an important proportion were workers and peasants. Together these account for almost one third of the total enrollment. In addition, a relatively high proportion of people reported that they were working in the service sector (25 percent).[7] Overall, at least two thirds of the students enrolled in the system could be considered part of the economically active population. Some of these traits are in sharp contrast to the adult education system that was to replace the SNEA in 1981.

A critical view of the SNEA system points out most of its shortcomings:

> It is clear that an evaluation of the success of a program cannot be limited to a short period such as the one analyzed ... However, in analyzing the evolution of enrollment, we find a systematic and accelerated trend of slowing down enrollment; thus there is undoubtedly a high rate of dropout ... In other words, if the satisfaction of the potential demand could not be considered in and of itself as a safe indicator—due to the characteristics of the program—the negative evolution of enrollment already constitutes an indicator of failure. (Cuellar, 1981: 42-43. Our translation)

By 1981, the SNEA system was languishing. With fewer and fewer students applying for enrollment and with a very marginal impact on literacy training, in May 1981 the State decided to launch the National Program of Literacy Training (PRONALF) and by September of the same year created the National Institute of Adult Education.

THE NATIONAL PROGRAM OF LITERACY TRAINING (PRONALF) AND THE NATIONAL INSTITUTE OF ADULT EDUCATION (INEA): 1981-82

The government initiatives, outlined in five main policy objectives and expressed through 53 priorities, were the core of President López Portillo's educational program. The first recognized the need to offer basic education to the population, in particular "giving to the adult population the opportunity to receive or complete basic (primary or secondary) education" (SEP, 1982: 25). This educational program was aimed at reducing illiteracy to 10 percent by 1982. It implied, in practice, enabling 3 million adults to finish their primary education and another 2 million adults to complete secondary schooling. The achievement of such ambitious goals implied making one million people literate during 1981 and 1982 and providing educational services to 2 million people who had not been able to complete either primary and/or secondary basic education. The magnitude of this task became immediately clear, particularly in the area of literacy training. Even if the trends of the previous decade, during which 1.5 million adults became literate, were able to continue at the same pace, it would still take almost half a century to wipe out illiteracy completely (SEP, 1982: 27).

To tackle the problem of literacy training, in May and June 1981, the National Program for Literacy Training (PRONALF) began to operate within the Secretariat of Public Education.[8] This program, conceived as an "operative command," was a unit with abundant resources, relatively independent from the bureaucracy and the inner political struggle of the SEP, and had a concrete and fairly well-circumscribed task of achieving the goals of literacy in the shortest possible time. Street (1983) has pointed out that during Fernando Solana's tenure as Secretary of Education, the center of policy definition was shifted from the traditional General Directorates of the SEP, hierarchically dependent on a given Sub-Secretary of the SEP, to the Office of the Staff of the Secretary. This was achieved through the creation of several advisory councils such as the Council of Open Education, the Advisory Council of Teacher Education, and the Council of Technological Education. These councils were to coordinate and therefore control the General Directorates. Educational planning in this context became institutionalized as a legitimate activity directed to reorganize different areas of education under the close control of Secretary Solana (Street, 1983: 254-255). Although this analysis emphasizes the importance of these organizational changes that Street defines as a "strategy of modernization," it does not place enough emphasis on the organizational and political implications that this operative command brought about in the context of the SEP.

This operative command was aimed at dealing with well-defined problem areas of policy using an approach free of bureaucratic bounds. It operated with engineering methods of program organization and administration, and under close control and monitoring by the Secretary's staff. This implied that their activities were kept safely away from the day-to-day administrative and political bargaining with the teachers' union and other bureaucratic factions.[9]

The operative command of PRONALF had the objective of "offering to all Mexican illiterates older than 15 years of age who demand it the opportunity to become literate and to use reading and writing skills" (PRONALF-SEP, 1981: 7). This strategy was expected to work initially only in localities with 100,000 or more inhabitants, but gradually to include other smaller areas. The age group to be primarily served by PRONALF included the highest proportion of illiterates in the country. These were defined as those individuals between 15 and 49 years of age who were not monolingual and lived in localities with 500 or more inhabitants. PRONALF estimated this group to cover approximately 3 million people, out of which the program sought to enroll 60 percent. In terms of terminal efficiency, given the effective enrollment, PRONALF planned to make one million adults literate in a year. The goals proposed by PRONALF in 1981 are outlined in Table 5-6.

Table 5-6
Goals Proposed by PRONALF, 1981

Target	Quantity	Percentages
1. Total Population	69,915.5	
2. Population 15 years and older	39,147.5	56% of total population
3. Total Illiterate Population	6,594.4	9.4% of total population
4. Illiterate Population of 15-49 years of age	4,126.6	62.6% of total illiteracy
5. Illiterates living in cities of 500 and more inhabitants non-monolingual and in the age group of 15-49 years of age	2,937.6	44.5% of total illiterate population
6. Target Enrollment	1,672.3	57% of No 5
7. Target of Literacy	1,000.0	60% of No 6

Source: Dirección General de Programación, SEP, 1981. PRONALF-SEP, *Manual de procedimientos para la operación del sistema de estadística contínua de los servicios de alfabetización*. Mexico, July 1981: 10.

The Planning and Administrative Structure of PRONALF

The administrative structure of PRONALF was designed following new criteria of administrative deconcentration. There were five operational levels to carry out the National Literacy Campaign: the national central coordination, the state coordination, the regional coordinations that included the zone coordinators, the regional organizers of literacy training, and the literacy training group.

The *national coordination* was responsible for preparing the general program and the normative documents of the campaign. Among its specific tasks were the preparation of the national plan for the diffusion of the literacy campaign; the allocation of financial resources; the design, reproduction, and delivery of literacy materials; and the training of the personnel responsible for the program in the states throughout the country. It was also in charge of the evaluation of the program nationwide. The *state coordination* or the *General Delegation* was directly responsible for programming the different cycles of literacy training and preparing agreements with the state governments. It was expected to facilitate the operation of the program in their jurisdiction; organize the delivery of the program according to different zones; recruit, select, and train state personnel; take charge of the local diffusion and coordination of the literacy campaign; distribute literacy material; and evaluate the program at the statewide level. The *zone coordinators* were in charge of organizing, conducting, and supervising the implementation of the programs at the county level. They were also responsible for identifying the regions where programs were to be in place. At this level the coordinating responsibility was with the *regional organizers* of literacy training. They were in charge of operating, leading, supervising, and evaluating the work of the campaign at the regional level. These organizers were also responsible for detecting and enrolling illiterates into the program; sensitizing the population about the problems of illiteracy; forming the literacy groups; locating classrooms and sites for the operation of the literacy groups (e.g., schools, community clubs); organizing the literacy training material and equipment needed; and hiring, assigning, and advising the teachers and literacy training facilitators. The grassroots level of operations included the teachers, literacy training facilitators, and literacy pollsters.

The planning of PRONALF began in March 1981, and the first literacy training activity took place in early June 1981. During the first 13 months, the program was planned to carry out eight cycles of training, each with a duration of five months. A month after the beginning of each cycle the next would start. However, this plan was followed only until August 31, 1981, when the INEA was created. With INEA, PRONALF became a Directorate of Literacy Training within INEA together with Basic Education, Cultural Promotion, Work Training, and the Quality of Education and Administration Units (INEA, n.d.: 3).

Two organizational characteristics of PRONALF should be highlighted at this point. Since its inception, the organization of decision making and policy planning in PRONALF was highly centralized. At the same time, however, it was completely decentralized in the operation of its services nationwide. The diffusion, training of personnel, and distribution of didactic materials were controlled from the National Central Coordination.

PRONALF hired an impressive number of temporary personnel without tenure or a permanent administrative base in the educational system. One of the outcomes of this situation was that PRONALF was forced to operate using short-term contracts and personnel paid by honorarium. Most were hired for token wages or, as in the case of many literacy training facilitators, were volunteer workers. By September 1982, the literacy training personnel at INEA consisted of 200 officials at the National Central Coordination. Among them, 40 were at the Central Coordination and 160 were assigned to political delegations of the Federal District. The General Delegation had 16 coordinators, each with a salary slightly over 45,000 pesos ($600 US).[10] Personnel working at the administrative level in the delegations were receiving salaries ranging between $370 to $480 US per month. The 400 promoters were receiving salaries of $173 US a month, with the responsibility for creating and supervising 10 to 15 groups on literacy training, with a maximum of 30 work hours per week. Finally, the 3,000 "advisers" and literacy training facilitators were each receiving $18 US monthly, working fewer than eight hours a week.

The literacy training was organized following in part the method of the "generative word" inspired by Paulo Freire. Each literacy circle was planned to be developed over a five-month period. The first month was to identify, enroll, and organize the illiterates as well as to train the teachers and literacy facilitators. Part of this personnel were volunteers, some of them junior high school and university students fulfilling their social service requirements before graduating. The remaining four months of each circle were to be spent in literacy training. However, after the period between November 1981 and January 1982, and following internal debate and criticism at the level of the National Central Coordination, the timetable was changed to include one extra month to reinforce the literacy training.

The Literacy Training Method

The method used in PRONALF consisted of three stages outlined in the *Manual del Alfabetizador* (PRONALF, n.d.). The first stage covered the thematic discussion of 14 situations, including reading and writing of generative words. The generative words used were: shovel, vaccine, garbage, medicine, bar (cantina), work, guitar, family, milk, tortilla (corn bread), piñata (ornament for children's parties), house, market, education (PRONALF, n.d.: 16-18).[11] In the first stage of thematic discussion, the words were presented in posters and pictures representing specific situations. The second stage consisted of a minimum of four existential situations to be discussed within the group of students to reinforce reading and writing. The situations were grouped into four main categories including words and situations related to (a) means and activities of urban life; (b) rural life and the agricultural and craft industries; (c) rural activities of cattle raising and the craft industry; and (d) coastal areas, fishing, agricultural activities, and craft industries (PRONALF, n.d.: 18). These words were to be discussed in the order presented using pictures for the thematic discussion but without the words. At this stage, after the students finished reading and writing, they were expected to begin learning mathematics. Table 5-7 shows the grouping of the words.

The third stage was to address the thematic discussion and to reinforce reading and writing skills using a list of additional words, this time provided without any mandatory sequence, picture, or poster. The facilitator introduced directly the themes for discussion and wrote the words on the blackboard.[12] At this stage, the facilitator was advised to use printing for the students' reading, and cursive writing for the written part of the meeting. Originally, the process was planned to last four months, three sessions a week of one and a half hours each. Although closely resembling the formal structure of Freire's method, the approach used by PRONALF has some important differences (Freire, 1978: 139-72; Freire and de Oliveira 1980: 207-19; Torres, 1978: 433-49; 1981: 75-129).

Freire defined literacy training as a process of conscientization or raising the critical consciousness of the participants. In this process, there is an intimate link among a project political in essence (the literacy training project), a method for literacy training, and a process of educational research. PRONALF broke the link among these three components of the method. Although the logical-linguistic structure of Freire's method was retained, its critical component of conscientization was explicitly avoided, thus eliminating its more political-ideological dimension.[13] This was reflected in the selection of generative words and particularly in the organization of the methodological sequence of the teaching-learning process.[14] Freire's (1973) original method begins by discussing ten "strategic-existential situations" aimed at deepening the analysis of the relationships among human beings, culture, and nature. The pictures he proposes to lead the discussion include a human being in relationship with nature and culture; nature as an object of dialogue; culture and its historical dimension represented both by the image of an illiterate farmer or hunter, and his tools, weapons, and modern technology; an animal which is not a subject of culture; people transforming nature with their work as the first dimension

Table 5-7
PRONALF's Generative Words

factory	seed	cattle	fish
trade union	harvest	milking	machete
plumber	weave	weave	weave
television	midwife	midwife	midwife
midwife			

of culture; the product of such transformation represented by handicrafts and manufactured goods as the second dimension of culture; the word as a form of craft represented by poetry, the third dimension of culture; human beings reacting to something new, representing the phenomenon of social change; and a cultural circle in session with people discussing their purpose in being there.

In the 14 situations selected for the PRONALF's method, the relationship among human beings, culture, and nature was entirely absent. There was no clear methodological progression in the process, nor were the different cultural dimensions and the different relationships between human beings emphasized. The generative words selected followed only criteria of syllabic richness and phonetic difficulty and were not necessarily related to the existential problems of the communities, which in practice change according to their location, principal form of production, previous history, and so forth. Thus the issue of social change was diluted in a body of words whose value was primarily linguistic.

The organization of the teaching-learning sequence implicit in the PRONALF's method was to some extent in contrast to Freire's methodology. In the latter, each stage in the methodological sequence has similar importance and plays a particular role in the general process of literacy training and in the raising of the critical consciousness (Table 5-8 presents a brief schematic description of the Freirean method). In the PRONALF's method, the research stage on the generative themes and the detection of the generative words was done only once, and the outcome of this stage was

Table 5-8
Freire's Method

Stages	Tasks
First stage: oriented toward research	Delineation and initial knowlege and contact of area to work with, existential codification, existential decodification; creation of a research circle; verification of research findings.
Second stage: oriented toward programming	thematic treatment of the previous content detected in the community (by using a multi-disciplinary approach); reduction of the epochal themes to a significant themes; thematic codification within the research circle, elaboration of the didactic material.
Third stage: oriented towards pedagogy	Publicity of the Program in the community; thematic decodification: the dialogue will begin in the cultural circles and the process of literacy training and conscientization will commence.

Source: Carlos A. Torres. *La praxis educativa de Paulo Freire*. Mexico, Editorial Gernika, 1978.

later systematized in the Manual of Literacy Training. The main implication of this approach was that the cultural, political, economic, and social peculiarities of each community remained unnoted and the method was thus homogeneously implemented all over the country.

A similar situation is found in the processes of reduction, codification, and decodification that are keys to Freire's method. These three processes were condensed into a set of simple prescriptions included in the Manual to be followed by those applying the method. In practice, however, without intense training, the method lost its linguistic and didactic power and appeared incomprehensible to the adult education teacher. This has been confirmed by research on the perceptions of the literacy facilitators. Studies have shown that teachers discovered "ambiguous messages" in the Manual, felt profound dissatisfaction and lack of understanding as to why students dropped out from the program, and finished devaluing the importance of the method and even questioning its validity for the task at hand (1982: 169-217). The teachers were thus facing a dilemma: to follow passively the directions in the different Manuals provided by PRONALF, or reject them completely and substitute or even invent their own method (De Lella, 1982: 170).

The method of PRONALF has also been considered extremely rigid. It did not provide room for creativity and it lacked alternatives that could be explored within the cultural circles between teachers and learners. De Lella indicates that "the method is not valued or implemented as an instrument of conscientization or organization of the population; it is only a method to achieve reading and writing, a technique restricted to achieving this central objective" (De Lella, 1982: 173).

In some cases teachers replaced the method and the Manual with books for children, arguing that the didactic materials required to properly implement the method were lacking. Occasionally, the method was replaced at the suggestion of the students or because the teachers considered it did not respond to the learning needs of the students (De Lella, 1982: 177). Among the main problems detected with the PRONALF's method were the slowness of the learning process, problems with retention of what had been learned, difficulties in using syllables to organize new words and sentences, and the presentation of a great number of letters that overwhelmed the students (De Lella, 1982: 182-183). In short, the pedagogical stage of the original Freirean method was overemphasized in PRONALF's approach. It is only in the technical sense that the method of the "generative word" of PRONALF followed a sequence similar to the method of the "thematic research" proposed by Freire. The method of the "generative word" as used by PRONALF was stripped of the political and ideological bark found in the original Freirean proposal, thus benefiting an alternative political project sustained by the Mexican State (Cuellar, 1983: 6-7).

An evaluation of the results of the method two years after its inception claimed that the method was weakened and profoundly affected in its execution by lack of appropriate training of the regional coordinators, teachers, and literacy facilitators. It has also been recognized that the method did not work well with some groups (Chaparro, 1983). In fact, the results of the first year of operation of PRONALF were very poor compared with expectations. In 1982, the expected enrollment target in PRONALF was set at 2,145,877 students, whereas only 1,188,233 or 55.4 percent were enrolled. The expected certification was set at 976,122 students. Among these only 360,348 or 36.9 percent were actually certificated as literate, which in turn represented only 30.3 percent of the actual enrollment (De Anda, 1983: 274).

The shortcomings of the initial stages of PRONALF-INEA can be attributed to many factors. Two of them, however, were particularly important: the method implemented by PRONALF and the criteria for the recruitment of personnel. Although the personnel recruited for the campaign had experience working for the Secretariat of Public Education, they were not teachers and above all they did not have expertise or experience in adult education. They were incorporated into the newly created system of INEA mostly because of their lack of ties to the teachers' union and because of their knowledge of organizational theory and administration. This, however, proved insufficient to achieve the expected objectives of the program.

THE PRONALF BUREAUCRACY: BACKGROUND, EXPERIENCE, AND EXPERTISE IN ADULT EDUCATION

It has been argued that the personnel hired to undertake the activities of planning and implementation in adult education at the INEA were young and inexperienced (Torres, 1984a: 202-237). A study of a sample of INEA personnel shows that 84 percent of the staff were younger than 35 years of age, and approximately 29 percent were younger than 18 years of age. By sex, 76 percent of the female personnel were younger than 25 years of age, while almost 50 percent of the male staff were between 26 and 35 years of age. Teachers and field coordinators, the bottom line of service operation, were younger than the upper echelon of the system. Approximately 81 percent of the teachers and 68 percent of the field coordinators were 25 years of age or younger. The members at upper levels of the INEA-PRONALF bureaucracy were all between 26 and 45 years old. While teachers' positions were occupied by very young women, higher officials' jobs were filled by middle-aged men from middle-class backgrounds. Overall, the INEA-PRONALF personnel had limited experience in teaching and research, even though these traits could be considered important hiring criteria in this institution. As many as 83 percent of the staff from the sample had no teaching experience, and 91.5 percent had no research experience.

These findings raise questions about the rationale used by PRONALF-INEA to hire personnel for the campaign. For example, was the need to implement the literacy program at an accelerated pace the main reason for not paying enough attention to the qualifications of teachers and field coordinators? Or was there some implicit restriction in PRONALF that impeded the hiring of personnel with teacher certificates and therefore linked to the teachers' union? Some answers to these questions can be obtained by reviewing the previous work experience of PRONALF's personnel.

For analytical purposes, the bureaucracy at PRONALF can be divided into an "organic bureaucracy" (i.e., higher officials) and a "subordinate bureaucracy" (i.e., field coordinators and teachers). Notable differences can be found between both groups in age structure, gender distribution, educational credentials, work experience, and family socioeconomic and educational background (Torres, 1984a: 202-237). Although the public sector is one of the most important employers in the country, an analysis of a sample of PRONALF personnel shows that 55 percent had no previous work experience with the federal government, and only 17 percent had worked for the Secretariat of Public Education before entering PRONALF-INEA. Among the latter, all were higher officials at PRONALF. This leads to the conclusion that most teachers and field coordinators participating in the campaign were almost entirely alien to the Secretariat of Education. Before entering PRONALF, 18.75 percent of the sample had worked for the private sector, 29.16 percent for the federal government but not within the SEP system, 16.7 percent had worked within the SEP system, and a large proportion (35.4 percent) had no previous work experience.

In summary, the PRONALF bureaucracy was young, with an average age of 35 years at the beginning of the program. By gender, women predominated in the lower ranks of the bureaucracy. The members of the organic bureaucracy had a predominantly urban middle-class socioeconomic and educational background, with average educational credentials equivalent to an incomplete B.A., although some individuals had done postgraduate study. In most cases, they had ample experience in administration and policy planning at SEP but no experience in research and/or in teaching adults. The subordinate bureaucracy was younger on average, mainly women with no work experience. They had lower levels of education than the members of the organic bureaucracy, in most cases only secondary education. In terms of family background, they belonged to peasant, worker, or low middle-class families. Overall, they lacked linkages to the formal structure of SEP or to the bureaucratic factions of the government. They did not attend teachers' colleges, and they did not belong to the teachers' union prior to entering PRONALF. This last feature brings to light an important dimension that merits further comment.

To avoid introduction of the SEP bureaucratic struggle into the new structure of PRONALF and INEA and to prevent possible conflicts due to corporatist economic demands, including demands for better work stability and higher salaries, the PRONALF executives opted to avoid the traditional pool of candidates for teaching positions in their recruitment practice. This excluded teachers trained at the teachers' colleges or *normales* who could bring into PRONALF trade union's demands for controlling the policy planning process and the institutional life of the program. Thus, at the expense of teaching quality and experience, a decision was made to incorporate junior high school and high school graduates as well as university students and young professionals into the program, even at the lower levels of policy operation. Engineering students, people with training in physics, mathematics, public administration, public accounting, sociology, communications, and arts or medicine were common among those hired by PRONALF. Personnel with teacher training were the rare exception.

This situation became even more critical as a result of lack of work stability. Short-term contracts and low salaries also affected the composition of the subordinate bureaucracy in the short run. Young professionals moved to better paying and more stable jobs, leaving PRONALF with postsecondary and young university students, some of whom served on a non-remunerative basis in order to fulfill their university or high school requirements for social service. This particular composition of the teaching force of PRONALF explains the high turnover of personnel that characterized the program since 1981. There seems to be enough evidence to argue that the configuration of the subordinate bureaucracy was the result of a deliberate decision from the organic bureaucracy, formed by members of the technocracy that responded to the Secretary of Education, not to hire teachers who were *normalistas*. The alternative explanation, that the rationale for recruitment responded to the urgency to begin the program with the proper human resources, seems not to be valid at least in the case of the Federal District.[15] Despite some evidence indicating that in certain regions of the country PRONALF found it more difficult to hire qualified personnel as a result of the expansion of the services (Cuellar, 1983), the configuration of PRONALF's personnel was more the result of political decisions at the central level than the outcome of scarce human resources.[16]

The Profile of Human Resources at PRONALF

In September 1982, an evaluation meeting of 132 higher officials of PRONALF took place. A short questionnaire was distributed among those attending the meeting,[17] its object to explore and gather information about two substantive issues: how these functionaries distributed weekly time in their jobs, and what current knowledge they had about relevant information and events on adult education.

This survey found that these functionaries had limited knowledge of the different institutions working in adult education in the country and of the academic events that had taken place in the area of adult education and literacy training. The data also showed that they had limited information about the literature on the subject published in Mexico in the previous three years. Although the members of the organic bureaucracy seemed to have had good knowledge of PRONALF's didactic materials and normative documents, and could handle information on the laws and decrees related to adult education, the data in Table 5-9 show that they had only an average knowledge of the historical antecedents of adult education and academic events in Mexico and a deficient knowledge of adult education as a discipline and field for research, policy planning, and teaching.

Additional information can be found by looking at the educational profile of PRONALF personnel. An analysis of the 60 most prominent positions in the central coordination of PRONALF shows that 20 percent of the personnel hold a B.A. in basic sciences and engineering, which provides a type of training quite different from training in education. About 47 percent hold a B.A. in social sciences and humanities, 12 percent had a B.A. in administration, 3.3 percent had a B.A. in sciences and graphics and art design. Only 18 percent had a B.A. in education or teacher training (Torres, 1984a: 231). By level of functional and hierarchical responsibility, those holding engineering degrees were in charge of the principal divisions of PRONALF (i.e., general coordination, programming, planning, and administration). Thus the General Director of PRONALF, afterwards General Director of Literacy Training at INEA, holds a B.A. in civil engineering from a private university, and the General Director of INEA holds a B.A. in electrical and mechanical engineering from the National University (UNAM), with a M.S. in operational research and planning from an United States university.

In general, 35 percent of PRONALF personnel in the National Coordination hold degrees other than social science or education. This is perhaps an indicator that the selection of higher officials was based on their knowledge of system theory, linear programming, and administration and on their loyalty to the Secretary rather than on any solid background in literacy training or adult education. Those who were trained in the social sciences, humanities, and education (65 percent) worked mainly in research, opera-

Table 5-9

PRONALF's Organic Bureaucracy Average Value of Knowledge of Different Areas of Adult Education

Areas of Knowledge	Average Value*
Knowledge on Juridical Dispositions on Adult Education	2.2
Knowledge on Historical Antecedents of Adult Education in Mexico	3.2
Knowledge and Command on PRONALF's Didactic Material and Normative Documents	1.9
Knowledge on Periodicals and Journals on Adult Education	3.9
Knowledge on Other Publications, Books and General Literature on Adult Education	3.8

* Scale presented: (1) very good knowledge; (2) good knowledge; (3) average knowledge; (4) deficient, poor knowledge; (5) no knowledge at all.

Source: Pescador, *Algunas reflexiones sobre las características del personal directivo del INEA*. México, CNTE-SEP, 1982 (mimeographed) page 20.

tions, and in some cases in policy planning but not in policy making. The lack of representation of people graduated from teachers' colleges or *normales*, less than 9 percent of the total, shows how carefully PRONALF was devised to avoid hiring personnel with *normalista* background. Moreover, of those trained in education, slightly more than half were trained at the university and not at teachers' colleges.

Overall, the lack of familiarity found among the members of this organic bureaucracy with some of the most fundamental adult education issues is striking. Although they were familiar with the basic documents and laws of PRONALF, they did not have a solid background in adult education because of lack of extensive experience on the subject or because they belonged to professions outside the field of the social sciences and education. The latter allowed them to adjust easily to the normative and administrative aspects of the PRONALF bureaucracy, but it made it very difficult for them to play a competent role in the more academic and educational aspects of the program.

Pescador has summarized this phenomenon as follows:

> In the case of INEA, the problem is that having many of its administrators a great deal of administration and planning experience in education (in some cases in adult education), it seems, however, that the deficiencies are of general theoretical nature (for example those related to the social sciences, and to the relationships between education, society, the job market and the political life, in short, all those areas which are represented by the political economy of education, the sociology of education, philosophy of education and educational anthropology), and those more particular in nature (i.e., adult education curriculum, participatory research, didactic materials for adults, and participatory communication) which are nonetheless important to the personnel of INEA . . . To judge from the results of the questionnaire, PRONALF has incorporated young and highly qualified professional people. This is potentially important for a process of accelerated apprenticeship. However, the analysis of their knowledge of the history of adult education in Mexico is very disturbing, showing as it does that in general the previous experiences in adult education are not known. (Pescador, 1982b: 10-11)

The lack of familiarity with adult education is further reflected in their lack of knowledge of previous evaluations of plans and programs of adult education implemented in the country. The majority of respondents to Pescador's survey (70 percent) recognized that they were not aware of any previous evaluation in adult education, and half of the members of the organic bureaucracy declared that they did not know of previous studies or evaluations. It is also striking to note that the majority of teachers and 60 percent of the field coordinators lacked such knowledge.

There are thus important organizational traits rooted in the origins of PRONALF. It was a highly centralized program, devised with a similar rationale to the SEP's program for administrative decentralization (Pescador and Torres, 1985). The administrative organization of PRONALF-INEA was organized with great emphasis on autonomy of the institute's operations in the states. There was also a clear attempt to modify the criteria for hiring personnel. The INEA-PRONALF moved from full-time unionized teachers to part-time unionized young students and professionals. One of the outcomes of this situation was that the political and cultural background of this personnel was different from that which prevails in the SEP's structure (Torres, 1984a: 235).

PRONALF's Efficiency and the Adult Education Clientele

A general profile of the adult education clientele of PRONALF can be drawn on the basis of data from several sources. In a survey of 9,918 respondents conducted between September 1981 and June 1982 by a private consultant hired by PRONALF (PRONALF-SPAC, 1982), 65 percent of respondents were found to be between 20 and 49 years old. Approximately 74 percent of those surveyed were women. In occupational terms, 62.4 percent of the students reported they were housewives, and 60 percent were not receiving salary or remuneration at the time. These findings were confirmed by another survey conducted between 1982 and 1983 among 400 students in three states of central Mexico (Torres, 1984a). These students were completing their PRONALF program in the Federal District, the state of Morelos, or the state of Tlaxcala. In this case, a higher proportion of students were women (87 percent), and 65 percent of the students in this sample were born and lived in states other than the one where they were residing at the time of the interview.

The clientele of PRONALF typically came from an intermediate, semiurban background, usually small towns located in the countryside. Students from rural populations, however, were represented by only approximately 20 percent of the sample in the second survey. Urban social background among PRONALF students was uncommon. In fact, less than 4 percent of the sample originated in cities or a large metropolis. Almost half of those interviewed had family incomes below or equal to one legal minimum salary for workers in Mexico, and 37 percent had a family income between one and two minimum salaries.[18] The condition of poverty of PRONALF students was also characterized by the fact that they tended to come from large families. Thus 24 percent of the students lived in families of 3-4 persons, 27 percent lived in families with 5-6 members, and 23.2 percent were from families of 7-8 persons (PRONALF/SPAC, 1982).

According to this study, the majority of the students of PRONALF were part of the economically active population, despite the fact that 69 percent of the sample were not working at the time of the survey and of those who were only 81 percent received some kind of payment. Among students who were employed, 40 percent worked in domestic service (e.g., housework or laundry for other families), 18.7 percent were peasants working in agricultural activities, and 12.5 percent were in the service sector (e.g., janitors, watchmen, office employees). Only 11.3 percent of the sample worked in manufacturing industries, while the remaining 17.5 percent were working in construction, as nonrural laborers, or self-employed.

Among the students interviewed between August and September 1982, the predominant motive for choosing to enroll at PRONALF was their desire to learn to read and write in order to obtain a primary school certificate (51.5 percent). Only 3 percent suggested that they wanted to become literate to get a better job or because they considered literacy to be useful for their current jobs. Almost 20 percent of the students were unable to explain why they had enrolled in literacy training. Concerning the particular skills that were sought from a literacy program, 44.7 percent of the students were seeking to learn to read; 25.5 percent were seeking to learn to read, write, and to acquire basic arithmetics skills; 15.3 percent were interested in learning basic mathematics; and only 8.7 percent were primarily seeking to learn to write. Only a very small percentage did not know what they wished to achieve.

In terms of the literacy training outcome of the program, given the students' expectations and the goals of PRONALF, it is important to discuss some additional findings. Among the students from the sample completing their program, a reading test consisting of a list of common words was applied. The results show that 23.5 percent of those who had completed the program could not read at all, 25.5 percent needed help to read, 23 percent could read with difficulties, and only 24 percent could read fluently without help. Thus half the students were not able to read or needed substantial help to do so, while the other half could read either with difficulty or fluently.

A follow-up survey was conducted in the spring of 1983 with a subsample of the students in the Federal District.[19] The results indicate that more than six months after the students had finished their program, there were no significant changes in their occupations, working conditions, or in their principal economic activity (Torres, 1984a: 238-278). The results of this follow-up were not encouraging. Students who could read fluently in the follow-up were only half the number of those who could read fluently six months earlier. Conversely, those who could read with difficulty in the follow-up were 13 percent more than in the original test. Those students who needed help to read in the follow-up (22 percent) were 10 percent fewer than in the original test (32 percent), and those who could not read had increased 10 percent at the time of the follow-up test. There are thus reasons to believe that the reading ability of PRONALF's graduates diminished over time and that the cognitive returns of the program were low.

Although the writing follow-up test showed that only 6 percent of the sample could successfully pass, 23 percent could finish it only partly, and an overwhelming majority (71 percent) could not pass it at all, it should be stressed that this study did not attempt to evaluate the educational effectiveness of the program. The analysis showed important aspects of the program in light of the education model of the State and its process of educational decision making discussed earlier. The fact that the program may or may not have worked made no difference to the political rationale underlying its organization and implementation. It did indicate, however, an important shortcoming of the proposed "technocratic strategy" challenging the corporatist and clientelist strategy predominating in the Secretariat of Public Education as a result of the participation of the teachers' union (Pescador and Torres, 1985). According to the teachers' union, the achievement of a high degree of efficiency in policy operation (measured by conventional educational standards) was one of the major political and technical claims of the new technocracy in its political struggle with the traditional bureaucracy. Thus the fact that a program intended to provide new avenues for policy making and did not efficiently achieve its goals of literacy training and adult education increased the contradictions of technocratic strategy within the Secretariat of Public Education.

Literacy Training Statistics

After almost seven years in operation, the INEA boasted high success in meeting the demands of literacy training in Mexico. Among the main claims of the Institute was reduction of the national rate of illiteracy to 7.7 percent by 1986. The working assumption was that by making 4.1 million adults literate in the period 1984-88, a national illiteracy rate of 4 percent was to be reached by 1988. Table 5-10 offers the INEA's estimates on the reduction of illiteracy.

However, this information raises some serious reservations. The poor quality of data gathered in the national census of 1980 precludes any systematic extrapolations to estimate the actual state and national illiteracy rate. At the time this was estimated, in 1987, it was a pre-electoral year and these figures could have been used to enhance the administration of the Secretary of Education, Miguel González Avelar, within the political spectrum of the PRI. No one will be at all surprised to find the next administration challenging and redefining some of these figures to support its own political strategy.

At the same time, as the definition of illiteracy (i.e., who is an illiterate) is a very difficult task (Bhola, 1984a), it is difficult to determine what, in practice, the official statistics represent. The illiteracy rates provided by the government refer to a notion of "absolute" illiteracy. This usually means the incapability to read and to sign one's own last name. Such an assessment of illiteracy is based on individual opinion and not on a systematic test of basic reading, writing, and numeracy skills. Because of this, it risks relying on information given to avoid the stigma of illiteracy, as Jonathan Kozol in the United States has demonstrated (Kozol, 1985). Because of obvious inaccuracies of some estimates based on defective census data, the vague definitions of illiteracy, and the shortcomings of self-declaration of illiteracy, other variations in the understanding of illiteracy are often used in contemporary societies as a means to avoid the absolute notion of illiteracy. Thus, in the case of Mexico, it is possible to find functional illiteracy for those who have finished four years of schooling but did not retain the basic reading and

Table 5-10
Illiteracy and Literacy Training in Mexico of a Population of 15 Years or Older, 1980-1986

	1980	1981	1982	1983	1984	1985	1986
Illiterate adults[1]	6,435,721	6,371,780	6,012,324	5,564,307	5,011,228	4,413,329	3,669,365
Newly literates[2]	-	54,315	481,133	511,658	687,216	747,906	1,002,609
Illiteracy rate	16.3%	15.7%	14.3%	13%	11.5%	9.9%	7.7%

[1]INEA, Acción Educativa 1981-1986, SEP Mexico, 1987.

[2]INEA, Serie Histórica 1981-1986, INEA, Mexico, 1987.

Source: INEA, Plan de acción del programa de alfabetización para 1987, Dirección de Alfabetización, January 1987, page 89, annex 3.

writing skills (UNESCO, 1982). It is also possible to speak of marginal illiteracy or semiilliteracy to refer to those who have completed the sequence of basic mandatory schooling but still fail to match their own qualification with, for instance, the requirements of a job as stated in a newspaper advertisement (Kozol, 1985; Gee, 1986: 126-140). Absolute, functional, and marginal illiteracy may constitute a pervasive phenomenon in Mexico which is not reflected in the self-serving estimates of the National Institute of Adult Education.

CONCLUSION: POLICY FORMATION IN ADULT EDUCATION IN MEXICO

Several approaches to policy formation have been explored so far. One is the concept of the "motion of the bureaucracy." From this perspective, the origins and dynamics of public policy formation as in the case of education, could be fundamentally—though not exclusively—interpreted as resulting from several factors. These include the needs of self-legitimation and expansion of a bureaucracy, the dynamics resulting from its organizational routines, and the conflicts and contradictions between factional bureaucracies in educational institutions. Indeed, sometimes these interbureaucratic factional clashes and contradictions follow parallel lines related to the basic political and social conflict in civil society. Another approach is the "purposive action." This results from rational policy planning by distinct social agents and state apparatuses or agencies which do not necessarily rely on the central State bureaucracy as their originator. The approach of purposive action is related to the assessment of conflict areas in civil society, the anticipation of further threats and conflicts, and, in the case of literacy training, the perception of failure of previous programs such as those of the SNEA. Finally, there is the "participatory consensus building" approach that tries to establish mechanisms of political bargaining and policy participation among the basic social actors in the political system. It is important to emphasize here that the legitimacy of the system is ultimately based on a higher, continuous, and massive inclusion of the social agents, including social movements and political parties, which are in confrontation on basic issues or are representative of the basic conflicts in civil society (Offe, 1974: 31-56; Oszlak & O'Donnell, 1976; Torres, 1987, 1988).

To study the process of public policy formation, it is important to characterize the political regime in which the policy making process takes place, as well as its principal patterns of political change. It is therefore important to study the general characteristics of the State and the political regime, especially modes of political control, organization, and political resources. Without such a background, and without a systematic political framework such as the notion of the Mexican state as a corporatist State, it is difficult to understand and assess the political rationale behind the use and allocation of resources, or the underlying motives for the creation and/or elimination of institutions, plans, programs, services, or specific policies.

From this perspective, it can be argued that education policies in Mexico have been used as part of the corporatist political network and the politics of interest groups. It is necessary to look at the role of education from a three-dimensional angle. First, education is the biggest cultural organization in the country and consistently fills a gap between the popular masses and the State. In such a context, the proposed massive approach of PRONALF or the ambitious tasks allotted to the INEA are examples of a new effort of the State to address the differential needs and demands of socially subordinate classes. Similarly, the process of institution building and the new policy for nonformal and adult education constitutes new political resources for the State and the ruling party.

Second, education also constitutes an important dimension in the attempt to articulate the relationships between the corporatist State and civil society. Because of the actions of the teachers' union, education has provided a place to organize the teachers' political constituency; win their acquiescence, support, and consensus toward the government's programs and policies; and to coopt their leadership. The expansion of employment in the educational sector, besides showing the importance of education within the overall context of welfare policies promoted by the corporatist State, also shows a trend toward strengthening the cooptation of the masses. In this regard, the teachers' union has been a key actor in the process of political mobilization, acting as an intermediary between the popular masses (particularly the peasants sectors) and the State. Although education has been an important setting for the organization of resistance activities, particularly due to the role of the *Coordinadora Nacional de Trabajadores de la Educación,* a salient worker's organization was strengthened by the teachers' political unrest and by a dissident movement that challenged the hegemony of the official teachers' union in the early 1980s.

Third, education is a contested terrain where some of the main contradictions of the State are displayed and the clashes between factional bureaucratic ideologies, political projects, and antagonistic political groups have underpinned the process of policy formation (the conflict of SEP-SNTE is a case in point). Education plays an important role in the process of public policy formation of the bureaucracy, particularly its dominant ideology and its modus operandi under the organizational rules of the corporatist State. The general framework of organizational rules in the Mexican State is built on two main elements. The first is the so-called historical legitimacy of the Revolution. The second is its contemporary expression into bureaucratic norms, codes, laws, rules, regulations and prescriptions embedded within the Constitution (i.e., which seems to sum up the ideology of the State) and National Laws and Presidential Decrees; and the production of rules that cause public policy to rely heavily on "allocative modes" of policy making, and, at least until 1982-83, on an abundance of money.

During the administrations of President Echeverría (1970-76) and President López Portillo (1976-82), the State followed a policy of constant increases in educational finances and expansion. This implied the commitment of a substantial and increasing amount of federal funds devoted to education. The financial setbacks after the crisis of 1982 resulted in a reduction of funds in several key areas, due to the rationalization of the economy and public sector expenditures carried out by the administration of President Miguel de la Madrid. Education and public health, however, were not affected by this financial retrenchment. Moreover, during 1984-85 the federal educational budget not only retained its real value but surpassed the rate of inflation by one or two points.

There also was a noticeable shift of priorities in educational policy formation after 1970, whereby a system heavily oriented toward formal schooling allowed nonformal education to acquire new dimensions and importance. The scope of the SNEA services (the predecessor of the PRONALF-INEA) has shown that even though these services were organized nationwide, they did not constitute a massive system, and enrollment in the program seemed to be insignificant in comparison with the potential demand. Between 1975 and 1980 the SNEA's enrollment figures declined, indicating that it was less attractive to its target clientele. Its operations were not even efficiently measured through objective indicators such as enrollment-graduation or levels of real demand.

The new policy of literacy training and adult education took place in the context of a modernizing educational administration with a technocratic outlook and an abundance of fiscal resources. In fact, the peculiar political and administrative organization of PRONALF, and later the INEA, could be seen as a policy outcome of the interbureaucratic and political struggle within the Secretariat of Public Education. It is obvious that in the organization of PRONALF, the possibility of a massive participation of human resources connected to the teachers' union was ruled out. This precluded, in the view of PRONALF-INEA higher officials, the incorporation and perpetuation of the ongoing power conflict in the formulation of educational policies related to PRONALF-INEA. Similarly, the incorporation of personnel under fairly unstable labor conditions precluded the introduction of old habits that could lead to the development of a self-expanding, ever-enlarging bureaucracy like that of the Secretariat of Public Education. This was a decision based on administrative decentralization, linear planning, and a fast and supposedly effective new method for literacy training. It was an attempt to control the process of policy formation in adult education by giving power of coordination to the new technocracy. Hiring university and high school students as volunteers was another option to achieve the goal of making the program cost-effective. This option resulted in employing personnel with perhaps higher levels of general education but lacking any experience or specialization in adult education.

At the organizational and political level, the administrative deconcentration and decentralization of educational policy and the training of adult education teachers and field coordinators within the emerging new structure of INEA deeply undermined the power base of the teachers' union. In the context of the new policies, the union had no say in the training of adult education teachers. The union is a highly centralized and hierarchical organization with decision making power resting in the hands of the Executive Council (Pescador and Torres, 1985). The new adult education policy handicapped the union in its capacity to deal with the higher officials at INEA, without a strong labor base within the institution. The process of decentralization thus created serious difficulties for the union in designing and implementing a unifying policy nationwide, at least at the beginning. The upper echelons of the INEA and PRONALF were filled with bureaucratic cadres connected with the Secretariat of Public Education, trained at the university level, with a predominant emphasis on technical-administrative professions and scientific administration as the main bureaucratic tools to handle the task outlined for adult education.

The fact that after 1970, and more so after 1981, adult education policy formation became a priority of the State raises a number of questions regarding the reasons behind this policy. During the decades prior to 1970, adult education in Mexico may be thought of as an expression of compensatory education closely related to the relative autonomy of the educational system. This is particularly so if the educational system is seen as an expression of the "national" component of the class-based capitalist state. As Poulantzas argues in this regard,

> If the State still maintains its character as a national State, this is due among other things to the fact that the State is not a mere tool or instrument of the dominant classes, to be manipulated at will.... the task of the State is to maintain the unity and cohesion of a social formation divided into classes. (1969: 78)

This relative autonomy, owing to the need to socially reproduce and legitimate the capitalist State, also underscores policies such as the new adult education policies devised by the Mexican State in the early 1980s. The policies formulated at this time were more than compensatory legitimation. They may be seen as tools for experimenting with new forms of policy making and policy operation. They also may have served the hidden purposes of building a network for political control, and political mobilization in the long run, among significant segments of the subordinate social classes, particularly the poorest of the poor.

The specific characteristics of the adult clientele are central to understanding the policy making process. The adults reached by the PRONALF-INEA belonged to the most impoverished and powerless groups in society. They were disenfranchised from the network of services and control of the State, and they were unable to contribute substantially, as a commodity form of labor, to the production of surplus value in the society. Although they were not taxable labor for fiscal purposes, a sizable proportion of those enrolled at PRONALF were part of the economically active population and engaged themselves in economic exchanges.

Adult education policies should not be seen only as a policy laboratory or as the result of a corporatist contradiction between bureaucratic groups in the State. They could be understood as an attempt by the State to integrate more directly an important segment of the labor force into the labor market as a commodity (Torres, 1983; 1987). This process of administrative "re-commodification"[20] (Offe, 1973) could contribute to the overall technical division of the labor force, with potential impact on income distribution, labor force productivity, social and occupational mobility, labor force discipline, citizenship building, and so forth. In fact, such an attempt might also have been related to a political rationale to bind together, through a new set of policies and programs for adults, some social sectors disenfranchised from the political, organizational, and mobilization control of the State and the ruling party. In this respect, the policy may not have been effective, given its intentions. The literacy training services conducted by PRONALF-INEA reached mostly women working as housekeepers or working part time in service jobs. It also reached a population of semirural origin living on the outskirts of the cities, and therefore related with many other services and urban demands, and a population of underemployed-unemployed with a high tendency to migrate within the country, and therefore difficult to include in mobilizations or further activities of political control.

The economic contribution of adult education does not seem to have been an issue from the perspective of the bureaucracy that made decisions or from the perspective of the adult clientele who become incorporated into the program. From the perspective of the adults who successfully finished literacy training, their expectations when they had entered the program were more cultural or educational than economically oriented. Thus the notion of setting up policies for the purposes of improving the quality of economic exchanges of a segment of the population, although this cannot be ruled out definitively, cannot be seen as having carried decisive explanatory weight in assessing the determinants of adult education policy formation in Mexico. This conclusion is especially true in the context of extremely heterogeneous labor markets where there is a high degree of monopolistic intervention from the State, or in the context of the 1982 crisis that drastically reduced the creation of jobs in industry and services as well as in the public sector.

At the time the PRONALF-INEA was created, the presidential succession was under way. The Secretary of Education, Lic. Fernando Solana, was considered a serious candidate to be nominated by the PRI for the presidency. Many have suggested that the new policies in adult education may have been related to the possible candidacy of Solana for the Presidency in 1982. Many also suggested that Solana succeeded in devising a system of equality of educational opportunity to all school-aged children through the program of "education for everybody," and that if a million people had been made literate in the year of 1981, from a political point of view, this could have been a substantial goal achieved in a short period of time. It has been argued that this was also the reason behind the appointment of the director of the very successful program of Education for Everybody, first as chairman of the PRONALF administrative command, and later as its general coordinator.

However, from a more theoretical point of view, this short-term political and somehow ad hoc explanation of policy formation does not seem to be persuasive enough. The broader picture of an expanding system of education, with inner contradictions between bureaucratic factions, and the need to provide a more solid political control of specific sectors of the educational clientele, seems to have more explanatory weight than short-term political interests. Overall, it seems that, given the trends operating in the State, the process of policy making in adult education represented a policy laboratory for trying a possible strategy for a long-term process of educational policy formation. Hence it is possible to view this new policy as a State response to some highly conflictive trends already present in civil society. It may be seen either as a direct response to a clearly identified ad hoc social problem, such as the growing urban marginality, unemployment, and undereducation, or as an indirect assessment of social threats and problem areas in civil society. Given that some of these problems became exacerbated after the economic crisis of 1982, the new policy in adult education may have been an attempt to devise a long-term avoidance strategy to deal with further threats and conflicts from different social sectors.

At the organizational level, this approach of the bureaucracy was expressed in the conflict between political-technical projects represented by the modernizing technocracy of the Secretariat of Public Education and the corporatist-clientelist political project of the teachers' union. In such a context, it can be argued that the lack of participation of the clientele of adult education in PRONALF and INEA, or the lack of participation of the social and political actors with some degree of meddling in the political system, ruled out the possibility of a rationale of participatory consensus building through adult education. The way the method of the "generative word" was designed and implemented seems to have prevented any real participation of teachers, field workers, and adults downstream of the system. Even the more political issues involved in the Freirean approach to literacy training that could have influenced the PRONALF's method were carefully deleted from the method of the generative word and from its teachers' training strategy.

The INEA changed general directors three times in less than seven years of operation, and the personnel turnover, even at the upper levels of decision making, remained high. The claim that between 1981 and 1986 the program made 3,447,233 persons literate, and that by 1987 the national rate of illiteracy would be less than 7 percent of the total population, cast some doubts on the reliability of these data. While INEA was again at the service of the political aspirations of a PRI potential presidential candidate in 1987, its most significant policies continued to be associated with a "new" political clientelism, with a technocratic flavor in the setting of a slightly more decentralized corporatist state.

NOTES

1. The major educational laws in Mexico are the National Organic Laws enacted December 31, 1941 that resulted from the third article of the Constitution, the Federal Law of Education, and the National Law of Adult Education.

2. According to UNESCO data, for example, in 1960 Argentina had an illiteracy rate of 7.7 percent compared to 33 percent in Mexico. In 1970 the rates were 7.1 and 23.8 percent respectively. These differences are even more significant given that information provided by the Mexican census shows higher rates for the country. Argentina also had a more even distribution of illiteracy between males and females. In 1960 the distribution was 7 percent for males and 8.5 percent for females in Argentina compared with 29.4 and 36.5 percent in Mexico. By 1970 this situation remained the same, 6.3 and 7.8 percent in Argentina, and 20.4 and 27 percent in Mexico (UNESCO, 1982).

3. Unfortunately, it is not possible to estimate accurately functional literacy in Mexico (i.e., those who have less than four years of schooling). However, Muñoz Izquierdo has noted that the average education of the labor force by the end of the 1970s was less than four years of schooling (CEE, 1982: 366). It is also important to indicate that according to the Economic Commission for Latin America, ECLA, almost half of the total active economic population (ages 15 to 60) in the region should be considered functional illiterates (CEPAL, 1976). It is equally difficult to estimate marginal illiteracy or semiilliteracy as suggested by Kozol when he refers to those whose reading skills are not equal to societal demands (1985: 10-11).

4. President Echeverría explained the creation of the National Law of Adult Education in the following terms: "It was a question of preparing a society using a different model of development, a wider political culture, a new intent. In my six years in office, more was done politically in education than in any other area except, perhaps, highway development. But you can see for yourself the number of secondary technical and farm schools (700-800) we created, the rural teachers' colleges in the desert so that farmers' children could study to be rural teachers and then remain in the area. The development of the Misiones Culturales was strengthened as was the development of universities." He also argued that one of the problems he faced was that the Mexican State had switched priorities between 1940 and 1970 toward expanding the school system, while forgetting the meaningful experience in nonformal education. He indicated that "illiteracy was a budgetary problem, always present and perhaps more acute in an atmosphere where development approached a general concept of a wider idea of social development which caused a return to more scholastic forms of education, ignoring the experiences of adult education, although the literacy campaign initiated by Torres Bodet during the administration of Avila Camacho was very important." This argument, made by Echeverría in a private interview in 1982, is also consistent with his public statement as Honorary President of the International Council of Adult Education (*Convergence*, 1981: 9).

5. This analysis draws heavily on several statistical sources, including the Dirección General de Certificación (Torres, 1980).

6. The analysis presented by Cuellar is based on data obtained by Vergara (1981). The information has some shortcomings and the figures should be used as rough information on trends and not as reliable, fully-fledged statistics. A main problem with the data refers to the total number of adults who submitted registration forms, which constitutes the basis for these statistics. Between 1975 and 1978 a total of 1,417,005 students were registered. The Secretariat of Public Education, however, has complete information for only 893,152 students, or 63 percent. The remaining application forms were lost and cannot be accounted for. It is, therefore, not possible

to assess which type of students are missing in the calculation. It is not known if those missing correspond to a random group of students, or to students at a particular educational level, such as literacy training, primary education, or secondary education for adults.

7. The poor quality of the statistics collected by the SNEA is shown in the high number of responses grouped under "other" and "non specified" of which 7.6 account for 12 and 15 percent of economic activity and occupation respectively.

8. It is interesting to compare the organization and planning of the literacy campaign and the National Institute of Adult Education in Mexico with the organization and planning of MOBRAL in Brazil ten years earlier. The experience of the Brazilian literacy movement has been extremely influential in Latin America (Morales-Gómez, 1979: 203-30). MOBRAL was established by Law 5379 of September 9, 1967. The mandate was signed in December 1967 by the Brazilian president at the time. Three years later, in September 1970, MOBRAL was reorganized with a new mandate to begin its operational phase (Bhola, 1984b: 120-137). Thus it took three years between decision making, planning, and implementation in the case of Brazil, while in Mexico the same process took less than six months.

9. One of the main, although relatively unknown, operative commands was created in 1979 to solve the bottleneck in teachers' salaries in some regions of the country (i.e., the state of Chiapas). This command, operating within the framework of administrative deconcentration, solved in three months the problems of salaries that in some cases had been unsolved for over two years, thus helping to reduce teacher unrest.

10. The peso at the time was affected by a constant devaluation. Between August and December 1982, the peso devalued 60 percent, while salaries increased only 12.5 percent.

11. In Spanish the words were: pala, vacuna, basura, medicina, cantina, trabajo, guitarra, familia, leche, tortilla, piñata, casa, mercado, and educación.

12. The words suggested for this stage were the following: dress, shoes, windmill, chile, sweet corn, banana, papaya, wood, palm roof, hammock, hospital, insurance, latrine, medicine chest, road, committee, cooperative, ejido, fertilizer, dam, henhouse, pigsty, insecticide, forage, watering place, thief, waiter, bootblack, kingfisher, sugarcane, mechanic, carpenter (PRONALF, n.d.: 20).

13. Felix J. Chaparro Pelassi, the technical and pedagogical deputy director at the National Institute of Adult Education at the time and the person responsible for the research team that designed the method used by PRONALF, indicated that some of the members of the team did not agree with Freire's views about consciousness raising. He also argued that the method to be adopted by PRONALF ought to be suitable for a nationwide literacy campaign, implying that Freire's methods were suitable at the community levels but needed some adaptation to be applied in the entire country.

14. In Freire's method, the selection of the generative words should consider three important aspects: the syllabic richness of the words selected, their phonetic difficulty, and their practical and existential content. The latter needs to be in tune with the social, political, cultural, economic, and ethical themes of the communities in which the literary process is taking place (Torres, 1978: 89).

15. The data used to illustrate this situation are based on a series of interviews done in the Federal District 14 months after PRONALF had begun nationwide. With the exception of higher officials, who were in the program since the beginning, the average seniority among the interviewees, including teachers and field coordinators, was three months or less.

16. Fifty percent of the teachers and field coordinators in the sample of the study worked in the Federal District or in the states of Morelos and Tlaxcala in the center of Mexico. It is important to emphasize the fact that these are not the states with the highest shortage of teachers or qualified personnel for the positions required for the PRONALF program.

17. This evaluation meeting was organized by PRONALF-INEA, September 8-11, 1982, in Hacienda Mansión, Galindo in the state of Querétaro in commemoration of the World Literacy Day proposed by UNESCO. The group attending the meeting included 22 general state delegates of PRONALF, which represented 69 percent of the total number of delegates constituting the highest PRONALF-INEA authority in the states; 32 coordinators; 8 zone coordinators, 25 coordinators responsible for several different units, departments, areas, or projects; 6 advisors of central units; 16 chief trainers; 10 support personnel; and 12 unidentified staff members. The composition of this group was representative of the high and intermediary levels of responsibility at PRONALF. The questionnaire applied was considered to be an exploratory instrument rather than an actual survey (Pescador, 1982b).

18. The concept of family income in this case included any salaries, wages, or personal income earned by the working members of the family. The legal minimum salary at the time was estimated at 6,083 pesos per month (approximately $81 US in 1982). This represents a simple average of the minimum monthly salary paid in the Federal District (7,000 pesos or $94 US), and the states of Morelos and Tlaxcala (5,625 pesos or $75 US). See also data from the National Commission for Minimum Salaries (January-December 1982) and the newspaper *Uno más Uno*, December 31, 1981, pp. 12-13.

19. The original survey in the summer of 1982 included 111 students from the Federal District. In the follow-up, a sample of 37 of these students were again tested in their reading skills using the same instrument originally applied. The test could be finished in approximately 10 minutes by a newly literate person. It included two paragraphs in the form of a letter applying for a job. Those who finished both paragraphs in legible writing were considered to have finished the test successfully. Those who completed a substantial part of the test were considered to be partially successful. No consideration was made in assessing the results of the test of grammar, spelling, or style.

20. The neologism *decommodification* refers to the thesis that *decommodified* forms of social organization of labor and of the value produced by a society are growing quantitatively. These *decommodified* life forms tend increasingly to become a problem of social stability to be dealt with by political means, insofar as such social groups, excluded from the social life form of wage labor, yet nevertheless subject to relations of capitalist domination, represent a potential for social unrest (Torres, 1984b; 26-33).

6 Adult Workers' Education: The Case of Producer Cooperatives

INTRODUCTION

Education in Mexico can be best described as a key social institution responsible for transmitting and legitimizing the State's ideology established by the Revolution. In doing so, education has been instrumental in reproducing the knowledge, skills, and social, economic, and political behavior desirable to perpetuate the structure of power and the pattern of class relationships sustaining the model of associated-dependent development. The use of education as a means to reach a political clientele increasingly discontented with the prevailing distribution of wealth and political power has shown the inherent contradictions to the hegemonic corporatist State. Despite this, education is still primarily responsive to the needs of the political bureaucratic elite in government. Education in all its forms is instrumental in securing an effective political socioeconomic device in the hands of government to cover and lessen the effects of the crisis of the model of *desarrollo estabilizador* (stabilizing development, Cotler, 1979), without altering the class structure of the society.

The experiences with formal and nonformal education discussed in previous chapters show that the technopolitical elite has become involved in the identification, design, and implementation of educational policy alternatives. The ultimate aim of these policies is to strengthen the legitimacy of the capital accumulation pattern underlying the development objectives of the Mexican government. Particularly relevant in this regard are the efforts of the State during the 1970s and early 1980s in the area of nonformal adult education.

The formation and implementation of educational policy in Mexico in this area have shown the dual character of education when planned in the context of a capitalist State. Education has been designed and implemented to facilitate the reproduction of the corporatist State. As such, it has assisted, first, in the reproduction of the labor force, particularly among the most disadvantaged groups, thus reinforcing an existing pattern of capital accumulation and political hegemony and, second, in the legitimation of a political structure that needs to respond to demands from civil society for greater participation in the benefits of economic growth and modernization.

There are strong indications, however, that the efforts to make education readily available to the adult working population have not been as successful as expected. A large proportion of this population is still without the benefits of formal schooling or unable to become actively integrated into the labor market. The education they have received has not been sufficient to enable them to increase their participation in society or to compete in the world of work.[1] Education outside the formal school system has been plagued with contradictions. These have seriously limited its effectiveness in filling the gap between revolutionary rhetoric and the practice of an economic and political system that is losing its nationalistic character at an accelerated rate. Few attempts have been made to create conditions to implement educational alternatives for adults in the workplace. Even in those types of producer organizations that may offer more appropriate structural conditions to bring into practice some of the social principles established by the Constitution of 1917 there has been little success.

The purpose of this chapter is to discuss the pattern of correspondence and contradiction found in education in Mexico beyond the scope of direct interventions of the State in the utilization of educational alternatives for adults already involved in the production system. The chapter discusses the educational potential of producer cooperatives (PCs) by looking at a sample of these organizations in the Federal District.[2]

The study carried out between 1978 and 1980 corresponded with a period in Mexican development when serious signs of a crisis had begun to appear and when new efforts were being made to strengthen nonformal education for adults. Retrospectively, the study shows the failures to effectively integrate into the implementation of adult education policies the conditions that may have existed outside the educational main stream to ensure their success. It also shows that in the process of policy planning the State has applied a rather narrow approach in the identification of nontraditional alternatives to assist educational planners and policy makers in their attempts to compensate for the failures of existing programs to reach the adult population. Instead of reaching the adult population in their most immediate environment, the workplace, adult education policies intended to bring adults into predesigned programs narrowly structured around basic literacy training.

THE CONTRADICTIONS OF WORKERS' EDUCATION IN MEXICO

Implicit in the model of development and modernization permeating the State after the Revolution there has been a tendency not only to periodically readapt some of the major social institutions, such as education, to better reflect the predominant paradigms of capitalist development, but also to create mechanisms that explain and legitimate such changes. This has responded to one of the key characteristics of the postrevolutionary State: the need to maintain control over the institutional reproduction process, making all sociopolitical agents operate within State policies. In fact, over the last 60 years the revolutionary tradition has called for the education of working-class adults as a means to integrate them into the society. During the postwar period, public policy in education, as in many other sectors, was directed toward the consolidation of a pattern of urban industrial growth. Education outside the formal system was aimed at expanding the benefits of modernization among those sectors of the poorer population represented by the rural poor that recently migrated to the cities and by the growing marginalized segments of the urban population.

Because most working-class adults, particularly those not organized under a union, form the social group that has historically suffered the most socioeconomic and political inequality and is a potential source of political unrest, the educational alternatives capable of reaching this sector have been a political means to maintain the corporatist structure of the State and its development strategy. The types of educational opportunities open to working adults have reinforced the belief that conditions of inequality affecting them are not a circumstantial outcome of isolated phenomena, but the manifestation of structural factors permeating the relationships between the State and civil society. Educational policies designed to reach working adults have reflected contradictions in the text of the Constitution, claiming that education should be "socialistic," while it "glorified private property in a nation where the proletariat had no say in governing" (Liss, 1984: 209).

Despite attempts to improve delivery, educational policies in Mexico have been designed and implemented as a means to ameliorate social conflicts and not to increase social participation or to open new avenues for sociopolitical mobility. Formal and nonformal education have played a legitimization role as if political and economic inequality and lack of opportunities were separate issues. Inequality in this sense has been dealt with by attempting to redistribute traits and skills valued in the productive system. It has been argued in this regard that schooling and adult education have served to reinforce the class structure, to maintain a hegemonic pattern of political control, to socialize individuals into the world of work, and to consolidate the social division of labor to reproduce the dominant mode of production, thus securing the material platform of class formation controlling the State.

In Mexico, as in many developing countries, adult education has been a major factor determining workers' productivity (La Belle, 1986; Carnoy and Shearer, 1980). Educational policy planners have operated under the assumption that by developing educational alternatives to provide the larger sectors of the adult Indian and peasant populations with the tools to perform in the world of work, many of the problems resulting from lack of political participation and poverty will be minimized and potential social conflicts will be defused. In practice, this has translated into high investments in education, further expansion of educational services within the formal system, and the provision of literacy training programs that create the illusion of social and economic equality of opportunities and mobility.

Little has been done to explore alternatives outside the formal system that go beyond the government-sponsored literacy programs to reach the large population of unskilled, poorly educated workers. This has created tensions, with the apparently preferential place of labor as a driving force in society according to the rhetoric of the government. The attempts in this direction have been the efforts coordinated by the INEA to implement programs of community basic education, particularly at the rural and sub-urban level, and the attempts to take basic education to the workplace. However, it can be argued that these efforts have been relatively isolated, poorly coordinated, framed within traditional views of adult education, and poorly connected to the productive sector (Pravda, 1984: 99-114).

In addition to the political motives leading the expansion of educational services, education has been planned primarily according to criteria of capital accumulation and reproduction. Education has been perceived as one of the main tools to bring together the economic objectives of a development process built on deep class differences and on a political tradition struggling to maintain an image of service to the workers and to low income sectors. In fact, the value of education has been seen by the State technopolitical elite in terms of rate of return to individual investments, direct costs, and income forgone. The individual's contribution to society has been ultimately measured in units produced in relation to the output of the overall system. Disguised under a rhetoric of "self-learning," the possibility of becoming better off through education is left to individual choice to make use of the opportunities offered by the State within the formal and nonformal educational streams.[3]

This concept of investment has played a key role in determining the ways in which workers' education has been perceived in Mexico. The idea that labor is paid according to its marginal productivity, and that productivity is a commodity that can be expanded and improved by individual decisions has led the technopolitical elite to hold the assumption that socioeconomic and political inequality among the poor can be reduced through education and training. In practice, however, aggregated data on working adults on productivity and income give no indication that the variations on both can be accounted for by the effects of formal schooling or adult education. In real terms, the quantity and quality of the education workers receive depend on the complexity and quality of the capital accumulation process. In this context, only a few politically organized production units may be in a position to provide the labor-oriented training that in the short run results in concrete economic benefits for the workers. A basic hypothesis in this regard is that, despite efforts to improve educational services and to wipe out illiteracy, there is still a gap between what the education provided by the State does and what most working-class adults need to compete under equal conditions in the labor market.

Over time, the selectivity and survival factors within Mexican education, both formal and nonformal, have changed only slightly. In previous chapters it was argued that the volume of dropouts continues to grow, and educational and development policies remain a key determinant in expanding the gulf between intellectual (educated) and manual work. Observing the contradictions in the process of educational policy formation, and between these and the performance of the prevailing mode of production in the current crisis, educational policies have failed to fully incorporate productive work into the government social strategy as a means to integrate working adults into the main streams of the development project of the State. Nonformal education experiments have been characterized by several factors. They have focused on literacy and literacy upgrading for the urban poor and for rural and Indian populations.[4] In some cases, they have emphasized training as a learning process of basic technical knowledge and skills to increase productivity related to specific functions, ignoring the need for a wider approach to the education of workers. They have also been determined by the views of society held by the technopolitical elite in government, which respond in part to the economic growth strategies designed to minimize the development crisis which has deepened in recent years. Most such initiatives have ignored the workplace as a viable setting for the education of working adults.

At least three basic principles have been ignored in planning education for working adults that could be of relative benefit to this sector of the population. First, the planning of workers' education has ignored that literacy and specific job training do not necessarily address needs for personal development and wider participation in society. Second, education for workers cannot be effectively developed away from the workplace, even if general educational attempts are framed within an overall community-driven approach. Third, in societies regulated by a hegemonic State bureaucracy as in Mexico, the education of workers is primarily determined by the needs for political control of labor rather than by the individual needs of personal growth and social participation. In this regard, the education of working adults has served a dual purpose as an instrument of the State. It has served to give the appearance of a State playing the role of mediator among classes unequally fitted to compete for the benefits of development, and it has provided the State with a powerful tool to maintain control over those who can reach positions of power in the society.

EDUCATION FOR ADULTS IN THE WORKPLACE

In this discussion, the analysis of the role of education among working adults focuses on the conditions found in the workplace in producer cooperatives. This type of producer organization was chosen because it reflects more closely some of the socioeconomic and labor principles favoring the education of workers established by the Mexican Constitution. In the context of urban settings, producer cooperatives may present conditions which correspond more closely with some of the principles underlying the community-based approach developed by the State in its attempt to reach the adult population through education.

To provide a framework and a rationale for the analysis of the educational role of producer cooperatives (PCs), the following factors were taken into account: (1) the characteristics of the pattern of economic growth and capital accumulation established in Mexico since the late 1920s that have determined the process of educational policy formation and its relation to the social reproduction process; (2) the role of the mechanisms implemented by the State to determine the content and role of education vis-à-vis the existing social and material relations of production; (3) the material and ideological effects of class stratification and power distribution reproduced by the political elite; (4) the relationships of correspondence and contradiction characterizing the labor movement and its political participation in society; (5) the ways in which the educational system has responded to the fluctuating demands of the production system and the mismatch between the functions of formal and nonformal education and the type of demands of working class sectors on the State.

The workplace as an alternative setting for the education of adults was approached by looking at the dialectical interaction between education and work in relation to national educational policies. The correspondence between the trends in policy formation and the requirements of the model of sociopolitical and economic development has implications for the attempts made by the government in adult nonformal education, and on the structural conditions of different production units in the economy. Given the latter, the focus of inquiry was directed toward the educational role of PCs as one of the most viable forms of worker-controlled organization under the existing mode of production compared, for example, with private firms.

It has been argued in the literature that, in contrast to privately owned firms, cooperatives have a greater potential to fulfill a critical educational role in capitalist societies (Anton, 1980; Balay, 1976; Bernstein, 1976; Greenberg, 1978). According to this argument, meeting workers' educational needs could lead in turn to workers' participation in decision making and ultimately to workers' control (Garson, 1977; Derek, 1977; Selucky, 1975). Carnoy and Shearer indicate that workers' control at the plant level is a crucial element in developing means for democratic decision making in society (1980: 127). In this regard, the productive organization of cooperatives has characteristics that present short-term advantages for the sociopolitical integration of working adults in societies where conditions of unequal participation prevail. However, this implies acceptance of two assumptions. First, in microsystems of social ownership of the means of production, it is possible to find more egalitarian labor conditions. And, second, microsystems may minimize the negative effects of the unequal social and material relations of production inherent in class societies. If this is correct, finding alternatives for the education of workers based on the potential of the workplace may assist in reducing the sense of powerlessness, meaninglessness, isolation, and self-estrangement that affects working-class adults in hierarchical capitalist societies such as Mexico. Experiences like those documented in the case of cooperatives in Mondragón, Spain, provide empirical support for this assumption (Carnoy and Shearer, 1980).

Given that in practice urban PCs tend to represent only a minimal contribution to the economy, their educational potential is not a direct result of their economic role. Educationally, their potential rests primarily on a mode of organization of work based on the principle of self-governance (Greenberg, 1978). It is therefore the environment in cooperative organizations that becomes conducive to the development of educational processes. Their social and labor relations are the factors providing the workers with the conditions to teach each other specific job skills and to share knowledge, because they are not operating in a competitive environment (Carnoy and Shearer, 1980: 177). This lack of competitiveness in the workplace has two types of implications in terms of workers' education. On the one hand, workers are not competing in economic terms. They are not, therefore, as easily driven by the predominant trends inherent in the development models promoted by the State. On the other hand, political competitiveness is reduced because workers are not under the direct pressure of a union system that could be closely linked to the government and in which the labor movement may find itself trapped. The following section discusses some of these ideas in the context of the Mexican society.

THE LABOR MOVEMENT AND WORKER ORGANIZATION

Labor organization in Mexico was a late product of the Revolution. Until 1910, workers in the agricultural sector were unorganized because of a semifeudal system of land ownership and of the complete political isolation of the peasant population. In the industrial sector, workers depended on small groups organized by occupation.[5] With the overthrow of Díaz, steps were taken toward the organization of workers under different forms of associations. Three major types of unions emerged during the government of Madero (1911-12): unions by occupation with members of specific professions; unions that included several occupations; and unions of workers within particular enterprises. However, all three forms were affected by serious organizational problems that made them ineffective as means of workers' representation and participation. This situation began to change in the late 1920s with the creation of the official party and later with the policies of Cárdenas that favored strengthening labor and peasant organizations.

The first stable labor organization was the Regional Confederation of Mexican Workers (CROM). This replaced the House of the Workers of the World in 1918 and controlled the labor movement until 1928. Between 1933 and 1936 the control of workers was under the General Confederation of Mexican Peasants and Workers (CGOCM) which in turn ended with the formation of the CTM in 1936, the most powerful labor organization in the country to this day. After its inclusion in the official party, the CTM became an integral instrument in government policies, thus losing its autonomy and its bargaining power (Adler Hellman, 1978: 42).

The CTM defines itself as a mass organization structured on the basis of a model of democratic participation. Its major aim is economic vindication of workers and mediation between them and the government. In practice, however, the CTM is primarily an instrument of government to control the labor movement and therefore a key player in the corporatist model of the State. As part of the PRI, the CTM is in fact a means to carry out government policies with a minimum of disruption by the working class sector. To do so, it uses a complex system of organization in unions and federations to eliminate potential opposition within the party. This serves as a political device to keep the labor movement internally divided. It is not unusual, therefore, to find workers who actually do not know their union affiliation (Leal and Woldenberg, 1976: 35-53). This type of organization also allows a wide range of flexibility to union leaders, often coopted by the party, leaving workers with no direct access to decision making. However, this pattern of labor organization is not a casual outcome of Mexican politics. On the contrary, it responds to the corporative strategy of the State which keeps the labor movement under the control of the technopolitical elite.

Restricted working-class political participation in Mexico is thus a mechanism to reproduce the one-party system and to maintain political stability among the poorest sectors of society. Such a pattern of labor organization gives the PRI control over political participation channels and over workers' decision making in the workplace. This in turn facilitates the State's actions to neutralize workers' demands and to maintain at the top a labor bureaucracy useful to the government's political objectives. Labor thus becomes controlled by an elite of union leaders perpetuated in power who play an intermediary role between the workers and the technopolitical elite. In this context, labor organization is not a means to eliminate class conflicts, but only to diminish them.

From the point of view of union affiliation, worker participation does not follow a consistent pattern. Large differences exist in geographical location, occupation, and degrees of political power of particular labor federations. Thus, in 1971, the five largest states in concentration of economically active population did not correspond to the largest states in terms of concentration of wage earning workers or to the states with the largest union affiliation.[6] In all cases, the Federal District had the highest concentration of wage earning workers and the largest union affiliation in the country. This phenomenon is explained by the high urban concentration and centralization of political power that exist in Mexico.

By economic sector, industry concentrates the higher number of workers who belong to a union. However, two aspects need to be taken into account. Over the years there has been a decrease in union affiliation in the primary industrial sector, despite government efforts to develop peasant organizations in rural and marginal urban areas. There is enough evidence to argue that, in terms of labor participation and political organization, the current pattern of development has negatively affected this sector of the economy. This reinforces the fact that the model of associated-dependent development rests on the expansion of industry at the expense of the rural sectors where the largest proportion of poorly educated workers still remain. A second aspect to consider is the low level of union affiliation found in the service sector with the exception of the teachers' union, even though this constitutes one of the strongest arms of government political support.[7]

The control of political organizations and the influence of private capital over economic development and its association with members of the technopolitical elite are some of the factors conditioning workers' participation in society. The hierarchical hegemonic structure of the State is a key factor in isolating workers from labor organizations. However, over the last few years there has been a growing awareness about the ineffectiveness of labor organizations as means to represent workers' demands. At the same time, increasing attention is being paid to alternative forms of arrangements in the workplace that do not depend on the union bureaucracy. In this sense, producer organizations such as cooperatives acquire a new dimension as microenvironments for the coordination of workers in the workplace.

COOPERATIVES AND ADULT WORKER EDUCATION

The attractiveness of PCs as settings for the education of working-class adults results from the characteristics of this type of production unit. They are formed following principles of self-help and participation in decision making that theoretically could facilitate workers' education and personal development (Vanek, 1970; Berg, 1971; Brembeck and Thompson, 1973; Carnoy and Levin, 1976; Leonor, 1985). In the context of Mexican society, a work environment such as a PC where workers may have access to the control and management of the means of production is more likely to facilitate the development of nonformal educational activities. This may help compensate for the lack of similar opportunities in society at large, and therefore benefit workers in terms of education and political development.

Cooperatives in Mexico have been associated with reform of article 123 of the Constitution that protects workers' rights to participate in the distribution of profits and in decision making. Workers' involvement in the workplace by assuming direct responsibility for production gives PCs a key role in the labor strategy of the State beyond the power of the major labor unions and federations. In 1978, the government argued that

> we cannot see, from now on, the cooperatives as isolated entities, suffocated within the capitalist type of relationship, but we have to see them as a fundamental part of the social economy of this country . . . as one of the fundamental arms of the mixed economy of the Mexican society in its transformation process. (*El Día*, October 24, 1978)

However, this attempt to create conditions for workers' participation in the workplace by supposedly recognizing their rights is also a means to minimize the effects of several phenomena affecting the Mexican economy.

In the rhetoric of the government, PCs are presented as a means to reduce unemployment, wage inequality, lack of social security, adverse changes in labor conditions due to the predominance of large-scale industries invading key sectors of the economy, and the negative effects of urban concentration.[8] Cooperatives were defined by a member of the Ministry of Labor as an alternative and hope to solve lack of employment, housing, food, and education (Vásquez Torres, 1978). PCs are also seen as a means to promote the expansion of small industries, to create new jobs, and to absorb unskilled and poorly educated workers. The creation of labor-intensive work in which workers are able to participate in the distribution of profits is presented as a mechanism to compensate for the general conditions of social inequality affecting low-income adults.

Cooperativism in Mexico was born in the 19th century under the influence of European doctrines. In the beginning, it attempted to imitate foreign legislation rather than to promote a social movement (Cárdenas, 1970). In 1889 cooperativism was included in the Code of Commerce as an alternative to promote redistribution of wealth "without class struggle" and without contradicting capitalist development. In 1916 the first consumer cooperative with stores in the Federal District was created to facilitate the supply of basic consumer goods affected by the destruction of the transportation system during the Revolution. In 1917 the first PC was established in the state of Yucatán for direct commercialization and export of fiber products. However, all these attempts were motivated by specific situations and by the interest of large producers and not by a widespread interest in the development of the cooperative movement itself. Thus the consumer cooperative in the Federal District disappeared when supply conditions improved a few years later, and PCs became an association of farm owners looking for ways to market their products.

In 1927 President Calles began a campaign to stimulate the expansion of cooperatives without attention to the specific conditions of society at the time. The general Law of Cooperative Societies reinforced ideas about cooperativism imported from Europe that emphasized the benefits of cooperativism without derogating regulations of the Code of Commerce that made cooperatives dependent on the private enterprise model. Although under the law cooperatives were protected by economic exemptions and benefits to promote their expansion, this law became an instrument for private interests to avoid labor legislation and to receive the benefits prescribed for cooperatives. In 1933 a new law was enacted to regulate cooperatives under special legislation that derogated their dependence on the Code of Commerce and created a system of internal administration under State control. This law, however, was idealistic and without much effect over the situation of abuse that already existed. Thus in 1938, under the presidency of Lázaro Cárdenas, a new law for cooperatives was approved, establishing that cooperatives were to be formed by "individuals from the working class that contribute to the association with their personal work" (Cárdenas, 1970).

In the 1970s cooperatives were controlled by the general Law of Cooperative Societies, the By-Law of Cooperative Societies, and the regulations of the national Act of Cooperativism. PCs were defined as associations in which their members work and own the enterprise in a collective way, producing for the market and sharing the profits according to the time and quality of their work. To operate a cooperative, the law required a minimum of 10 members. Their income must come from the product of their work and not from ownership of capital. They must function under equal conditions of rights and duties, with equal participation in decision making (one member, one vote), and must work for the socioeconomic improvement of the organization, their families, and the community.

According to the law, there are three main types of cooperatives. The first are those formed by individuals on the basis of an equal contribution of capital. Second are associations formed under special concession of local or federal authorities for the exploitation of public capital. These are classified as cooperatives of official intervention. Third are associations working in the exploitation of government goods under the concession of the federal government, state governments, departments of the Federal District, or by the National Bank of Cooperative Patronage. All three forms of cooperative must be organized under regional federations which in turn must be members of the National Confederation of Cooperatives, the main government institution for the control of cooperatives in the country. A key aspect established by law is that *all cooperatives must have the means to provide training and education to their workers according to their specific activities.*

THE CASE OF PRODUCER COOPERATIVES IN MEXICO, DF

The case study in this chapter attempts to assess the extent to which the principle of education in cooperatives takes place in practice. It examines some of the effects of the work environment and the activities within PCs and private enterprises (PEs) on the educational development of working adults. This issue was approached bearing in mind that the integration between education and work in the workplace is not a purely educational or a purely economic phenomenon. The education of working adults in societies characterized by deep class differences and political contradictions does not occur only within the boundaries of formal or nonformal education. The workplace, where workers transform the material base of the society through their daily work, plays a key role in their sociopolitical and human development.

Originally, it was expected to find a high variety of activities among PCs suitable to be classified as systematic learning experiences within a nonformal education framework compared with PEs. However, given the specific characteristics of PCs in Mexico and the broader sociopolitical and economic environment in which they operate, the findings indicated that the adult education potential of PCs is not fully used. The study did show, however, that PCs offer particular conditions, compared with PEs, that may help to transform the workplace into a more effective educational environment. In fact, PCs offer more opportunities than PEs for the implementation of nonformal education activities, particularly in areas related to workers' political participation within the job setting and to the development of workers' occupational skills.

The literature on out-of-school activities indicates a wide variety of opinions in connection with the traits used to distinguish among types of education. A key distinction among most types of out-of-school education is the extent to which individuals are active agents in their learning (La Belle, 1976, 1986). In PCs, most educational activities are not systematically organized, they do not provide certification, and they take place among peers. In this regard, they can be labeled informal education. However, activities also exist with a certain degree of organization on the basis of predefined educational and cultural objectives, even leading in some cases to some form of certification.

The identification of educational activities in PCs was made, first, by looking at those actions having a definite educational or cultural purpose oriented to the acquisition of knowledge and to the improvement of specific production skills. These were activities intentionally programmed, with a specifically defined content, and taking place under relatively formal class-room conditions. Included in this group were programmed training, political education, education on cooperativism or trade unionism, basic education, and lectures on current social, economic, or political issues. A second group of activities included those that were systematically organized and responded primarily to production or administrative concerns inherent in the organization of production rather than to explicitly established educational objectives. Their primary purpose was not educational, but their effects contributed to the workers' participation and personal development in a broad sense. These included participation in settings such as assemblies, workers' councils, and work committees.

Education in the Workplace: Some Findings

The case study discussed here is based on research using two independent populations, one of PCs and the other of PEs. In each case the unit of analysis was the single productive organization physically located in one productive plant in the urban area of the Federal District of Mexico City. PCs were identified using the National Registry of Cooperatives of the General Directorate of Cooperative Development and other sources.[9] PEs were identified using data from government and private sources.[10] The information gathered for each unit included number of workers, the main type of production, the year in which they began operation, and their location.

Following verification, the selected units were stratified into non-overlapping and internally homogeneous subpopulations according to type of production and size.[11] For sampling purposes, each unit was considered to be a *cluster* of individuals. From each cluster a random sample of workers was selected. The final sample from PCs included 224 workers and 24 leaders or workers' representatives. The sample of workers from PEs included 121 individuals.[12] The distribution of the sample is shown in Table 6-1.

Data were gathered using structured interviews.[13] The survey was oriented to detect conditions in the workplace that could favor workers' education. Information about changes in workers' attitudes toward specific aspects of Mexican society and their labor and political participation was also collected. The study of each production unit permitted the gathering of information on the type of educational benefits received by the workers, the existence and use of facilities for educational purposes, and the attitudes of management toward the education of workers in the workplace.

In terms of schooling background, only a small number of workers had no formal education (7 percent in PCs and 3 percent in PEs). Among them, only 3.8 percent in PCs and 1.6 percent in PEs were illiterate. In both cases the differences in formal education were relatively small (see Table 6-2). Although the average number of years of formal schooling was 6.8 in PCs and 7 in PEs, this could be considered above the average schooling of the Mexican labor force as a whole. Among PEs, the number of workers with secondary education or more was slightly higher, while among PCs the workers with a higher level of formal schooling were mainly those occupying leadership positions. In both types of organization, male workers had more years of schooling than females, but female workers were better off with regard to complete primary or complete secondary education.

Workers with lower levels of education were concentrated among smaller organizations, while the higher percentage of workers with secondary education was found among large PEs. Similar differences were also found in relation to the type of production of the units. In this case, the higher number of more educated workers was found among firms in which production involved a higher degree of technological knowhow, such as printing and textiles, and workers with the lower levels of education were in units in the construction business. Overall, however, the combined effects of size and type of production of the units accounted for up to 33.8 percent of the differences in education of workers between PCs and PEs.

With this information in mind, an attempt was made to identify specific activities with educational effects in each group of production units. Having found that the level of formal education was relatively low across the units, and that PCs were more suitable work environments in terms of workers' involvement in their own personal development, it was expected that a higher number of educational activities were taking place in PCs. Prior field observations had suggested that PC workers were more interested in developing activities that bring educational benefits to the workers' collective. The findings showed some significant differences between PCs and PEs

Table 6-1
Samples of Workers from Producer Cooperatives and Private Productive Units (percentages)

STRATA	PC Members			PC Leaders			PE Workers			Totals	
	N	% of Sample Members	% of Total Sample	N	% of Sample Leaders	% of Total Sample	N	% of Sample Workers	% of Total Sample	N	%
Type of Production											
Printing	103	45.9	27.9	9	37.6	2.4	44	36.4	11.9	156	42.3
Handicrafts	16	7.2	4.3	2	8.3	5	10	8.3	2.7	28	7.6
Food	16	7.2	4.3	2	8.3	5	13	10.7	3.5	31	8.4
Construction	24	10.7	6.5	3	12.5	8	18	14.8	4.9	45	12.2
Clothing	43	19.2	11.7	6	25.0	1.6	29	24.0	7.9	78	21.1
Textiles	22	9.8	6.0	2	8.3	.5	7	5.8	1.9	31	8.4
Total	224	100	60.7	24	100	6.5*	121	100	32.8	369	100
Size											
Small	61	27.2	16.5	8	33.3	2.2	41	33.9	11.1	110	29.8
Medium	69	30.8	18.7	7	29.2	1.9	36	29.8	9.8	112	30.4
Large	94	42.0	25.5	9	37.5	2.4	44	36.3	11.9	147	39.8
Total	224	100	60.7	24	100	6.5	121	100	32.8	369	100

*approximated

Table 6-2
Formal Schooling of the Workers in Producer Cooperatives and Private Productive Units, by Gender (percentages)

| | No School | | Formal Schooling — Primary | | | | Secondary | | | | Post-Secondary | |
| | | | Incomplete | | Complete | | Incomplete | | Complete | | | |
	PC	PE	PC	PE	PC	PE	PC	PE	PC	PE	PC	PE
Sample												
N	16	4	51	33	84	40	32	22	31	16	10	6
%	7.1	3.3	22.8	27.3	37.5	33.1	14.3	18.5	13.8	13.2	4.5	5.0
Gender												
Over Total per group												
Male	6.9	4.3	23.3	26.6	36.5	31.9	14.5	17.0	12.6	13.8	6.3	6.4
Female	7.7	0.0	21.5	29.6	40.0	37.0	13.8	22.2	16.9	11.1	0.0	0.0
Over Total Sample												
Male	4.9	3.3	16.5	20.7	25.9	24.8	10.3	13.2	8.9	10.7	4.5	5.5
Female	2.2	0.0	6.3	6.6	11.6	8.3	4.0	5.0	4.9	2.5	0.0	0.0

in the workers' knowledge of the existence of activities in the workplace suitable to play an educational role (see Table 6-3).

PC workers were found to be more interested in developing and participating in activities perceived to be educational in their effects, especially actions perceived to have impact on the survival of the cooperative and on the workers' personal development. Such a finding is important given the role that participatory activities in the workplace may play in strengthening aspects such as political development, a critical factor in the education of working adults in countries like Mexico where other alternatives for their political development are considerably limited. Activities with clearer educational outcomes, mainly among PCs, were those administrative in purpose involving the direct participation of workers, such as assemblies and workers' councils.

Overall, a clear pattern was found between the two types of organizations. Approximately 89 percent of the PEs did not have educational activities for their workers. Only 1 percent of PEs were found to have on-the-job training and 14 percent sports-related activities, compared with 31 and 48 percent respectively among PCs. From the point of view of the benefits workers perceived in educational activities, 41 percent of the respondents in PCs saw benefits related to the development of cooperativism, 19 percent to their basic education, 16 percent to on-the-job training, and 11.9 percent to community development. Among PE workers the perceived benefits were limited to on-the-job training and community development, and only a small number saw some benefits in the area of trade unionism.[14]

Another aspect examined was the extent of workers' involvement in activities in the workplace that might have educational potential such as those discussed above. Three specific aspects were considered: knowledge of the source of decision making to determine the content of education, the type of participation workers had in these activities, and the reasons explaining the lack of worker involvement in such activities. Table 6-4 indicates that, overall, PCs show a higher degree of workers' participation in educational activities in the workplace.

Cooperatives were found to be a more suitable environment for the organization of education in a broad sense. In terms of organization and content of educational and participatory activities in the workplace, PC workers were found to be more independent in the decision making processes taking place in this regard. Only 4 percent of the PCs depended on sources external to the production unit for decisions about the type of educational activities that could be organized and implemented in the workplace, compared with 46.5 percent in PEs. Similarly, PCs were more participatory in the workers' involvement in the actual organization of activities. In fact, 46 percent of PC workers reported they were involved in some type of educational activity in the workplace compared with only 1 percent in PEs.

Table 6-3
Types of Educational Activities in the Job Setting in Producer Cooperatives and Private Productive Units (percentages)

Educational Activities	PCs N = 224			PEs N = 121		
	Yes Answers (a)	No Answers (b)	Don't Know (c)	Yes Answers (a)	No Answers (b)	Don't Know (c)
Assemblies, Meetings and/or Committees	71.0	29.0	0.0	10.0	88.0	2.0
Training Activities	31.0	63.0	6.0	1.0	97.0	2.0
Activities on Political Education, Cooperativism and/or Unionism	14.0	79.0	7.0	0.0	98.0	2.0
Activities related to basic Education	5.0	79.0	16.0	0.0	98.0	2.0
Lectures	15.0	6.0	79.0	1.0	97.0	2.0
Group Activities	14.0	83.0	3.0	0.0	98.0	2.0
Sports Activities	48.0	50.0	2.0	20.0	78.0	2.0

(a) Includes only answers indicating direct knowledge about the existence of the activity.
(b) Includes only answers indicating direct knowledge about the nonexistence of the activity.
(c) The "don't know" answers do not necessarily indicate that the activity does not exist.

Table 6-4

Worker Involvement in the Development of Educational Activities in the Workplace by Groups or Units (percentages)

	Productive Units	
	PCs	PEs
Sources of Decisions About the Contents of Educational Activities	N = 224	N = 121
Don't Know	2.0	12.3
Assembly/General Meeting	20.0	1.2
Council/Committee	46.0	0.0
A Worker's Representative	28.0	3.5
Someone from outside the unit	4.0	46.5
No answer	-	36.5
Worker Participation in Educational Activities	N = 224	N = 121
No Direct Participation	53.0	99.0
Preparing Materials	11.0	0.0
As Member of a Team	34.0	1.0
Teaching	2.0	0.0
Reasons for no Direct Participation in the Organization of Educational Activities	N = 24	N = 81
No Interest	13.3	15.4
Don't Know How	30.0	18.3
Not Appropriate Conditions	33.3	58.1
Didn't Have the Opportunity	6.6	2.5
No answer	16.8	5.7

Workers' Education and the Mexican State

Despite the efforts of the Mexican government to encourage the education of working adults, it may be argued that, given the conditions under which PEs and PCs operate, they do not meet the workers' demands for education. In practice, these units do not have the necessary material and human resources to carry out educational activities in the workplace. This situation reduces workers' initiatives and limits the independence of PCs in their attempts to develop activities involving the participation of workers that may result in their further educational development.

Four types of facilities were identified as the minimum required by PCs and PEs to develop educational activities in the workplace. These were trained personnel, space, economic resources, and organization. Overall, it was found that in spite of the comparatively poorer material condition of PCs, they were considerably better off than PEs. Among workers in PCs, 21 percent indicated they were involved in some type of educational or training activities with peers, compared with only 4 percent among PEs. In both cases, however, workers felt they were not adequately prepared to perform educational roles and saw the need to receive external assistance for this purpose (79 percent in PCs and 80 percent in PEs). In terms of physical facilities, 46 percent of PCs had some kind of facility to carry out educational activities compared with only 17 percent of PEs. A similar difference was found in available economic resources. Among PCs, 25 percent had the financial means to organize educational programs compared with 4 percent of the PEs. This, however, is still very low if it is remembered that PCs, according to their bylaws, must allocate a percentage of their earnings to the education of their members. In terms of organization, PCs had a better structure in place but their effectiveness was jeopardized by their limited resources.

Availability of facilities in the workplace was found to be dependent on resources external to the organization. However, in practice, access to external sources of assistance is poor and limited to a few government programs which in many cases are largely political in purpose. Only 48 percent of PCs received some form of assistance from external sources, and no PEs in the sample were receiving such assistance. Among PCs, 63 percent considered this assistance to be poor and with few or no practical benefits for the organization or for the workers. Given that most of the assistance received by PCs originated in the government, this particular finding reinforces the assessment of other government sponsored educational activities for adults discussed in previous chapters.[15]

It has been indicated that the use of standard definitions to identify different forms of out-of-school activities presents some difficulties when applied to PCs. Keeping this in mind, the concept of "reciprocal nonformal education" was used to identify work relationships among individuals that might bring some educational outcomes to those involved. Operationally, this concept emphasizes the interactive character of mutual and diffuse teaching-learning processes that may occur in the workplace as a result of the dynamics of production. These relationships are dialectical and spontaneous, and their content reflects the experience, needs, and interests of the persons involved mediated by the requirements of production. This type of education was analyzed in relation to activities that involved the adoption of a teaching role by some workers to transmit their experiences and knowledge to others in their everyday work. It also involved the learning role of other workers in the process of material production. The data indicated that workers in PCs had fewer opportunities for this type of education than workers in PEs, with the exception of PCs with over 100 members. Smaller PCs tend to be less sophisticated in their production techniques and more concerned with their survival than PEs that are more diversified, have a higher flow of new workers, and rely more on workers' specific training and skills.

Education and Political Participation in the Workplace

Perhaps one of the most interesting outcomes of this study was the differences found between PCs and PEs in workers' political development. Given workers' isolation from the centers of political power, and the correlation that exists in societies like Mexico between class origin and political participation (Scott, 1970: 330-95; Basañez, 1981), the workplace becomes the most immediate setting in which workers develop forms of participation that may break their isolation from other members of their class and generate conditions for participation in society at large.[16] Two aspects were studied in regard to the potential educational effect of PCs on workers' political development: their political participation in society and their critical attitudes toward the sociopolitical system.

The analysis of political participation was directed to detect differences in the degree of political involvement outside the workplace, workers' political militancy, and the degree of continuity in their political participation in their jobs.[17] Workers' political participation was analyzed by looking at participation in a political party and in labor organizations, and by estimating a general indicator of participation. Political militancy was studied by looking at militancy before and after the present job. Political involvement was also studied by analyzing participation in political elections in the workplace, in the Federal District, in state elections, and at the national level. Table 6-5 shows the findings in this regard for workers in both PCs and in PEs.

The data on workers' political membership within groups were actually lower than expected. This was particularly evident in membership in political parties which at the national level was lower than membership in labor organizations. Only a relatively small percentage of workers had actual militancy in a political party. Female PC workers had the highest participation in both groups. Participation in labor organizations was higher among PE workers (19 percent compared with 8.5 percent in PCs).[18] The general indicator of political militancy shows that 11.6 percent in PCs and 24 percent in PEs are actually politically militant.[19]

The analysis of the continuity of workers' political militancy before and/or during their present job supported the argument that when workers enter the PC, they tend to become politically nonconformist and reject the political system by withdrawing their direct participation in the party. Thus, among workers without current political militancy, 22 percent in PCs and 12 percent in PEs did have political militancy before their job. This shows that among PCs there was a greater tendency to discontinue formal militancy after beginning to work in a cooperative. This also may indicate that PCs tend to attract workers with a higher political culture than PEs. When militancy before the present job was considered among those who had political militancy at the time of the study, it was found that a higher number of PC workers had previously participated more actively in politics. Among this group, participation in political elections as a whole was higher, particularly in the workplace. In general, 69.2 percent of PC workers participated in politics through elections compared with 37.9 percent of PE

Table 6-5
Worker Political Participation in Producer Cooperatives and Private Productive Units

Political Participation Variables	Male	Female	PCs Total	Male	Female	PEs Total
Membership in a Political Party	2.5	4.6	N=224 3.1	6.4	0.0	N=221 5.0
Leadership in a Labor Union Organization	10.1	4.6	N=224 8.5	19.1	18.5	N=221 19.0
General Political Membership	12.6	9.2	11.6	25.5	18.5	24.0
Political Membership Before Present Job if Do Not Participate Now	23.4	18.3	N=205 22.0	15.7	0.0	N=92 12.0
Political Membership Before Present Job if there is Present Participation	35.7	50.0	N=18 38.9	58.3	20.0	N=29 51.7
Participation in Elections in the Workplace	85.5	76.9	N=224 83.0	8.7	14.8	N=119 10.1
Participation in Election in the Federal District	74.2	67.7	N=224 72.3	62.4	44.4	N=120 58.3
Participation in Election in the State	8.2	6.2	N=224 7.6	44.4	31.8	N=94 41.5
Participation in Presidential Elections	88.7	75.4	N=224 84.8	77.7	63.0	N=121 74.4
General Participation in Political Elections	72.3	61.5	N=224 69.2	35.9	47.1	N=95 37.9

workers. In the workplace, participation in elections was substantially higher in PCs with 83 percent of the workers compared with 10 percent in PEs.[20]

Education and Workers' Critical Attitudes

The data on workers' critical attitudes toward the values, beliefs, and the formal institutions of society also showed some interesting findings related to the specific job setting.[21] To identify the differences between critical attitudes of PC and PE workers, four aspects were considered: their attitudes toward the model of development promoted by the government, the role of labor organizations, the political system, and the educational system.[22]

The idea of development and what it represents is a key component of the language of the State's technopolitical elite, who use it as a value element to give a raison d'être to the policies of modernization and to the pattern of distribution of economic and political power (Torres, 1988). In fact, this concept has an ideological connotation that serves to distort reality and generate a false perception of the future, and also to unify the people behind a common goal. Workers in PCs showed an overall higher critical attitude than those in PEs (see Table 6-6 for the general distributions). Interesting to highlight is the fact that being in a PC or in a PE was a strong factor explaining the deviations of the group averages, and that workers in PEs were more directly affected in their attitudes by factors such as formal schooling, participation in decision making in the workplace, and by political participation.[23] Given the specific data gathered to assess this particular critical attitude, it may be argued that workers in PCs had a wider perception of the idea of development as presented by the government. Development was perceived not to be exclusively associated with economic factors and going beyond the nationalistic overtone of the government rhetoric.

The findings regarding the attitude of workers toward the role of labor organizations were similar. Among PCs, 27.2 percent did not show critical attitude compared with 33.1 percent among PEs, whereas 24.6 percent of PC workers showed "average" criticism and 11.6 percent showed "high critical" attitude compared with 19.8 and 1.7 percent respectively in PEs. The higher critical attitude among PC workers corresponded with their lower formal participation in this type of institution and with their perception that cooperatives represent an alternative to government controlled labor organization. The differences between PC and PE workers can be basically accounted for by the type of workplace rather than other independent factors. These findings were closely related to the differences in workers' critical attitudes toward the political system. The overall distribution showed that 35.5 percent of PE workers and 22.8 percent of PC workers had no critical attitude toward the political system. Even larger differences in favor of PC workers were found in the category "high" criticism (29 percent in PCs compared with 12.4 percent in PEs). The fact that higher

Table 6-6
Workers' Critical Attitudes in Producer Cooperatives and Private Productive Units by Gender (percentages)

Critical Attitudes Toward	PCs			PEs		
	Males	Female	Total	Male	Female	Total
Development						
None	42.1	27.7	37.9	54.3	14.8	45.5
Low	25.2	46.2	31.3	23.4	70.4	33.9
Average	22.0	23.0	22.3	14.9	11.1	14.0
High	10.7	3.1	8.5	7.4	3.7	6.6
Labor Orgnization						
None	24.5	33.8	27.2	31.9	37.0	33.1
Low	35.2	40.0	36.6	45.7	44.5	45.5
Average	28.4	15.4	24.6	20.3	18.5	19.8
High	11.9	10.8	11.6	2.1	0.0	1.6
Political System						
None	26.4	13.8	22.8	30.8	51.9	35.5
Low	23.3	21.5	22.8	31.9	18.5	28.9
Average	23.9	29.2	25.4	21.3	29.6	23.2
High	26.4	35.5	29.0	16.0	0.0	12.4
Education						
None	8.2	6.2	7.6	18.0	18.6	18.2
Low	54.1	53.8	54.1	51.1	44.4	49.6
Average	37.1	40.0	37.9	29.8	37.0	31.4
High	0.6	0.0	0.4	1.1	0.0	0.8
General Critical Attitude						
None	1.1	0.0	0.8	5.6	4.8	5.4
Low	11.3	10.2	8.0	13.9	4.8	11.8
Average	35.5	15.4	32.6	31.9	33.3	32.3
High	52.1	74.4	58.6	48.6	57.1	50.5

critical attitudes were found among PC workers although they have lower political militancy tends to indicate that political participation and critical attitude toward the political system is inversely related in PCs.

The analysis of workers' critical attitudes toward education provided key information about the perceptions working adults have about the potential of education as promoted by the Mexican State. The previous chapter indicates that the pattern of economic development and modernization followed by the State has been built on the assumption that education by itself can play a key role in formation of human resources required to achieve the objectives of nation building, economic growth, and social and economic equality. Historically, this has been particularly relevant for the government educational strategies in adult and rural education. These findings show that, in spite of the identifiable problems plaguing the government's attempts to successfully use education to respond to the demands of the working-class sector, workers do not express similarly high degrees of criticism toward the role of education as they do toward other social institutions. In the distribution within groups, very small differences were found in the "medium" and "high" categories of critical attitudes between PC and PE workers.[24] Both categories combined included only 38.3 percent of PC and 32.2 percent of PE workers, being in fact the lower percentages of workers among those with higher critical attitudes of the four scales in the study. These findings reinforce the idea that the development of working adults is limited by the value that the sociopolitical system in Mexico has been able to attribute to the formal and nonformal educational alternatives generated from government initiatives.

CONCLUSION

Contrary to what could be expected given the emphasis of the Mexican government on the education of adults, education and work continue to be seen as sequential rather than interacting processes: Individuals are first expected to go through the school system and later perform as producers. The planning and implementation of adult education have been carried out assuming that State-controlled education presents substantial advantages in economic and political terms. Economically, education for adults has been planned to ultimately integrate them into the production system, thus reinforcing the process of capital reproduction within the model of associated-dependent development. Politically, adult education has served to socialize individuals perceived to be outside the main streams of the political legitimation process, and thus ensure the reproduction of the corporatist power structure of the State.

One purpose of the study presented in this chapter was to determine the extent to which participatory work environments like producer cooperatives may represent alternative advantages to the education of adults outside the traditional educational streams. In particular, this approach looked at the extent to which conditions of participation in decision making in the workplace and direct involvement of workers in decisions concerning their role as producers may result in a greater involvement of working adults in society in regard to political participation and the development of critical attitudes toward the social system.

The findings showed that given the differential conditions that exist in cooperative organizations, workers have greater opportunities for personal development as a result of the type of work environment. This comprises not only the existence of more opportunities for the development of activities leading to the implementation of nonformal education activities, but also to the development of informal education that results in their better understanding of the conditions for participation in society. Workers in PCs perceived that, because of the type of work setting, they can obtain greater educational benefits from activities developed in the workplace, particularly in basic education, on-the-job training, and community development. The overall social and material relations of production in PCs represent a potential setting for further development of the education of working adults, although PCs had considerably poorer economic conditions than PEs and even fewer mechanisms available to them at the societal level for their development as settings for worker control.

The linkages between education and work as far as adult education is concerned have been seen by government planners and policy makers within a linear, incremental, and quantitative-functional path. From this perspective, the efficient operation of both education and work are perceived to be essential for the achievement of particular objectives of the State. In practice the planning of adult education has been a means to secure control over the legitimation and reproduction functions of the corporatist State. Education has thus become an instrument in maintaining the unequal social and material relationships among classes, in the structural formal and nonformal education streams, and in the world of work. Planning the role of adult education has been transformed into an exercise in social engineering. By politically assessing the needs of the process of capital reproduction, the education of the adult population has been designed to produce individuals with the attitudes and skills necessary to achieve political and economic short-term objectives of the technopolitical elite in power. In this regard, the design, planning, and organization of adult education in Mexico has been carried out not only without paying the necessary attention to the role of the workplace, but also seeking a continuous adaptation of the needs of working adults to the political and economic goals of the government. The analysis of participatory work environments and their implications in terms of the education of working adults suggests that the planning of adult education is in need of a careful review by focusing on the dialectical interaction between the education and work processes in society.

NOTES

1. By the mid-1970s the educational system was serving approximately 17 million people. Around the same time, 11.9 million people over 14 years of age had not finished

primary education. Among them 6.2 million had not received in practice the necessary basic instruction that would allow them to actively participate in the economy. See also in this regard the discussion in Chapter five.

2. See also Morales-Gómez, 1985 and 1986a.

3. The National Law of Adult Education of 1975 encouraged a "self-learning system, without schedules, but [adapted] to each person's time . . . under programs and materials produced by the Secretariat of Public Education itself" (Mexican Government, 1976).

4. By the end of 1987, the INEA had shifted its focus of literacy training for native minorities and had devised a new program for training first in the students' mother tongue and later in Spanish. In February 1988 materials in 16 basic native languages were printed and distributed among students.

5. Labor organizations were found among handicraft occupations oriented by objectives of mutual aid, adopted by the new industrial proletariat given the constraints for the formation of union coalitions. The strikes of 1906, 1907, and 1908 were a result of these organizations, many of them influenced by anarchist ideas. See Leal and Woldenberg, 1976.

6. The five largest states in concentration of economically active population were the Federal District (17.2%), Veracruz (7.7%), State of Mexico (7.7%), Jalisco (6.9%), and Puebla (5.2%). The five largest states in percentage of wage earning workers were the Federal District (77.9%), Nuevo León (72.8%), Tamaulipas (67.5%), State of Mexico (66.9%), and Jalisco (64.6%). The five largest states in terms of union affiliation were the Federal District (38.7%), Nuevo León (21.8%), Tamaulipas (16.5%), Sinaloa (12.8%), and Jalisco (9.3%); see Mexican Government, 1971.

7. The Federation of Civil Service Unions (FSTSE) groups most public employees and is the basis of the popular sector of the PRI, acting independently of the main body of the labor movement.

8. A key factor affecting labor conditions in Mexico in the 1970s was the combined effect of industrialization and urban concentration. Large-scale industries control 81 percent of the net invested capital and 76 percent of the value of production, and employ 60 percent of the total industrial labor force. Accordingly, industries fall into two categories. The first is traditional industries that produce nondurable consumer goods, of which five products (food, textiles, shoes and clothing, drinks, and tobacco) employ 37 percent of the work force and generate 32 percent of the total value of production. The second group consists of the modernized industries producing durable consumer and intermediary goods. This can be divided into chemical products and metal and machinery, employing 22 percent of the labor force and generating 21 percent of the value of production, and industries including basic metals, transport materials, oil and petrochemical, electricity, and rubber products employing 17 percent of the labor force and generating 29.5 of the value of production (Osorio Urbina, 1975: 6-23).

9. Sources used to gather this information included the National Registry of Cooperatives, the Office of Statistics and Studies of the General Directorate of Cooperative Development, the Bank for Cooperative Development (BANFOCO), and the Secretariat of Industry and Commerce, the National Institute for Cooperative Education (INECOOP).

10. These sources included the Chamber of Commerce, the Confederation of Private Owners of the Mexican Republic (COPARMEX), the National Confederation of Industrial Chambers (CONCAMIN), and the National Confederation of Chambers of Commerce (CONCANCO).

11. Type of production was defined as the main type of economic activity of the production unit. According to this criterion, both PCs and PEs were grouped into six types: printing, handicraft production, food production, building construction, clothing production, and textiles. The size of the production unit was defined according to the number of workers. Following this criterion, three groups were established: small (10-49 workers), medium (50-99 workers), and large (over 100 workers). The minimum of 10 workers for the small units followed the criteria used by the Mexican government that required a minimum of 10 workers to form a PC.

12. Owing to the larger number of PEs in the original population compared with the population of the PCs, the selection of the sample of individuals from PEs was made by matching the number of production units to those of the final group of PCs selected for the study. The matching was done according to type of production and size of unit.

13. Three pretested questionnaires were applied by interviewers to leaders of cooperatives, cooperative members, and workers from private firms.

14. The activities originally considered in the study were: basic education, vocational development, political development, cooperativism, community development, trade unionism, on-the-job training, sports, and arts. Approximately 74 percent of PC workers identified at least one of these activities in terms of actual educational benefits, compared with only 14 percent among PE workers.

15. The most common source of financial assistance to PCs in Mexico is government organizations. Among them the National Bank of Cooperative Patronage is perhaps the most important. Most leaders of PCs indicated, however, that access to this source is conditioned by political factors, including in some cases the relationship of the cooperative to the PRI. They also indicated that the bureaucratic structure of government is a major factor limiting access of PCs to existing funds, particularly for small PCs which do not have the means or expertise to negotiate their request with the branches of government involved in the processes of approval and assistance.

16. Three situations, however, must be taken into account. First, the development of conditions and mechanisms for participation in the workplace are not a guarantee in themselves of effective worker control, or the only necessary element required to change the social and material relations of production in the workplace. Second, the creation of these mechanisms must be undertaken together with the creation of mechanisms for education that could assist in developing the workers' class consciousness and critical attitudes toward the system in which they live. Third, a possible outcome of the integration between education and work may be the political development of the workers that in turn may contribute to increase their participation in society.

17. Several aspects were taken into account in the analysis. Among them were the unique pattern of traditional political institutions that exists in Mexico; the traditional lack of formal political participation of members of the working class; the influence of the political culture that rests in the rhetoric of the revolutionary tradition; the perception of political participation as a means to legitimize rather than to change the existing political structure; and the pattern of cooptation that exists among political and labor leaders in society.

18. In many cases, however, workers do not know if they actually have formal political militancy in a party or in a labor union, given the close link between their labor organizations and the structure of the PRI.

19. A few aspects could be considered to explain these findings among PC workers. On the one hand, political participation in Mexico tends to be higher in urban centers. However, lack of participation tends to be a more direct indicator of political dissatis-

faction than in rural areas (González Casanova, 1970: 123). Participation in politics, both in the party system and in the labor organization, on the other hand, are perceived as a form of commitment with government policies and therefore not beneficial for the cooperative organization.

20. The general differences in political participation between PC and PE workers are to a large extent explained by the type of workplace where they operate. At the same time, however, part of these differences also account for other intervening variables such as the size of the production unit, the type of production in which it is involved, and the degree of worker job satisfaction. The difference between groups regarding participation in elections in the workplace shows an F-ratio of 336.83 in the one-way analysis of variance. This was reinforced through the analysis of covariance which indicated that PC workers have less involvement in political organization outside the job setting but higher involvement in the workplace.

21. A basic assumption is that workers' capacity to question and change their roles in society and in so doing change the socioeconomic and political system in which they live is directly related to the conditions of structural power at the micro- and macrolevels. At the microlevel this capacity is subject to the conditions under which workers sell their labor as producers and their degree of participation in decision making. At the macrolevel this capacity depends on the development of a class consciousness given the conditions of power that exist in society in regard to political participation (Olsen, 1970: 72).

22. Each of these aspects was measured using pretested attitudinal scales developed using Guttman Scalogram Analysis. Each scale was unidimensional in which the component items measured movement toward or away from the single issue associated with a particular attitude. To build the scales, three separate runs of scaling analysis were done, one for each sample and one for both samples combined. This allowed the formation of the optimum scales with the higher coefficients of scalability and reproducibility.

23. Analyses of variance and covariance were used to identify deviations within and between groups when the main effects were controlled by selected covariates.

24. The scale applied to measure critical attitudes toward education included the following items: "To acquire a good education only depends upon individual capacity," "education is the best means to create conditions for social change," "education is a means to transmit the ideas of the social group in power," "the workers must attend school if they want to improve their conditions of living," and "work is a good means for the education of workers."

Conclusion: The Corporatist State and Educational Policy Planning

THE CHANGING TRENDS IN THE ROLE OF THE STATE

The evolution and characteristics of educational policy formation and implementation in Mexico need to be understood in the context of the political history of the country since the early 1900s. The unique character of the Mexican State, which has claimed its origin as the offspring of the first social revolution of this century, is still a determinant factor shaping public policy planning in education.

The earlier expression of the State formation known today in Mexico was born out of a revolution. This was a process of transformation fundamentally contradictory in its multiclass structure and led by a complex coalition of forces seeking to bring radical social changes within capitalism. The Institutional Revolutionary Party (PRI), which ruled the country without substantial political or social interference until the late 1980s, has been a key instrument in maintaining the contradictions of the postrevolutionary State within a politically manageable framework. However, the decline in the State's capacity to control the power coalition that is witnessed today marks perhaps the beginning of a new period in Mexican history. Over the last two decades, traditional attempts to maintain sociopolitical cohesion through different means, including the use of education by the State, have begun to show signs of serious deterioration.

The model of associated-dependent development was highly successful in achieving its short-term objectives until the unfolding of the fiscal crisis in the early 1970s, further aggravated by the external debt crisis in the 1980s. These events have shown that this model underestimated the longer-term negative impact of associated-dependent policies on both Mexico's development goals and the base of popular support of the State. However, in spite of the grave economic and sociopolitical crisis faced by the country after the Revolution, Mexico still remains one of the newly industrialized powers of the world and an important political actor in the Latin American scenario (Lowenthal, 1987: 66-102).

It has been argued in this book that a key to the secular political stability of postrevolutionary Mexico and its high rate of economic growth is found in the nature of the corporatist State. The State is based on a complex network of interest groups comprising, among others, a bureaucratic bourgeoisie, industrialist groups, and the labor unions. This political class alliance has underscored not only the processes of interest representation, political control, and social participation that make the unique Mexican democracy governable, but also the processes of public policy formation including education.

STATE AND EDUCATION

A central hypothesis in this book is that educational expansion and the development of the educational system at large has been dependent on the consolidation of the corporatist State as a mode of governance and political legitimation. The success of the model of dependent economic development from the 1940s through the 1960s, with rates of economic growth ranking among the highest in the world, allowed the Mexican State to have enough economic surplus to support increasing educational financing well above the rate of inflation. In addition, educational investment was subsidized by keeping teachers' salary increases below the level they had achieved in the early 1920s. By and large, educational expansion has been controlled, regulated, and financed by the federal public sector with little, if any, participation of the states, the municipalities, or private individuals.

The rationale for educational expansion has been justified not only as educational investment per se but also as part and parcel of the political commitment of the postrevolutionary corporatist State. Given that the Revolution committed itself to provide every citizen with free, compulsory, and secular education, formal education was expected not only to put human capital into the development model but, and above all, to input political capital aimed at the consolidation of the postrevolutionary system. Hence education became a central dimension in the public policy of the State, and the expansion, diversification, and improvement of elementary education have been basic elements in the constitution of modern Mexico.

Particularly relevant in this context are the nature and characteristics of the processes of policy planning. Studying the role of planning in Mexico, Benveniste asserts that "if a national plan is to be implemented, planners need to generate their own sources of social power" (1970: 1). In other words, they are obliged to foster belief in the feasibility of their plans. Traditionally, this has been done by three means: stressing the technical and scientific validity of the plan; acquiring and using information to influence and alter policies; and organizing coalitions of planning implementors to increase the probability of success of the planning outcomes (Benveniste, 1970: 11). After reviewing evidence in Mexico, Benveniste concludes that "one can think of planning as part of the overall control system which insures the participation and desirable behaviors of the members of a complex social system" (1970: 117). He goes even further by arguing that there has been "a discrepancy between the concept of planning prevailing among the actors . . . and the process of planning which seemed in fact to be taking place" (1970: 111).

In this context, educational planning has been no exception. The evolution of the relationship between education and the State has shown that within the framework of the government's public policies, educational planning has been not only an exercise in optimism, but also a mechanism of social control. For those at the top of the technopolitical ladder, educational planning has been a means to control a basic social process. For those in middle-level positions it has been a means of participation in educational policy making, and therefore a means to influence future social participation.

However, this discrepancy between planning and implementation in education cannot be explained if the framework for analysis separates politics and administration. Throughout the discussion of the contradictory relationships between education and the corporatist State in this book, such separation is challenged. In the previous chapters, the politics of educational planning and educational planning as a political process are critically analyzed. Both are reviewed in the light of the overall hegemonic role of a State formation claiming to be a legitimate successor to the Revolution, while it is permeated by interbureaucratic struggles for power and resources. Thus the process of planning underlying educational change has been understood as an expression of the political struggle and manipulation characterizing public policy formation.

The analytical separation between politics and administration as two independent processes can be attributed to the influential work of Weber (1947 [1970]). Although Weber recognized that the modern State "claims the monopoly of the legitimate use of force" (Gerth and Mills, 1970: 78) and therefore is the expression of social relationships of domination, it requires "a system of continuous administration in order to maintain its organized domination" (Bates, 1985: 5). Within this line of argument, the development of an official bureaucratic structure, based on expertise to perform purely technical functions within the State apparatus becomes a prerequisite for the development of the modern, rational capitalist State.[1] This identifies what is perceived as the necessary and continued role of the career bureaucrats that stands in sharp contrast with the dispensability of the politician:

> The development of politics into an organization which demanded training in the struggle for power, and in the methods of this struggle as developed by modern party policies, determined the separation of public functionaries into two categories, which, however, are by no means rigidly but nevertheless distinctly separated. These categories are "administrative" officials on the one hand, and "political officials" on the other. The "political" officials, in the genuine sense of the word, can regularly and externally be recognized by the fact that they can be

transferred any time at will, that they can be dismissed, or at least temporarily withdrawn. (Gerth and Mills, 1970: 90)

Several characteristics identified by Weber to define bureaucracy do not necessarily apply in the case of the Mexican State, and even if they do they are conditioned by the nature of the coalition controlling the State.[2] The absence of a career civil service in Mexico strongly conspires against the notion of career bureaucrats. Weber's contrast between the nature of politics as a vocation—with its element of passion, value judgement, and subjective leadership—and the nature of administration—based on a scientific vocation, objective judgment, impartiality, and exclusive personal responsibility for decision making and administration—cannot be easily verified in the performance of the Mexican State, particularly in public policy formation and planning processes.

Until now Mexico's State administration has been able to rest on a one-party structure. In this setting, the highest levels of the technopolitical bureaucracy are closely connected to the highest party cadres. Over time, this makes possible the exchange of key positions in decision making. Top political and administrative appointments in the government follow the rules of power distribution among corporatist interests and power groups participating in the class and political alliance. This also serves to balance the regional power blocks and interests within the party which are struggling to be part of the decision making process in the national arena.

Political bargaining is thus carried out within the corporatist structure under a veil of institutional anonymity. The rational-legal structures recognized by the State as acceptable settings for decision making in practice are often overridden by top level decisions aimed at balancing power demands. In the practice of public policy, impartiality in the examination and treatment of specific policy decisions is often a rare commodity in Mexico's political arena. In most cases, it becomes subsidiary to the overwhelming power of the top ranks of the *oficialía mayor* (the comptrollers' offices in the administrative structures of the State), of the differential power of the corporatist partners, especially labor unions, and particularly of the presidential nature of politics and its patrimonial traditions. The technical rationale expected to be found in policy decisions is thus easily subsumed under a political corporatist rationale of policy formation (McGinn and Street, 1982).

As in other spheres of the State within the corporatist structure, there is no clear distinction in education between the political and administrative cadres dealing with policy formation and implementation. Frequently decisions about appropriation of educational resources, implementation of educational innovations, ideological orientations in educational objectives and content, and alternative political loyalties within the aims of the party are characterized by serious conflicts and contradictions among the bureaucratic factions of the technopolitical elite.

EDUCATIONAL POLICY AND COMPENSATORY
LEGITIMATION

The discussion in this book about the relationships between the State and education has shown that the provision of mass, compulsory, and free education on a continuous and incremental basis is primarily an expression of the legitimacy needs of the State. This point has been reinforced by the work of other scholars (Latapí, 1976; Vaughan, 1982; Hamilton, 1982). In the context of such relations, educational planning has been utilized by the powerful technopolitical elite as an instrument of modernization and development, and as an alleged means to respond to the basic needs of the poorer sectors of society. In practice, however, there is enough evidence to argue that, first and foremost, the planning of schooling and nonformal education have played a central role in the process of social reproduction and political control exercised by the State.

The analysis of the role of elementary education, adult education policy and planning processes at the national level, and the lack of response of the State to the needs for workers' education outside its direct sphere of influence shows a consistent use of education for political and legitimation purposes. Changes in education as a component of corporatist development strategy reflect relations of correspondence and contradictions inherent in a capitalist State seeking to reproduce its labor force for capital accumulation purposes within a hierarchical division of labor. They also reflect the structural and ideological relations between the social relations of education in terms of its rationale and policy outcomes and the State's need for economic and political legitimacy.

Since formal education has been a key element in the formulation of educational policies, nonformal education instead, in spite of its high profile in the 1930s and 1940s, languished in modern Mexico, with less and less support from the State. Adult education policies only emerged again as a priority when the possibilities for further expansion of schooling were exhausted in the context of the fiscal crisis of the State and the increasing pressure from the teachers' union to intervene, manipulate, and control educational policy formation. In fact, when the pressure of the latter became unacceptable to the State, because the governability of the education system was being affected and education has become more costly, adult education received special attention.

Despite improvements in the provision of elementary, higher, and technical education, all fueled by heavy borrowing first and by the oil boom later, it was the nonformal education system that began to receive more attention during the time of fiscal constraints. However, the pace, style, scope, and organizational routines developed in the 1980s were primarily the result of the conflict built into the bureaucratic structure of the Secretariat of Education. This conflict took place between the teachers' union that has been pursuing clientelist-oriented policies for more than three decades and the technobureaucratic elite at the SEP that pursued modernization policies since the early 1970s. In this context, the teachers' union involvement in policy formation was maintained by a political rationale, while the modernization of the educational structures pursued by the decision making elite was maintained by a technocratic rationale. The latter was aimed at undermining the power of the teachers' union by keeping it away from the formulation of nonformal education policies. In the midst of this conflict a third actor emerged between 1979 and 1989: the movement of democratic teachers. Challenging the authority of the teachers' union and, to a lesser extent, the modernizing project of the State bureaucracy, democratic teachers attempted to create an autonomous project of educational reform. This third actor will make political negotiations in education much more complex in the 1990s. Since the main gains of the democratic movement occurred in 1989, the focus of analysis of this book, which centers on the period 1970-1988, remains the conflict between the teachers' union and the Secretary of Public Education.

The process of educational policy formation witnessed over recent years, including the practice of educational planning inspired by a technocratic outlook, has been part of a process of compensatory legitimation. The remains of the revolutionary ideology of the Mexican State can no longer compensate for the growing contradictions emerging in society at large. The current economic and political crisis exacerbates the effects of social inequality, the lack of services to satisfy basic needs, and the negative effects of regressive policies in income distribution. Education has thus become, more than ever before, the means that allows the State to keep alive some of the principles and rhetoric of the Revolution. It also allows the ruling elite to articulate new forms of political enfranchisement and cooptation of new social actors. The political capacity of the State to compensate for the growing pauperization and marginalization of wide sectors of the society, particularly women, nonunionized workers, and peasants, can no longer rely exclusively on the role of the one-party political system. The outcome of the process leading to the presidential election in 1988 was a vivid demonstration of the crisis faced by the corporatist State in maintaining its traditional role toward the most disadvantaged sectors of the society.

The internal deterioration of the political ideology that maintained a cohesion in the power structure over several decades is showing more frequent signs of conflict and contradictions in the process of policy formation. In education there is a growing mismatch between the premises supporting the rational paradigm of educational planning and the requirements of the corporatist State to maintain political cohesion among the poor. The practice of educational policy planning has been permeated by ongoing and growing conflicts between technocrats and *normalistas*, and between the political will and capacity to mediate the rising of a more militant opposition.

Despite the characterization of the development model in terms of modernization of the social structure, quality of education and equality of educational opportunities for the vast majority of Mexicans are still expensive commodities. Dropout and attrition remain critical problems. By 1986 school efficiency had reached only 51.3 percent in elementary education and

74.4 percent in junior high school. Throughout the system, there are still large differences between the quality of education available to the poor through public schooling and the quality of teaching to which middle- and upper-class children can have access through private education. The distribution of opportunities regarding access, retention, mobility, and type of education continues to favor the wealthier sectors of society. Paradoxically, the social sector that has benefited the most from the educational expansion of the last two decades is the urban middle class and not the true subjects of the Revolution: peasants and workers, especially those in rural Mexico.

In the context of such trends, the contradictions of educational planning are not an outcome of competing technical forces within the educational arena, or the result of a mismatch between educational resources and outcomes. In practice, they are the expression of the contradictory role that education is expected to play at the service of the State. Public education continues to be primarily an instrument of modernization and a tool for social and political control. However, at the same time, it is expected to be a constitutional means for maintaining and expanding economic and political democracy. Although education is expected to produce human capital, in practice it is designed to produce political capital for the State and the elites. Higher education in particular has been used as a State response to counteract some of the radical trends resulting from growing political conflicts in society and to contain differences among the corporatist factions within a dominant elite. Although formal education appears to be closely associated with economic development, in practice it is used as a substitute for the lack of more substantive distributive reforms for the masses. While nonformal education is justified as an effective low-cost approach for literacy training and adult basic education, its implementation makes it primarily an instrument for political franchise and control of the labor force and those sectors which are marginal to the corporatist network of loyalties and services. Even adult education had been used as a policy laboratory to test alternatives for educational decentralization and as a means to compensate for policies which have increased the privatization of technical-vocational training.

Economic and educational policies have been an expression of the political objectives of the bureaucratic bourgeoisie which is a key actor in the State. They have been used to mediate social conflict, maintain the dominant mode of production, and reproduce the class structure and the relations among classes in a society historically characterized by deep cultural and economic divisions. Education has also been an important instrument in the process of political socialization and ideological legitimation inherent in the sustainability of a nationalist project. It has contributed to the reinforcement of political stability and the legitimation of the image of a revolutionary tradition providing a historical frame for corporatism.

Historically, education was conceived as a complement to the legalization and support of trade unions, and to land and political reform. Throughout the process of educational development, however, this has been contradicted by the actual role of working-class, middle-, and upper-class schools. The study of schools in Mexico City presented in this book, for example, shows that their differential performance is still intimately related to the socioeconomic traits of the social classes they serve. Similarly, the study of workers' education shows that the educational development of working adults is constrained by the value that the State has attributed to formal and nonformal educational alternatives generated under government initiatives. Contrary to what could be expected, education and work continue to be seen as sequential rather than mutually complementary processes.

THE STATE AND PUBLIC POLICY IN EDUCATION

The class alliance supporting the political system is one of the most important factors in the formulation of educational policies. The capacity of education to respond to the demands of the dominant class in a political formation is critical in shaping the pattern of social reproduction. Education is thus an important instrument to gain access to higher positions within the State bureaucracy, to develop mechanisms of political representation, to establish alternative forms of legitimation, and to respond to the socioeconomic and political concern of those receiving educational services.

To understand the role of the State in educational policy in Mexico, it is necessary to look at Mexico's economic development as built on the basis of four broadly defined sectors. These are a monopoly sector, a competitive sector, a public sector, and a residual labor force sector. These sectors interplay in the context of capitalist and precapitalist forms of production within the social formation giving place to policy and planning practices including those in education.

The political economy of the Mexican State has traditionally been organized to support primarily the development of a social formation in which the mode of production is commodity oriented. In this context, State economic interventionism through its service policies is directed toward performing those functions that capital is unable to perform alone due to its many factions and mutually antagonistic parties. But State intervention is also oriented toward strengthening the legitimacy of the current ruling alliance as a prerequisite to sustaining a pattern of capital accumulation. In Mexico, the State's central paradox in public policy follows the dual character of any capitalist State. On the one hand, it determines the class relationships with its policies aimed at constituting and reproducing the capitalist system. On the other, it performs as the official representative of the nation pursuing a revolutionary nationalist project.

In this book, the Mexican State is viewed as a pact of domination and a set of institutional apparatuses, bureaucratic organizations, and formal and informal norms and codes seeking to represent the public and private spheres of society. The class character of the State does not reside in the social origin of the members of the technopolitical elite or the ruling classes, but in its internal structure and its political institutions including the educational system. Policy making is thus the combined product of various interacting factors. These include (1) the actions of a bureaucratic bourgeoisie that, despite its internal fragmentation and conflicts, actively participates in the corporatist network and processes of conflict and bargaining in policy; (2) a network of legal, institutional, and ideological norms reproduced by the revolutionary tradition; and (3) a pattern of interaction in the relationship between the State and the political and social clienteles.

This structural framework of policy formation and implementation permits the State to perform its principal functions, particularly in the area of basic services. These include the execution of a preventive strategy of crisis management, the establishment of a system of priorities with respect to social needs and threats, and the creation of a long-term avoidance strategy to defuse future threats to political stability and social consensus as a result of unfulfilled social demands. From this perspective, the contradictions in educational policy formation cannot be interpreted as a result of class antagonism or the product of interbureaucratic struggle. They are in fact the necessary by-products of an integral system of political control and reproduction. What is still to be seen in the future evolution of the country is how the Mexican State will deal with the growing deterioration of its capacity to maintain social and political control. This is a critical aspect to observe in the evolution of Mexico in the 1990s, particularly when its political cohesion begins to disintegrate, its fiscal revenues continue to diminish, the easy ways of educational expansion are almost exhausted, and the people continue to demand fulfillment of the promises of the revolution for more and better free public education. In the educational context, attention should be given to the growing complexity of policy formation brought about by the democratic teachers' movement and whether its members will be incorporated into or excluded from the policy framework. If they are integrated, the question is how it will be done, and how this would affect policies of compensatory education. If they are excluded, the question is then at what cost for the political system.

SCENARIOS FOR THE FUTURE

To speculate about possible scenarios for changes in education, it is necessary to picture the structural and political conditions that would make such scenarios viable. Between 1982 and 1988 the Mexican State allocated over $89 billion to service the external debt. With an external debt of $108.5 billion, all trends indicate that fiscal resources will continue to be deeply affected. This is reinforced by current developments. In the last three years, approximately 50 percent of total public expenditure has been allocated to service the debt; inflation has risen between 60 and 80 percent per year; and with devaluation maintained at a minimum, the peso by January 1989 was overvalued at least 8 to 10 percent. If the price of a barrel of oil does not drop below $15 it could be expected that economic growth will continue at a slow pace, below 2 percent per year.[3]

Given such an economic framework, Mexico's political conditions may not experience significant changes. The regime will continue to be civilian in character, with a parliamentary system and the army having no direct intervention in policy making. The Church will continue its struggle to modify article 130 of the Constitution without any more success than increasing pressure on the government. The bulk of the working class and the large peasant population will maintain a position at the side of the government, despite the threat posed by the Cardenista new democratic party heavily supported by sectors of the middle class and a few trade unions. If all the conditions to sustain this framework are met, then it is possible to conceive several possible scenarios.

The first scenario is characterized by *electoral chaos with deterioration of public education*. In spite of the PRI's efforts, if the right-wing opposition obtains sound gains in the next elections or even forms a new government, there will be increasing union militancy against government educational policies, with boycotts, misuse of resources, and clashes at every level of policy formation and implementation. There might be a shift toward private education, with important Church support, and a clear deterioration of public educational services, particularly in rural areas. This will mean growing support for private universities, and less financial support for public universities that eventually will become much more conflictive. Under such circumstances, there will be a decline in the support for adult education and on-the-job training programs, and to technical-vocational education.

The second scenario will be set by a *corporatist reorganization and the end of the modernization project*. This would imply that the PRI holds power giving room to maneuver to the hegemonic faction of the union in exchange for political support nationwide. This will be the end of the modernization efforts. It would imply an end to the process of decentralization, the return of teaching training institutions to union control, a new philosophy of back-to-basics in public education, and repression of union dissidents in some areas such as the states of Mexico, Oaxaca, Chiapas, and Morelos. There will be increasing financial support for education but eventually lower input due to the cessation of modernization measures; growing predominance of factions linked to technical education and the polytechnic institutions in public education, and diminishing importance of the National university.

This scenario could take place only if the PRI is able to reconstitute its electoral and political power. Past history has shown that in facing profound crises, the main factions of the PRI, including the populist, traditional, and technocratic factions, have set aside their differences and have been able to establish new political pacts. This will steady the situation in education, with the union reaffirming its power and interest in policy formation, the factions in favor of privatization pressing to give more power to the private initiative including the Church, and the State acting as a balancing mechanism in the midst of the political confrontation, setting aside any significant modernization or reformist projects. In this context, no significant changes or educational reforms could be expected, except for rhetorical changes. Some of the most recent developments in adult education and in workers' education could be brought to an abrupt end, with formal schooling becoming more predominant in the State's policies. Teachers, workers, and peasants will become, once again, the backbone of the PRI political domination strategy. The teachers' union will be vehemently opposed on the basis of nationalist trends seeking to rescue Mexican political culture from the revolutionary past.

The third scenario comprises a *populist outbreak and the development of a charismatic leadership*. If the electoral power of the PRD (Partido de la Revolución Democrática) Cardenist factions continues to grow, there is a clear possibility that both the welfare system and educational policies will come under the control of more left-wing elements. This will bring about a bitter struggle with the conservative Revolutionary Vanguard factions who are more concerned with the revitalization of union dissidence that most probably will be promoted by the State. The result will be increasing union conflicts and strikes, growing mass participation in the states but, at the same time, deterioration of the quality of education due to experimentation, lack of funding, and growing political turmoil. Education will become over-politicized at every level.

The fourth scenario will be characterized by an *authoritarian technocratization and imposed modernization*. Several factions within the prevailing ruling alliance have been pursuing authoritarian policies in dealing with their opposition. If authoritarianism becomes the centerpiece of the new government policies, particularly if this takes place together with economic policies in favor of the creation of a common market with the United States, this will meet strong resistance from teachers and the leadership of the teachers' union that advocates nationalist policies. In a context of increasing repression there will be a drop in support to public education, particularly at the elementary level, and attempts to create new systems of technical education and on-the-job training to meet the requirements of the new economic conditions. Educational decentralization will be pursued at the cost of seeking educational innovation, quality of education, and control and regulation of the educational output.

The previous discussion represents a modest overview of the wide range of scenarios that Mexico could face in the 1990s. In any of them, education will play a central role in shaping Mexico as a nation. A deep process of change has already begun in postrevolutionary Mexico; what form it will take in the next decades and at what social, political, and economic cost is something worth observing.

NOTES

1. Christopher Ham and Michael Hill in their book *The Policy Process in the Modern Capitalist State* argue that "Weber regards the development of bureaucratic administration as intimately associated with the evolution of a modern industrialized society. Bureaucratization is seen as a consequence of the development of a complex

economic and political system, and also a phenomenon that has helped to make these developments possible" (1984: 48).

2. Weber identified five major characteristics of a bureaucracy: (1) a continuous organization with specified functions bound by rules that ensures consistency and continuity; (2) clearly specified levels of authority within a hierarchy; (3) a separation between the individuals and the means of administration and production; (4) the appointment of individuals on the basis of qualifications and their promotion on the basis of merits; and (5) the tenure of positions within fixed terms ([1970] 1947: 329-41).

3. Despite the critical character of these trends for Mexico, they are still better than for the rest of Latin America. The regional GNP growth in 1988 was 0.7 percent, with the GNP per capita close to that in 1978, while inflation for the region was 472.8 percent.

Bibliography

Aboites, Hugo. "El salario del educador en México: 1925-1982." *Coyoacán*. Revista Marxista Latinoamericana. Mexico City: VIII, no. 16 (January-March 1984): 63-110.

———. "Sesenta años del salario del educador (1925-1985)." *México. Los salarios de la crisis. Cuadernos obreros*. Mexico City: CDESTAC (1986): 84-87.

Adler Hellman, Judith. *Mexico in Crisis*. New York: Holms and Meier, 1978.

Ahumada, Jorge. *La planificación del desarrollo*. Santiago: Ediciones Nueva Universidad, 1972.

Alavi H., and Shanin, T., eds. *Introduction to the Sociology of a Developing Societies*. London: Macmillan, 1982.

Alba, Victor. *The Mexicans: The Making of a Nation*. New York: Praeger, 1967.

Amin, Samir. *Accumulation on a World Scale: A Critique of the Theory of Underdevelopment*. 2 vols. New York: Monthly Review Press, 1974.

Anton, Frank. *Workers' Participation: Prescription for Industrial Change*. Calgary, Canada: Detselig Enterprises Limited, 1980.

Apple, Michael. *Ideology and Curriculum*. London: Routledge and Kegan Paul, 1979.

———., ed. *Cultural and Economic Reproduction in Education. Essays on Class, Ideology and the State*. London: Routledge and Kegan Paul, 1982.

Arriaga, María de la Luz. "El magisterio en lucha." *Cuadernos Políticos*. Mexico, DF: Ediciones Era. 27 (1981): 79-101.

Bailey, John. "What Explains the Decline of the PRI and Will It Continue?" *Mexico's Political Stability: The Next Five Years*. Ed. Roderic Ai Camp. Boulder, CO: Westview Special Studies on Latin America and the Caribbean, 1986: 159-183.

Balay, Esteban. *Bases del ordenamiento cooperativo de la economía social*. Buenos Aires: Artes Gráficas Bartolomé U. Chicsino, SA, 1976.

Bambirra, Vania. *El capitalismo dependiente latinoamericano* Mexico: Siglo XXI Editores, 3rd ed., 1976.

Basañez, Miguel. *La lucha por la hegemonía en México (1968-1980)*. Mexico, DF: Siglo XXI Editores Editores, 1981.

Bates, R. *Public Administration and the Crisis of the State*. Victoria, Australia: Deakin University, 1985.

Baudelot, Ch., and Establet, P. *La escuela capitalista.* Mexico, DF: Siglo XXI Editores, 1975.

Belligni, Silvano. "Hegemonía." Eds. N. Bobbio and N. Matteucci. *Diccionario de política.* Mexico: Siglo XXI Editores, 1981: 772-775.

Benveniste, Guy. *Bureaucracy and National Planning.* New York: Praeger, 1970.

Berg, Ivar. *Education and Jobs: The Great Training Robbery.* New York: Praeger, 1971.

Bernstein, Basil. *Class, Codes and Control,* Vols. I and III. London: Routledge and Kegan Paul, 1971 and 1975.

Bernstein, Paul. "Necessary Elements for Effective Workers' Participation in Decision-Making." *Journal of Economic Issues* 10, no. 2 (June 1976), 490-522.

Bhola, Harbans S. "A Policy Analysis of Adult Literacy Promotion in the Third World: An Accounting of Promises Made and Promises Fulfilled." *International Review of Education* 30, no. 3 (1984a): 249-64.

———. Campaigning for Literacy. Paris: UNESCO, 1984b.

Bobbio, Norberto. "Gramsci y la concepción de la sociedad civil." *Actualidad del pensamiento político de Gramsci.* Ed. F. Fernández Buey. Barcelona: Grijalbo, 1977: 150-176.

Boli, John, Ramirez, Francisco, and Meyer, John. "Explaining the Origin and Expansion of Mass Education," *Comparative Education Review* 29, no. 2 (May 1985): 145-70.

Boron, Atilio. "El fascismo como categoría histórica: En torno al problema de las dictaduras en América Latina." *Revista Mexicana de Sociología,* 39, 2, 1977: 481-528.

Bowles, Samuel, and Gintis, Herbert. *Schooling in Capitalist America.* New York: Basic Books, 1976.

Brandenburg, Frank. *The Making of Modern Mexico.* Englewood Cliffs, NJ: Prentice Hall, 1964.

Brembeck, Cole, and Thompson, Timothy. *New Strategies for Educational Development: The Cross-Cultural Search for Nonformal Alternatives.* Lexington, MA: Heath, 1973.

Bulnes, Francisco. *El verdadero Díaz y la revolución.* Mexico, DF: Editora Nacional, 1952.

Camp, Roderic Ai. "The Role of the *Técnico* in Policy Making in Mexico: A Comparative Study of a Developing Bureaucracy." Ph.D. dissertation, University of Arizona, 1970.

———. *Mexico's Leaders. Their Education and Recruitment.* Arizona: University of Arizona Press, 1980.

———., ed. *Mexico's Political Stability: The Next Five Years.* Boulder, CO: Westview Special Studies on Latin America and the Caribbean, 1986.

Cárdenas, Lázaro. "Exposición de motivos del proyecto de ley de sociedades cooperativas." *Ley general de sociedades cooperativas.* Mexico, DF: Ediciones Andrade, SA, 1970.

Cardoso, Fernando H. "Associated-Dependent Development: Theoretical and Practical Implications." *Authoritarian Brazil: Origins, Politics, and Future.* Ed. Alfred Stepan. New Haven, CT: Yale University Press, 1973.

———. "Las contradicciones del desarrollo asociado." *Desarrollo Económico,* 53, 14, 1974.

———. "Notas sobre el estado actual de los estudios de la dependencia." *Problemas del subdesarrollo latinoamericano.* Eds. Sergio Bagú et al. Mexico: Nuestro Tiempo, 1975, 2nd ed., 90-125.

Carnoy, Martin."Workers' Triumph: The Meridan Experiment." *Working Papers* (Winter 1976): 47-56.

———. *The State and Political Theory.* Princeton, NJ: Princeton University Press, 1984.

———. "The Political Economy of Education." *International Social Science Journal,* 37, 2, 1985: 157-173.

Carnoy, Martin, and Levin, Henry. *The Limits of Educational Reforms.* New York: David McKay, 1976.

———. *Schooling and Work in the Democratic State.* Stanford, CA: Stanford University Press, 1985.

Carnoy, Martin, and Shearer, Derek. *Economic Democracy: The Challenge of the 1980s.* New York: Sharp, 1980.

Carpizo, Jorge. *El presidencialismo mexicano.* Mexico, DF: Siglo XXI Editores, 1978.

Centro de Estudios Educativos. *Revista del Centro de Estudios Educativos.* Mexico, DF: CEE 1, no. 1 (1971).

———. *Revista del Centro de Estudios Educativos* 5, no. 3 (1975).

———. *Revista del Centro de Estudios Educativos* 6, no. 3 (1976).

———. *Revista del Centro de Estudios Educativos* (1979).

———. "La educación y cambio social: Resultados obtenidos, su explicación y posibles alternativas." *La educación popular en América Latina: Avance o retroceso?* Mexico, DF: CEE (1982): 363-84.

CEPAL. *Indicadores del desarrollo económico y social en América Latina.* Santiago: CEPAL, 1976.

Chaparro, Félix. "Modelo y curriculum de la primaria intensiva para Adultos," *Educación de adultos: Nuevas dimensiones en el sector educativo.* Ed. María Luisa de Anda. Mexico, DF: CNTE-CEE-GEFE (1983): 27-44.

Cockcroft, James D."The Social and Economic Structure of the Porfiriato: Mexico 1877-1911." In *Dependence and Underdevelopment: Latin America's Political Economy.* Ed. James D. Cockcroft, Andre Gunder Frank, and Dale Johnson. New York: Anchor Books, 1972.

———. "Mexico." *Latin America: The Struggle with Dependency and Beyond.* Ed. Ronald H. Chilcote and Joel C. Edelstein. New York: Wiley, 1974.

Comisión Nacional del Salario Mínimo. Mexico, DF: (December-January), 1982.

Convergence. (Toronto). 14, no. 3 (1981): 5-17; 20-27; 52-63.

Cordera, Rolando and Carlos Tello. *México. La disputa por la nación. Perspectivas y opciones del desarrollo.* Mexico: Siglo XXI Editores, 1981.

Córdova, Arnaldo. *La formación del poder político en México.* Mexico, DF: Ediciones Era, 1972a.

———. "Las reformas sociales y la tecnocratización del Estado Mexicano," *Revista Mexicana de Ciencias Políticas* 17 (October-December), 1972b.

———. *La política de masas del Cardenismo.* Mexico, DF: Editorial Era, 1974.

———. "La transformación del PNR en PRM: El triunfo del corporativismo en México." *Contemporary Mexico.* Ed. J.W. Wilkie et al. Berkeley, CA: University of California Press, 1976.

———. *La política de masas y el futuro de la izquierda en México.* Mexico: ERA, 1979.

Cosío Villegas, Daniel. *Historia moderna de México,* Volumes 1 and 2. Mexico, DF: Editorial Hermes, 1965.

Cotler, Julio. "State and Regime: Comparative Notes on the Southern Cone and the 'Enclave' Societies." *The New Authoritarianism in Latin America*. Ed. David Collier. Princeton, NJ: Princeton University Press, 1979.

Cuellar, Oscar. "El sistema de educación para adultos: evolución del registro y características de la población inscrita (1975-1978)." Mexico, DF: (mimeographed), 1981.

————. "México: Estado y educación. Aspectos políticos del programa nacional de alfabetización (1981-1982)." Mexico, DF: Departamento de Ciencias Sociales y Políticas. Universidad Iberoamericana I, no. 4 (May) 1983.

Dale, Roger. "Learning to Be . . . What? Shaping Education in Developing Societies." In *Introduction to the Sociology of Developing Societies*. Ed. Hanza Alavi and Teodor Shanin. London: Macmillan, 1982.

De Anda, María Luisa, ed. *Educación de adultos: Nuevas dimensiones en el sector educativo*. Mexico, DF: CNTE-CEE-GEFE, 1983.

De la Madrid Hurtado, Miguel. *Cuarto informe de gobierno. 1986. Educación*. Mexico, DF: Presidencia de la República, 1986.

————. *Quinto informe de gobierno. 1987. Educación*. Mexico, DF: Presidencia de la República. 1987.

De Lella, Cayetano. "Evaluación del proceso de alfabetización por los alfabetizadores." Mexico, DF: PRONALF (mimeographed), 1982.

Delli Sante, Angela. "The Private Sector, Business Organizations and International Influence: A Case Study of Mexico." In *Capitalism and the State in U.S.-Latin American Relations*. Ed. Richard Fagen. Stanford, CA: Stanford University Press, 1979.

Derek, Jones. "The Economic and Industrial Relations of Producer Cooperatives in the United States 1791-1930." *Economic Analysis and Workers' Management*, 3-4, (1977).

Día, El. (Mexico, DF). Editorial, October 24, 1978.

————. (Mexico, DF). Editorial, December 2, 1982.

Eckstein, Susan. *The Poverty of Revolution. The State and the Urban Poor in Mexico*. Princeton, NJ: Princeton University Press, (1977) 1988.

————. *Power and Popular Protest. Latin American Social Movements*. Berkeley and Los Angeles: University of California Press, 1989.

ECLA. *Economic Survey of Latin America and the Caribbean, 1984*. Santiago: Economic Commission for Latin America and the Caribbean, 1985.

Epstein, Ervin E. "National Consciousness and Education in Mexico." Mimeographed, 1985.

Evans, Peter. *Dependent Development*. Princeton, NJ: Princeton University Press, 1979.

Expansión. XVIII: 435 (March), 1986.

Fagen, Richard R., and Nau, Henry R. "Mexican Gas: The Northern Connection." *Capitalism and the State in U.S.-Latin American Relations*. Ed. Richard Fagen. Stanford, CA: Stanford University Press, 1979.

Figueroa Unda, Manuel. *Methodological Explorations on Schooling and the Reproduction of the Social Division of Labor: A Case Study in Mexico City*. Ph.D. dissertation, Stanford University 1982.

Foxley, Alejandro. *Latin American Experiments in Neo-Conservative Economics*. Berkeley, CA: University of California Press, 1983.

Freire, Paulo. *Education as Practice of Freedom*. New York: McGraw-Hill, 1973.

———. "Investigación y metodología de la investigación del 'tema generador,'" *La praxis educativa de Paulo Freire*. Ed. Carlos Alberto Torres. Mexico: Gernika, (1978): 139-72.

———. *The Politics of Education, Culture, Power and Liberation*. Massachusetts: Bergin and Garvey, 1984.

Freire, Paulo and Rosiska, and Miguel Darcy de Oliveira, Claudius Ceccon. *Vivendo e Aprendendo. Experiencias do IDAC in Educação Popular*. São Paulo: Livraria Brasilense Editora, 3d ed., 1980.

Fuentes Molinar, Olac. *Política y educación en México*. Mexico, DF: Nueva Imagen, 1983.

García, Antonio. *Cooperación agraria y estrategias de desarrollo*. Mexico, DF: Siglo XXI Editores, 1976.

Garson, David. *The Democratic Enterprise: Workers' Self-Management in Western Europe*. New York: Praeger, 1977.

Gee, James Paul. "Literate America on Illiterate America." *Journal of Education* 168, no. 1 (1986): 126-40

Gerth, H.H., and Mills, C.W., eds. *From Max Weber*. London: Routledge and Kegan Paul, 1970.

Gill, Clark C. "Education in Changing Mexico." Washington, DC: Department of Health, Education and Welfare, 1969.

González Casanova, Pablo. *Democracy in Mexico*. New York: Oxford University Press, 1965 [1970].

———. *El estado y los partidos políticos en México*. Mexico: ERA, 1981.

González Casanova, Pablo, and Florescano, Enrique, eds. *México hoy*. Mexico, DF: Siglo XXI Editores, 1979.

González, Norberto. "Opening Address. International Colloquium on New Directions for Development Planning in Market Economies." *CEPAL Review* 31 (April), 1987.

Gramsci, Antonio. *Note sul Machiavelli, sulla politica e sullo stato moderno* Turin: Einaudi, 1949.

———. *La formación de los intelectuales*. Mexico: Grijalbo, 1967.

———. *Quaderni del carcere*. Rome: Edizione Critica dell Istituto Gramsci. A cura de Valentino Geratano, Giuliu Einaidi editore, 1975.

Greenberg, Edward. "Producer Cooperatives and Democratic Theory: The Case of Plywood Firms." Palo Alto, CA: Center for Economic Studies, 1978.

Ham, Christopher, and Hill, Michael. *The Policy Process in the Modern Capitalist State*. Brighton, UK: Wheatsheaf Books, 1984.

Hamill, Hugh M., Jr. *The Hidalgo Revolt*. Gainesville, FL: University of Florida Press, 1966.

Hamilton, Nora. "Dependent Capitalism and the State: The Case of Mexico." *Kapitalistate*, 3, Spring 1975: 72-82.

———. *The Limits of State Autonomy: Post-Revolutionary Mexico*. Princeton, NJ: Princeton University Press, 1982.

Hansen, Roger D. *The Politics of Mexican Development*. Baltimore, MD: Johns Hopkins University Press, 1971.

Huntington, Samuel P. *Political Order in Changing Societies*. New Haven, CT: Yale University Press, 1968.

Instituto Nacional para la Educación de Adultos (INEA). *Programa de educación comunitaria*. Mexico, DF: INEA, n.d.

————. *Programa de acción de alfabetización para 1986*. Mexico, DF: Dirección de Alfabetización. Mimeographed, 1986.

————. *Plan de acción del programa de alfabetización para 1987*. Mexico, DF: Dirección de Alfabetización. Mimeographed, 1987.

————. *Acción educativa 1981-1986*. Mexico, DF: SEP, 1987.

————. *Serie histórica 1981-1986*. Mexico, DF: SEP, 1987.

Iturriaga, José E. *La estructura social y cultural de México*. Mexico, DF: Fondo de Cultura Económica, 1951.

Jallade, Jean P. *Public Expenditures on Education and Income Distribution in Colombia*. Baltimore, MD: Johns Hopkins University Press, 1974.

————. "Financiamiento de la educación y distribución del ingreso." *Revista del Centro de Estudios Educativos*, 16:4, (1976).

————. "Basic Education and Income Inequality in Brazil: The Long-Term View." *Working Paper* 268. Washington DC: World Bank, 1977.

Kaufman, Robert. "Mexico and Latin American Authoritarianism." *Authoritarianism in Mexico*. Ed. José Luis Reina and Richard Weinert. Philadelphia: ISHS, 1977: 194-228.

Kozol, J. *Illiterate America*. Garden City, NY: Anchor Press/Doubleday, 1985.

Labastida, Julio. "Nacionalismo reformista en México." *Cuadernos Políticos*. Mexico, DF: Ediciones Era, 3 (January-March), 1975.

La Belle, Thomas. *Nonformal Education and Social Change in Latin America*. Los Angeles: UCLA, Latin American Center Publication, 1976.

————. "Liberation, Development and Rural Non-Formal Education." *Non-Formal Education and the Rural Poor*. Ed. Richard Niehoff O. East Lansing, MI: Michigan State University Program of Studies in Non-Formal Education, Institute for International Studies, (1977): 211-27.

————. *Nonformal Education in Latin America and the Caribbean. Stability, Reform, or Revolution?* New York: Praeger, 1986.

Labra, Armando. "El estado y la economía." *El estado mexicano*. Jorge Alonso (coordinador). Mexico: CIESAS—Editorial Nueva Imagen, 1982: 49-63.

Latapí, Pablo. *Política educativa y valores nacionales*. Mexico, DF: Editorial Nueva Imagen, 1976.

————. *Análisis de un sexenio de educación en México, 1970-1976*. Mexico, DF: Editorial Nueva Imagen, 1980.

Leal, Juan Felipe. "El estado en México." *Revista Punto Crítico*. 1:8 (August, 1972a): 38-41.

————. *La burguesía y el estado Mexicano*. Mexico, DF: Ediciones El Caballito, 1972b.

————. "The Mexican State: 1915-1973. A Historical Interpretation." *Latin American Perspectives* 2, no. 5: 2 (Summer 1975a), 48-80.

————. *México, estado, burocracia y sindicatos*. Mexico, DF: Editorial El Caballito, 1975b.

————. "The Mexican State, 1915-1973: A Historical Interpretation" *Modern Mexico. State, Economy, and Social Conflict*. Ed. Nora Hamilton and Timothy F. Harding. Beverly Hills, CA: Sage, 1986.

Leal, Juan Felipe, and Woldenberg, José. "El sindicalismo mexicano. Aspectos organizativos." *Cuadernos Políticos*, Mexico, DF: Ediciones Era, 7 (January-March 1976): 35-53.

Leff, Gloria. "El partido de la revolución: Aparato de hegemonía del estado mexicano." *El estado mexicano*. Jorge Alonso (coordinador). Mexico: CIESAS—Editorial Nueva Imagen, 1982: 201-223.

Lehmbruch, Gerard, and Schmitter, Philippe., eds. *Patterns of Corporatist Policy-Making*. Modern Politics Series, vol. 7. Beverly Hills, CA: Sage, 1982.

Leonor, M.D., ed. *Unemployment, Schooling and Training in Developing Countries*. London: Croom Helm, 1985.

Levy, Daniel C. *University and Government: Autonomy in an Authoritarian System*. New York: Praeger, 1980.

———. "The Political Consequences of Changing Socialization Patterns." *Mexico's Political Stability: The Next Five Years*. Ed. Roderic Ai Camp. Boulder, CO: Westview Special Studies on Latin America and the Caribbean, 1986: 19-46.

Liss, Sheldon B. *Marxist Thought in Latin America*. Berkeley, CA: University of California Press, 1984.

Livingstone, David. "On Hegemony in Corporate Capitalist States: Material Structures, Ideological Forms, Class Consciousness and Hegemonic Acts." *Sociological Inquiry* 46, nos. 3-4 (1976): 235-50.

Lowenthal, Abraham F. *Partners in Conflict. The United States and Latin America*. Baltimore, MD: Johns Hopkins University Press. 1987.

Manjarrez, Froylán C. "Editorial." *Diario Oficial*. Mexico, DF: 1930.

Marx, Karl, and Engels, Friedrich. *The German Ideology*. New York: International Publishers, 1970.

McGinn, Noel, and Street, Susan. "The Political Rationality of Resource Allocation in Mexican Public Education." *Comparative Education Review* 26 (June 1982): 178-98.

———. *La asignación de recursos económicos en la educación pública en México*. Mexico, DF: Gefe, 1983.

———. "Has Mexican Education Generated Human or Political Capital?" *Comparative Education* 20 (1984): 323-38.

Mexican Government. *Anuario estadístico de los estados Mexicanos, 1970-1971*. Mexico, DF: Dirección General de Estadísticas, 1971.

———. "México a través de los informes presidenciales. La educación pública." Mexico, DF: Presidencia de la República, 1976.

Meyer, John. "The Effects of Education as an Institution." *American Journal of Sociology* 83, no. 4 (July 1977).

Meyer, Michael, and Sherman, William. *The Course of Mexican History*. New York: Oxford University Press, 1979.

Miliband, Ralph. *Marxism and Politics*. Oxford and New York: Oxford University Press, 1977.

Morales-Gómez, Daniel A., ed. *Educación y desarrollo dependiente en América Latina*. Mexico, DF: Ediciones Gernika-C.E.E., 1979.

———. *Workers' Education in Latin America: The Educational Role of Producer Cooperatives in Mexico, DF*. Ph.D. dissertation, University of Toronto, 1982.

———. "La educación de los trabajadores en los centros de Trabajo. Una comparación entre las cooperativas de producción y las empresas privadas en México." *Revista de Educación de Adultos* 3, no. 1 (Enero-Marzo 1985): 6-19.

———. "Cooperativas de producción y participación de trabajadores: La experiencia Latinoamericana." *Apuntes*. Santiago: Consejo de Educación de Adultos de América Latina (May), 1986a.

———. "La situación de crisis y el papel de las ciencias sociales en el desarrollo de América Latina." *David y Goliat* 16, no. 50 (December 1986b): 60-66.

Muñoz Izquierdo, Carlos. "Evaluación del desarrollo escolar y factores que lo han determinado." *Revista del Centro de Estudios Educativos* 3, no. 3 (1973).

————. "Efectos económicos de la educación de adultos." *Ensayos sobre la educación de adultos en América Latina*. Ed. Carlos A. Torres. Mexico, DF: Centro de Estudios Educativos, 1982.

Nacional, El. (Mexico, DF). May 30, 1983.

Nacional Financiera, SA. *La economía mexicana en cifras*. Mexico, DF: Banco de México, 1974.

————. SA. *La economía mexicana en cifras*. Mexico, DF: Banco de México, 1978.

Navarrete, Ifigenia M. "La distribución del ingreso en México: Tendencias y perspectivas." *El perfil de México en 1980*. Mexico, DF: Siglo XXI Editores, 1970.

Neumann, Peter, and Cunningham, Maureen. *Mexico's Free Textbooks. Nationalism and the Urgency to Educate*. Staff Working Papers No. 541. Washington, DC: World Bank, 1982.

Niblo, Stephen R. "Progress and the Standard of Living in Contemporary Mexico." *Latin American Perspectives* 2, nos. 5, 2 (Summer 1975), 109-24.

Núñez, Iván. *Gremios del magisterio. Setenta años de historia 1900-1970*. Santiago, Chile: PIIE, 1986.

O'Donnell, Guillermo. *Estado y alianzas en Argentina, 1956-1976*. Buenos Aires: Centro de Estudios de Estado y Sociedad, October 1976.

————. "Corporatism and the Question of the State." *Authoritarianism and Corporatism in Latin Ameraica*. Ed. James M. Malloy. Pittsburgh, PA: University of Pittsburgh Press, 1977: 47-87.

Offe, Claus. "The Abolition of Market Control and the Problem of Legitimacy." *Working Papers of the Kapitalistate* I and II (1973): 109-16; 73-75.

————. "Structural Problems of the Capitalist State." *German Political Studies*. Ed. K. von Beyme. London: Sage, 1974.

————. "The Theory of the Capitalist State and the Problem of Policy Formation." *Stress and Contradictions in Modern Capitalism*. Ed. L. Lindberg et al. Lexington, MA: Lexington Books, 1976.

————. *Contradictions of the Welfare State*. London: Hutchinson, 1984.

Olsen, Marvin E., ed. *Power in Societies*. London: Macmillan, 1970.

Ornelas, Carlos. "The Decentralization of Education in Mexico." *Prospects* 18, no. 1 (1988): 105-13.

Osorio Urbina, Jaime. "Superexplotación y clase obrera: El caso mexicano." *Cuadernos Políticos*, Mexico, DF: Ediciones Era 6 (October-December 1975): 6-23.

Oszlak, Oscar, and O'Donnell, Guillermo. *Estado y políticas estatales en América Latina. Hacia una estrategia de investigación*. Buenos Aires: CEDES-G.E.-CLACSO 4 (March), 1976.

Padgett, L. Vincent. *The Mexican Political System*. Boston: Houghton Mifflin, 1966.

Padua, Jorge. *La crisis y la política educativa en México: Evaluación de algunos problemas y perspectivas para el futuro*. Villahermosa, Tabasco: Congreso Internacional sobre educación política. Política educativa en tiempos de crisis. Educación política ¿Una alternativa? Mimeographed, February 1987.

Paoli Bolio, Francisco José. *Ensayos de sociología y política*. Mexico: UAM-Azcapotzalco, 1982.

Parker F. and Parker, B. J. *Mexico: A Bibliography with Abstracts*. Troy, NY: Whitston Publishing, 1985.

Paz, Octavio. *The Labyrinth of Solitude: Life and Thought in Mexico*. New York: Grove Press, 1961.

Pereyra, Carlos. "México: Los límites del reformismo." *Cuadernos Políticos*. Mexico, DF: Ediciones Era 28 (July-September 1974): 52-55.

———. "Estado y sociedad." *México Hoy.* Ed. Pablo González Casanova and Enrique Florescano. Mexico, DF: Siglo XXI Editores, 1979: 289-305.

———. "Estado y movimiento obrero." *Cuadernos Políticos.* Mexico, DF: Ediciones Era. (April-June 1981): 35-42.

———. "Estado y movimiento obrero." *El estado Mexicano.* Jorge Alonso (coordinador). Mexico: CIESAS—Editorial Nueva Imagen, 1982: 151-166.

Pescador, José Angel. "Las universidades privadas toman el poder." *Revista Siempre.* Mexico, DF: 1980.

———. "Guía práctica para la formulación de programas de educación de adultos." *Ensayos sobre la educación de adultos en América Latina.* Ed. Carlos A. Torres. Mexico, DF: Centro de Estudios Educativos, 1982a.

———. "Algunas reflexiones sobre las características del personal directivo del INEA." Mexico, DF: CNTE-SEP. Mimeographed, 1982b.

———. "El balance de la educación superior en el sexenio 1976-1982." *Foro Universitario* 28 (March), 1983.

———. "El esfuerzo alfabetizador en México (1910-1985): Un ensayo crítico." Mexico, DF. Mimeographed, 1986.

Pescador, José Angel, and Torres, Carlos A. *Poder político y educación en México.* Mexico, DF: Uthea, 1985.

Portes Gil, Emilio. *Quince años de política Mexicana.* Mexico, DF: Editorial Botas, 1954.

Poulantzas, Nicos. "The Problem of the Capitalist State." *New Left Review* 58 (1969): 237-41.

Pravda, Juan. *Teoría y praxis de la planeación educativa en México.* Mexico, DF: Grijalbo, 1984.

PRONALF. *Manual del alfabetizador.* Mexico, DF: PRONALF, n.d.

PRONALF-SEP. *Manual de procedimientos para la operación del sistema de estadística continua de los servicios de alfabetización.* Mexico, DF: Dirección General de Programación. SEP (July), 1981.

PRONALF-SPAC. "Análisis de las opiniones y actitudes referidas al PRONALF. Resultados preliminares." Mexico, DF: PRONALF-SPAC. Mimeographed, June 1982.

Psacharopoulos, George, and Woodhall, Maureen. *Education for Development. An Analysis of Investment Choices.* New York: Oxford University Press, 1985.

Raat, W. "Los intelectuales, el positivismo y la cuestión indígena." *Historia mexicana.* Mexico, DF: Educación del Estado, n.d.

Raby, D. *Educación y revolución social.* Madrid: Sep-Setentas 1974.

Rama, Germán. "Estilos educativos." *Educación y sociedad en América Latina y el Caribe.* Ed. G. Rama. Santiago, Chile: UNESCO-CEPAL-PNUD-UNICEF, 1980.

Reyes Heroles, Jesús. *El liberalismo mexicano.* Mexico, DF: Fondo de Cultura Económica, 1983.

Reyna, José Luis, and Weinert, Richard., eds. *Authoritarianism in Mexico.* Philadelphia: Institute for the Study of Human Issues, 1977.

Reynolds, Clark. *The Mexican Economy: Twentieth Century Structure and Growth.* New Haven, CT: Yale University Press, 1974.

Rist, Ray. "Student Social Class and Teacher Expectations: The Self-Fulfilling Prophecy in Ghetto Education." *Harvard Educational Review* (August 1970).

Roman, Richard. *Ideology and Class in the Mexican Revolution: A Study of the Convention and the Constitutional Congress.* Ph.D. dissertation, University of California, Berkeley, 1973.

Rosenzweig, Fernando. "El desarrollo económico en México de 1877 a 1911." *Trimestre Económico* 32 (July-September 1965): 405-54.

Rothstein, Frances. "The Class Basis of Patron-Client Relations." *Latin American Perspectives* 6, 2 (1979): 25-35.

Saldívar, Américo. *Ideología y política del estado mexicano (1970-1976)*. Mexico: Siglo XXI Editores, 1980.

Schmitter, P. C. "Still the Century of Corporatism." *The New Corporatism: Social-Political Structures in the Iberian World*. Ed. F. B. Pike and T. Strich. Notre Dame, IN: University of Notre Dame Press, 1974: 85-131.

Scott, Robert. *Mexican Government in Transition*. Urbana University of Illinois Press, 1964.

―――. "Mexico: The Established Revolution." *Political Culture and Political Development*. Ed. Lucian W. Pye and Sidney Verba. Princeton, NJ: Princeton University Press, 1970.

Secretaría de Educación Pública. *Diagnóstico del sistema educativo nacional*. Mexico, DF: Dirección General de Programación, 1977.

―――. *Estadísticas básicas del sistema educativo nacional*. Mexico, DF: Dirección General de Programación, 1982.

―――. *Memorias 1976-82*. Mexico, DF: SEP, 1982 [1983].

―――. *Cuarto informe de gobierno*. Mexico, DF: SEP, 1986.

Secretaría de Industria y Comercio. *Agenda estadística*. Mexico, DF: Dirección General de Estadísticas, 1970.

―――. *IX Censo general de población, 1970*. Mexico, DF: Dirección General de Estadísticas, 1972.

―――. *Agenda estadística 1974*. Mexico, DF: 1974.

Secretaría de la Presidencia de México. *Mensaje presidencial 1980*. Mexico, DF: 1980.

Secretaría de Programación y Presupuesto. "Producción estatal de servicios." Mexico, DF: 1979.

―――. *Plan global de desarrollo, 1980-1982*. Mexico, DF: 1983.

Selucky, R. "Marxism and Self-management." *Self-Management*. Ed. Jeroslav Vanek. Baltimore, MD: Penguin Education, 1975.

Silva Herzog, Jesús. "La revolución mexicana en crisis." *Cuadernos Mexicanos*. Mexico, (1967).

―――. *El pensamiento económico, social y político de México 1810-1964*. Mexico, DF: Instituto Mexicano de Investigaciones Económicas, 1967.

Skocpol, Theda. *Los estados y las revoluciones sociales*. Mexico: Fondo de Cultura Económica, 1984.

Smith, Peter. *Labyrinths of Power. Political Recruitment in Twentieth-Century Mexico*. Princeton, NJ: Princeton University Press, 1979.

―――. "Leadership and Change, Intellectuals and Technocrats in Mexico." *Mexico's Political Stability: The Next Five Years*. Ed. Roderic Ai Camp. Boulder, CO: Westview Special Studies on Latin America and the Caribbean, 1986: 101-117.

Solana, F. *La política educativa de México en la UNESCO*. Mexico, DF: SEP, 1980.

Solari, Aldo. "La desigualdad educativa en América Latina." *Revista Latinoamericana de Estudios Educativos* 10, no. 1, 1980: 1-56.

SPP-CONAPO-WADE. *Estimaciones y proyecciones de población 1950-2000*. Mexico, DF: SPP, 1983.

Stavenhagen, Rodolfo. "Collective Agriculture and Capitalism in Mexico: A Way Out or a Dead End?" *Latin American Perspective*. 11, no. 5:2 (Summer 1975), 146-63.

Stepan, Alfred. *The State and Society in Peru in Comparative Perspective*. Princeton, NJ: Princeton University Press, 1978.

Street, Susan. "Burocracia y educación: Hacia un análisis político de la desconcentración administrativa en la Secretaría de Educación Pública (SEP)." *Estudios Sociológicos* 1 (1983): 239-62.

———. "Los distintos proyectos para la transformación del aparato burocrático de la SEP." *Perfiles Educativos*, 7, October-December 1984: 14-29.

———. "El magisterio democrático y el aparato burocrático del estado." *Foro Universitario*, 8, 11, 1989: 7-24.

Suárez Gaona, Enrique. *¿Legitimización revolucionaria del poder en México? (Los presidentes, 1910-1982)*. Mexico, DF: Siglo XXI Editores, 1987.

Tannenbaum, Frank. *Peace by Revolution after 1910*. New York: Columbia University Press, 1966.

Tello, Carlos. *La política económica en México (1970-1976)*. Mexico, DF: Siglo XXI Editores, 1979.

Trejo Delarbre, Raúl. "El movimiento obrero: Situación y perspectivas." *México hoy*. Ed. Pablo González Casanova and Enrique Florescano. Mexico, D.F.: Siglo XXI Editores, 1979: 121-151.

Torres, Carlos Alberto, ed. *La praxis educativa de Paulo Freire*. Mexico, DF: Editorial Gernika,1978.

———. "La educación de adultos en México: problemas y perspectivas." *Cuadernos de Trabajo*. Mexico, DF: Dirección General de Educación de Adultos (DGEA). Secretaría de Educación Pública 1 (March), 1980.

———. "La sociología de la cultura y la crítica pedagógica de Paulo Freire." *Sociología de la educación. Corrientes contemporáneas*. Ed. G. González and Carlos A. Torres. Mexico, DF: Centro de Estudios Educativos, 1981.

———. "Adult Education Policy, Capitalist Development and Class Alliances: Latin America and Mexico." *International Journal of Political Education* 6, 1983: 157-73.

———. *Public Policy Formation and the Mexican Corporatist State: A Study of Adult Education Policy and Planning in Mexico. 1970-1982*. Ph.D. dissertation, Stanford University, 1984a.

———. "The Political Economy of Adult Education in Latin America." *Canadian and International Education* 13:2, 1984b: 22-36.

———. "State and Education: Marxist Theories." *International Encyclopedia of Education*. Ed. T. Hussen and N. Postlethwaite. New York: Pergamon Press, 1985.

———. "Toward a Political Sociology of Adult Education: An Agenda for Research on Adult Education Policy Making." *CIED Occasional Paper*. Edmonton, Canada: Department of Educational Foundations, University of Alberta, 1987.

———. "The Capitalist State and Public Policy Formation. Framework for a Political Sociology of Educational Policy." *British Journal of Sociology of Education*, 10:1, 1989: 81-102.

———. "The Mexican State and Democracy: The Ambiguities of Corporatism." *Politics, Culture and Society*, 2, 4, 1989: 563-586.

———. *The Politics of Nonformal Education in Latin America*. New York: Praeger, 1990.

UNESCO. *Public Expenditure on Education in the World. Regional and Country Trends, 1970-1979*. Paris: Division of Statistics on Education, STE/FIN/4, 1982.

———. International Yearbook of Education. Paris: UNESCO, 1986.

United States Government. *A Review of Progress Goals*. Washington, DC: Government Printing Office, 1969.

Universal, El. February 9, 1922.

Universidad Autónoma Metropolitana (UAM). *Organo informativo*, Volume IX. January 14, 1985.

Uno más Uno. December 31, 1981.

Vanek, Jeroslav, ed. *The General Theory of Labor Managed Market Economies*. Ithaca, NY: Cornell University Press, 1970.

———. *Self-Management: Economic Liberation of Man*. Baltimore, MD: Penguin Education, 1975.

Vaughan, M.K. *The State, Education and Social Class in Mexico, 1880-1928*. De Kalb, IL: Northern Illinois University Press, 1982.

Vázquez, Josefina. *Nacionalismo y educación en México*. Mexico, DF: El Colegio de Mexico, 1970.

Vázquez Torres, Moisés. "El cooperativismo Mexicano." Mexico, DF: Seminario sobre Cooperativismo, 1978.

Vergara, Regina. "El sistema nacional de educación para adultos." Thesis, Universidad Iberoamericana, Mexico, DF, 1981.

Vernon, Robert E. *The Dilemma of Mexico's Development: The Roles of the Private and Public Sectors*. Cambridge, MA: Harvard University Press, 1963.

Vidal, Susana. "Experiencias en educación para adultos. Antecedentes históricos en México." *Educación*. Revista del Consejo Nacional Técnico de Educación 3, no. 35 (1981): 121-26.

Wall Street Journal, The. October, 31, 1986.

Weber, Max. *The Theory of Social and Economic Organization*. Glencoe, IL: Free Press, 1947 [1970].

Weiler, Hans. "Legalization, Expertise and Participation: Strategies of Compensatory Legitimation in Educational Policy." *Comparative Education Review* 27 (1983): 259-77.

———. "The Political Economy of Educational Planning." *Educational Planning in the Context of Current Development Problems*. Paris: UNESCO-IIEP, 1985.

Wilkie, James W. *The Mexican Revolution: Federal Expenditure and Social Change since 1910*. Berkeley, CA: University of California Press, 1967.

Wionczek, Miguel S. *Politics and Economics of External Debt Crisis. The Latin American Experience*. London: Westview Press, Special Studies on Latin America and the Caribbean, 1985.

World Bank. *Technical Education in Mexico: A Subsectoral Study of Training and Skill Development*. Washington, DC: Education and Training Department. 1986.

———. *Policy Choice and School Efficiency in Mexico*. Washington, DC: Education and Training Department. 1987.

Young, Michael, ed., *Knowledge and Control*. London: Collier-Macmillan, 1971.

Zedillo Ponce de León, Ernesto. "The Mexican External Debt: The Last Decade. *Politics and Economics of External Debt Crisis. The Latin American Experience*. Ed. Miguel S. Wionczek. London: Westview Press, Special Studies on Latin American and the Caribbean, 1985.

Index

About the Authors

DANIEL A. MORALES-GÓMEZ holds degrees from the Catholic University of Valparaíso in Chile, Stanford University in the United States, and the University of Toronto in Canada. Currently a senior program officer of the Social Sciences Division of the International Development Research Centre (IDRC) in Canada, he has taught in universities in Chile, Mexico, and Canada. He is author and editor of *Educación y Desarrollo Dependiente en América Latina* published in Mexico.

CARLOS ALBERTO TORRES holds degrees from the Universidad del Salvador in Argentina, the Latin American Faculty of Social Sciences (FLACSO) in Mexico, and Stanford University in the United States. Currently an assistant professor in the Department of Educational Foundations, Faculty of Education at the University of Alberta in Canada, he has taught in universities in Argentina, Mexico, and the United States. He is the author of *The Politics of Nonformal Education in Latin America* published by Praeger, and a number of books and articles on nonformal education, sociology of education, comparative education, and critical pedagogy.